It's OK to Talk to Animals

(and Other Letters from Dad)

by

nathan timmel

To Hilly

(naturally)

Prologue

September 3, 2014

Dear Hillary,

Like most good ideas under our roof, the project you are holding came from your mother's mind. She read a story about a parent writing letters to their infant and decided, "You should do that while you're traveling. Write to Hilly and tell her where you are, and what you're up to."

(Because creating projects and pawning them off on me is what your mother does best.)

So, I did as I was told and wrote, wrote away.

From August 2013 to August 2014, I dreamt up and scribbled down letters to you, the topics of which are as varied as can be. Sometimes I wrote to you in the present moment, you being a toddler, sometimes I imagined an age far in the distance and wrote to you as if you were reading my words in your college dorm room. I wrote about our daily activities, milestones in your existence, and my life, the last of which being done in the hope you may forgive me my nonsensical ways.

It's good I started at your first birthday, because to detail the first twelve months of any human existence wouldn't be the most exciting of tales: "Today you ate, pooped, and napped. Repeatedly."

Likewise, it might be best the writing has slowed now that you're two, because the "Terrible" age kicked in quickly after your second birthday. It's as if a switch was thrown, because you went from being my adorable little cuddle-bug to a tantrum-throwing monster almost overnight. Not that I don't still love you, and you are still my little cuddle-bug, but my God, some days you are almost Sybil in nature, given how quickly you can flip temperaments. Plus, tales that perpetually end "and then you threw a fit" might be as boring as repeated poop/nap letters.

Anyway, as the year passed, I dropped a couple of the notes on my blog and holy poop-on-a-stick was the response overwhelmingly kind. People laughed, cried, and spread the words around, telling their friends, "Hey, you need to check this out."

"So," you might be wondering, "why not just post them all on your blog? Why turn them into a book?"

Because college is expensive, and I don't have it in me to "Tiger Mom" you to death so you can get a great scholarship (and have no friends or life along the way). Also, to quote The Joker in one of my favorite movies, "If you're good at something, never do it for free." (Daddy has odd idols.) For all of the above reasons, and the fact that I flat-out enjoy writing letters to you, this book came into existence.

Also, I'm not ashamed or embarrassed by anything in here. The letters are personal, but they're not sensitive. Plus, given my ability to act the fool in public, I'm sure by the time you *do* read these you will have a thick enough skin to avoid being scarlet-cheeked by anything I've shared.

(Your teenage years will most likely play a great role in this "toughening up." Teenagers are already sensitive; having a comedian for a father will probably lead you to eye damage from all the rolling you'll be doing as I embarrass you. But, at the end of it all, you'll come out all the stronger for it. Promise.)

So.

With any luck, the pages that follow will help give you insight into what life was like in one of your earliest years.

I hope you enjoy it.

Love,
Dad

August 9, 2013

Dear Hillary,

I am in Ann Arbor, Michigan, and missing you dearly. Yesterday you turned one year old, and today we saw one another via the wonders of modern technology, or at least modern to 2013. By the time you are reading this, video chat may be old hat, and holograms the hip new trend. But for now, I'll take seeing you wobble as you attempt to walk any way I can.

You aren't really sure what a phone is, but you light up in smiles when I yell my exaggerated "Hello!" your way. And your smiles, little one? Oh, they are my fuel. They are as important to me as air, or food. They are a nourishment that pushes me through the long hours spent driving in my car, a seemingly endless slab of concrete continually spilling forth in front of me.

Traveling and missing you is difficult, but this is my job, and my job helps keep you in diapers, so travel I must. After the first show tonight, the doorman walked by me, paused, and offered this compliment: "I see too much comedy, but dude, you were funny." When a jaded worker tells you you're good, it's high praise.

The dream in all of this is to someday be a known entity, someone people specifically want to see, not just a warm body gracing the stage during an arbitrary visit to the local comedy club. Hopefully, if and when that day comes, I'll be able to choose fewer gigs, and be away from you less often.

Until that time, I will do my best to make people giggle, and wonder if you are noticing my absence while I am gone. Most likely you're too fascinated by the dog food to realize I'm not around, because those little kibbles are just oh-so-tempting, sitting right there in the bowl on the floor, waiting for you to pick up and gobble them down...

...but I can always pretend you are thinking of me.

Either way, I am absolutely thinking of you.

I always am, and forever will be.

Love,
Dad

August 16, 2013

Dear Hillary,

One of the best things any form of art—painting, literature, music—can do, is move us emotionally.

But does that mean it changes us?

I remember my days of teen angst and really enjoying J.D. Salinger's defining novel, *The Catcher in the Rye.* The book no longer speaks to me the way it once did, but certain scenes still remain in the cobwebbed corners of my mind. Case in point, the movie theater moment, where Holden is killing time before catching a drink with Carl Luce.

As it is written, there is a woman in the theater with her child. She is alternately crying—because she is so touched by the movie—and berating her child for being restless and having to go to the bathroom. In other words, she is scolding her child for being a child. The disparity being described is that of a person who probably believes she is "deep" and "kindhearted," because art moves her, yet in reality is a bit of a monster who is neglectful to the needs of her own son.

I wonder if we all don't have a little of that woman in us. We all see things that inspire us to be better than we are, art that tells us we can carry that emotion with us after the credits roll or turn the last page of a book. But how often do we actually live up to the ideals we set for ourselves? We see something in a theater that moves us, then roll up our window on the way home when we see a homeless person holding a "Hungry" sign at a red light.

The difference between who we think we are—caring, loving, connected—and who we really are—emotionless, cold, indifferent—has me thinking about Mommy. People always joke about their marriages—"I married up!"—but when I say I married my better, I mean it.

Mommy continually proves herself to be a genuinely good person.

A few years before you were born, we moved from a condo into a home. The subdivision we lived in had only one entrance, and to get to it we generally had to go through a four-way stop. There was a modest, one-car-garage house at the four-way stop, and we soon discovered that in every-season-but-winter, there was usually an elderly gentleman sitting on its front porch wearing cowboy attire. It didn't matter if it was sixty or ninety degrees, he'd always have on the same flannel shirt, the same deep-blue blue jeans, and naturally, a cowboy hat perched atop his head of grey hair. The faded-name "Carter" barely survived on the weathered mailbox in front of the dwelling.

For several years, Mommy waved every time she saw the cowboy sitting outside. Sometimes he would wave back; sometimes he wouldn't see her.

After a few months, Mommy's wave turned to interest.

"I want to talk to him," she told me. "I don't know why, I just want to go say hi."

When spring 2012 hit, with you growing inside her belly, Mommy started taking our doggy, Kitty, on a two-mile walk, one that looped right past the cowboy's house. She still waved as she passed, but it felt different. Waving from a car was one thing; being on foot and only a few yards away made her desire to actually speak to him burn a hole in her.

One day, Mommy finally mustered up the courage to walk right up and introduce herself. Turns out, the faded name "Carter" was accurate. Mr. Carter was a ninety-two year old widower, and a combination of friendly, happy, and maybe most important to this tale, lonely.

He missed his wife, never really got used to sleeping alone, and smiled a wide, semi-toothless smile whenever someone took the time to visit with him. Mr. Carter had kids, grandkids, and even great-grandkids, but many lived in other cities throughout the state and country.

Every time Mommy stopped to chat, he left her with the same parting invite: "You stop by anytime now. And tell that fella of yours he's always welcome to say hello, too!"

Maybe it was because she was starting to experience maternal instinct—your ever-growing self was spreading hormones soaked in love throughout her—in a very short period of time, Mommy grew to care for Mr. Carter. To her, the idea of anyone being lonely was painful to imagine. Because of this, when Mommy traveled for work, a new addition appeared on my "Honey Do" list:

- Water plants
- Send pictures of doggy
- Visit Mr. Carter!

Many moons ago, I wrote a blog where I quoted the movie *As Good As it Gets*, regarding what I was looking for in a partner, "You make me want to be a better man." I know two things: One, I absolutely found that in Mommy. Two, I may not be too great right now, "But I'm trying, Ringo. I'm trying real hard to be the shepherd."

Because I want to improve as a person, I did visit Mr. Carter while Mommy was away. It made me feel good inside.

Mr. Carter sees a lot from his porch, and notes, "Not everyone stops at those stop signs like they're supposed to... but motorcycles, they do every time. They know they gotta..." Everyone knows that when it comes to motorcycle vs. car, truck, or bigger, motorcycle loses. The only fistfight they win involves a bicycle.

Mr. Carter's favorite story involved a random moment that took him by pleasant surprise. "One day, I was just sittin' here," he began, smiling. "Wasn't really paying attention to anything, when I heard a woman yell. 'What do you think of these?' she shouted, and I looked up, and right there was a truck, and this girl leaning out of it, her shirt pulled all up! Her

12

boobies were hanging out all barefoot! Well, they drove off before I could yell back, 'Come a little closer so I can get a better look, then I'll tell you what I think!'"

Mr. Carter laughs every time he regales a listener with that tale.

Now you and Mommy, or the three of us, visit Mr. Carter. He laughs a gentle laugh as you grab everything within reach, and he calls you "Sissy," a combination of "Sister" and "Missy."

Sometimes we bring him cupcakes, sometimes ice cream. Mr. Carter doesn't get out of the house much, not since he sold his truck. Mr. Carter eventually gave up driving after going up over the curb and hitting a street sign. He had been on the way to McDonald's for coffee, and since neither he nor anyone else was injured, he got out of the cab and walked the final half-block to the restaurant, leaving the truck where it had crashed.

"I figured the police would be able to find me if they needed to," he explained.

Well, they did, and, as said, that was the end of his driving days.

Now Mr. Carter waits on visitors to fill his long days and nights.

I don't know how much longer he'll be around; I don't know if you'll be forming permanent memories by the time Mr. Carter departs this world. But when you're old enough, when you're a young woman or a mother yourself, my hope is you'll find someone in your neighborhood that you've always wanted to say "Hi" to, and knock on their door.

Because I hope that as you grow up, you become as much like Mommy as you can.

Love,
Dad

August 23, 2013

Dear Hillary,

"What have we here, laddie? Mysterious scribblings? A secret code? No! Poems, no less! Poems everybody! The laddie reckons himself a poet!"

~Pink Floyd, The Wall

According to the baby books Mommy devoured while pregnant, there are two different personality traits infants have while in utero. You administer a test by pushing on the belly, and the baby will either (a) try to wiggle away, frightened by whatever intrusive presence is pressing upon its home, or (b) start kicking away at the trespasser, basically saying, "Oh no you didn't!"

Waves baby index finger in the air

You, little one, were a kicker, a willfully belligerent little bugger who fought back when challenged. Now that you are a toddler, this persistence of mind is showing itself more and more. When you want something, you want it.

Mommy says that when your cousin Alaina was your age, she would cry easily. If she had her nose in something she shouldn't—"Look! An electrical outlet! I wonder what would fit in there?"—her Mommy would say, "Alaina, no," in a gentle tone...

...and Alaina would burst into tears for being scolded.

You, on the other hand? You are adamant about doing whatever it is you are doing. Whether digging in drawers locked by "child-proof" fasteners or investigating electrical outlets, if Mommy tells you "No," you don't even turn your head. If Mommy reaches over to you, you brush her off without looking, "I'm busy, Mommy. Go bother someone else." When Mommy tires of being ignored and finally picks you up, *that,* my dear, is when you burst into tears. But unlike Alaina, it's not because you've been scolded, it's because you are being prevented from putting peanut butter in the dog's fur. You only grow upset when your desires are thwarted.

So now I wonder, *is personality something we're born with, or do we develop into who we are?* It's the age-old question: Nature, or Nurture? To put it another way: can a street hustler become a Wall Street stockbroker with a little nudge?

("Looking good, Billy Ray!" "Feeling good, Louis!")

I have a friend whose earliest childhood ambition was to be a lawyer. In his own words, he didn't know what a lawyer was, but he liked the idea of dressing sharply and wearing a suit to work. One day in grade school, they went around the room announcing their dream jobs, and when my friend made his declaration, the teacher's response was, "You aren't smart enough to be a lawyer."

And that was that. My friend said the defeatist statement stuck with him, and in part he gave up on his dreams because of the lack of support from an authority figure. My friend was timid then, and is unassertive to a fault today. He genuinely worries about other people's feelings. Not that that's a bad thing, but he seems to sacrifice his opinions for the constant sake of not wanting to make ripples, much less waves.

I, on the other hand, have never been accused of taking into account what others think. I never intend harm—unless I'm dealing with an obnoxiously drunk heckler or severely obtuse and under-educated lout—but I'm also not shy about vomiting up my thoughts on any given subject. I don't take myself too seriously, but sometimes I forget that others might not understand that. When my lack of tact comes into contact with someone of less-than-stellar self-esteem, it can cause for an interesting oil-meets-water dynamic. Especially during online interactions. In person, tone and inflection can carry a joke, but online, all vocal lilts are absent. If I am bleating on like a sheep, words said in jest can be interpreted as cold, or even harsh.

I'm not sure what caused me to be an argumentative idiot, but it's been a part of me for as long as I can remember. Whenever I was ever told in life that I would be unable to achieve a dream or obtain a goal, I wanted nothing more than to prove the person wrong.

Like my friend's interaction with the teacher who shot down his lawyerly aspirations, I also had authority figures using their own unique brand of judgment to determine my future. In high school, an assistant principal said matter-of-factly and straight to my face that I would probably spend time in jail. Not because I had a lengthy record of starting fights, being drunk, or using drugs, he and I just didn't see eye-to-eye on the state of our school's education. Because I was young, it was assumed I was wrong.

I'll fully admit I did have a "bad attitude" in high school. I was surly and moody and had a chip on my shoulder because I wasn't part of the "in" crowd or popular with girls. In other words, I was a teenager. If I was going to jail because of my "attitude problem," then so was half the school.

But that's not my point. When told I would end up in jail, though I remained silent, I remember thinking quite clearly, "You can go straight to hell." I did not back down, cry, or cower from the authority figure in front of me. I dismissed him immediately. If anything, as if using an internal form of Judo, I used his words to make me stronger. "You think I'm going to jail? I'll show you that I can be better than you've ever given me credit for."

What made me confident the assistant principal was wrong while my friend took to heart he would never be a lawyer? Our childhoods were dissimilar, but not so much so that an easy form of psychological finger-pointing could be done; "This is why one pushes while the other shoves!" It's not as if I was raised under the wing of millionaire parents, never wanted for anything, and was raised to be as confident as a

Rockefeller. I just never liked being told, "That's outside your abilities."

The question is: did I kick back in the womb, and did my friend wiggle out of the way? I wonder why no discussion of a third type of baby exists, because there have to be babies who just sit there and do nothing when pushed against. What kind of person would this be? Would they be Zen, and immune to outside influence?

At the end of the day, this is all conjecture and isn't important. No matter who you are I love you. You are my belligerent little baby girl, and apparently have been this way since your time inside Mommy's belly.

Whoever we are in life is neither good nor bad (but thinking makes it so), it is what we have to accept about ourselves. If I didn't accept that some people aren't going to gel with my personality, I'd be either angry or depressed constantly. My friend's penchant for worrying about others is what makes him a good person.

And that is my note to you. Embrace who you are, because if you don't, no one will.

Love,
Dad

August 30, 2013

Dear Hillary,

By now, you are aware enough to see that not only do I speak and sing to you, I also tend to carry on conversations and sing to both our four-legged housemates: Simon the cat and Kitty the doggie.

A quick aside, "Doggie" is currently your go-to word for all things furry. When you see Simon, you point and squeal "Doggie!" When you see a bunny, squirrel, or guinea pig, you point and squeal "Doggie!" And when you see Kitty, you grow quite animated and squeal, "DOGGIE!"

So, something in you does recognize which one of the many creatures you label "doggie" is actually a dog, but it doesn't prevent you from calling anything with four legs "Doggie!"

Anyway, because you are a toddler, things that might not make sense to others still make sense to you. Case in point: how you see me interact with animals. "Daddy talks and sings to me, and that makes me happy. Daddy talks and sings to Simon and Kitty, that must make them happy."

And maybe it does, but who knows? The thing is, I believe most people talk and sing to animals when they are children. It's just that some people allow that side of them to wither and fade as they age.

When I was younger, I read an interview—or maybe a book jacket, I don't remember—containing a quote by Berke Breathed: "People ask me why I talk to animals, and the only reason is because they appear to be listening."

I liked that, and believed it to be true. And I figured if he was comfortable talking to animals as an adult, why wouldn't I be?

When we are kids, the world is "normal." We don't judge, we accept. It's only as we age that certain things change inside us, usually "values" instilled in us from our parents or society. We still enjoy inspirational quotes—"Dance like there's nobody watching. Sing like there's nobody listening"—but rarely do we actually allow ourselves these moments. We're too embarrassed to sing or dance in public, too driven by ego to allow ourselves a happy moment within view of others.

Fortunately, or unfortunately, I have never been cursed with the "embarrassment gene." I will act silly in public without a care in the world. Mommy accepts this for the most part, but it sometimes causes her to blush. (Ask her about our very first date, and how I went flailing across a field joyfully chasing bunny rabbits.)

We used to have a cat called Panda. (Yes, Mommy and I tend to name our animals after other animals. Don't ask why that is; we have no answer or justification.) Multiple times a day, sometimes upwards of 50 times, I would find Panda looking at me, so I would say, "Oh, Panda, I've been meaning to talk to you about that. I think we should schedule some face time, so we can sit down and discuss our options in moving forward."

Read that again if you'd like, but it won't make any more sense the second time through.

For absolutely no reason, when I looked at Panda, I saw in her face a "business" sense. So that's how I responded, as a coworker in an office setting might.

I would give my little soliloquy, and then scratch her ears and move on with my day.

I have to believe she enjoyed our interactions, because late at night I would awake to find her atop my pillow, purring and licking my hair. Cats give baths in that fashion; it's a sign of affection. So whatever I was doing with Panda, she enjoyed, and enjoyed enough to treat me as if I were one of her kittens, acting maternal toward me nightly.

I don't seem to have a fixed set of phrases for either Kitty or Simon. I tend to use nonsensical songs with Kitty and mock anger/finger-wagging with Simon. Sometimes I wonder what runs through Kitty's little mind as he sits on the floor, cocking his head delicately to the side, staring at me as I do a little shuffle dance for him. Maybe he is thinking, "What an idiot," but most likely he is wondering if I am going to give him a treat when I am finished making an ass of myself.

Either way, you love petting both Kitty and Simon, and I'm sure that as you find your words you will love talking and singing to them, too.

My hope is you'll retain that joy as you grow, and remain someone who has no problem with treating animals as equal, not lesser, beings. Who we are as people is reflected in how we treat those who need our care and affection, not what we demand of them.

Love,
Dad

September 6, 2013

Dear Hillary,

There is a scene in the movie *A Fish Called Wanda* where John Cleese is wooing Jamie Lee Curtis. He comically dances around the first floor of a flat in London, doing a striptease and speaking Russian—foreign languages are a fetish for the Jamie Lee Curtis character—as she writhes in ecstasy on a rope in the loft. This event is not occurring in either of their homes; they are in the apartment of a colleague of Cleese, someone currently on vacation.

As he ballets, Cleese grows ever more nude (nudity being the whole point of a striptease), and as he achieves the apex of his routine—a twirl that casts aside the remaining strip of cloth, his underwear—he finds himself face-to-face with the family currently leasing the apartment from its owner. There is a pregnant pause as a mother and father eye the naked man before them in shock, then their young daughter arches her eyebrows, leans in slightly, and takes a curious gander at something she's seeing for the very first time. It is, needless to say, hilarious.

I describe the above because that look of wonder is one I am exceedingly familiar with, as I see it on your face daily.

You have inched past one-year of age and are now discovering the world around you with much in the way of seriously inquisitive intent. When you notice something new, you stop in your tracks and focus on the object or happening Gimlet-eyed, a placid demeanor across the rest of your face. Nothing around you exists; the only item left in your world being the focus of your attention. In that moment, you become as alluring as the hypno-toad. While you analyze whatever has captured your attention, I can do nothing but be absorbed by you. As you learn, I learn.

(Albeit different lessons.)

This is an admittedly odd turn of events, seeing that one year and one month ago I didn't even want to be a father. Hell, for forty-three years and eight months I abhorred the idea of parenthood. Little time thieves, babies were, robbing adults of their independence and God-given right to the freedom to do whatever they wanted, whenever they wanted. It is the argument of the childless, "I enjoy my freedom!"

Thing is, once you lose said "freedom," you don't miss it; you become too distracted by the wonder that is your offspring. Now, instead of wanting to spend a morning sipping hot cocoa at Panera Bread, I actively desire spending an entire day following you around on the floor as you scurry hither and dither, to and fro.

You and I play games, such as "All my clean diapers must be strewn about, now!" and "Why are these clothes on the drying rack?!" To outside eyes these competitions must look tiresome, but they're not. Not by a mile. Your joy of discovery is infectious, intoxicating, and probably many other "i" words I cannot think of. I simply do not care that you are destroying the laundry, because you are having oh-so-much fun doing so.

During our playtime, I test your problem-solving abilities. I create little obstacles, such as closing a drawer you are currently pulling items from. You suspend your actions—*This isn't what it was a second ago... something is different*—and then you grasp at the handle until your grip firms, and you finish with a tentative pull. *Is this going to work?*

I admit in full parental embarrassment there is no accurate way to describe the immense gratification I feel when you do something entirely mundane, such as the aforementioned task. I get to actively observe the gears grinding away inside your wee noggin, then witness as you decide on a course of action and follow through. Trial and error, trial and error. It is, to use an understated word, amazing.

Once the drawer has been re-opened, you push up on your tippy-toes and peer over the ledge, examining the treasure within. THERE they are, the diapers! One by one they are again plucked and plopped on the floor.

Occasionally this game involves my picking up every diaper and dropping it back into the drawer as they are being withdrawn. This causes you to look at me funny, the thought, "But I just took that out, Daddy" written across your face. You will giggle and remove the diaper once more, an action somewhat reminiscent of James Woods continually grabbing at Reese's Pieces: "Oh, piece of candy!"

A game I enjoy (that you might not) involves messing with your sense of spatial relations. You happen to delight in splashing your hands in our pet's drinking fountain. You like to pound your hands in the water, actually stand in the base of the fountain, and pretty much do all you can to create as large (and as wet) a mess as possible. While I generally do not mind your moments of joyful destruction, when it comes to the water fountain I do attempt to restrict your damaging ways.

When I catch you headed toward the water fountain, I lay on the floor, blocking your path. I am an easily overcome obstacle, however, so you begin an expedition up and over my body as if I am a mini-Mount Everest. As you are crawling over my torso, however, I spin 180 degrees, so that by the time you are completing your descent you are back where you started and not a hair closer to your destination. Safely on firm ground once again, you look up, pause, and turn around. For reasons that beguile you, the water fountain is behind you once again. So, you climb up on me, bee-lining it for your favorite toy... and once again I spin, and once again you are confounded.

If such actions sound tedious, they are. But they're not trying. They are time capsules, moments that won't be repeated as you grow. Understanding this, I treat each idiotic action as beloved.

Over the past year, I can count on a closed hand the number of times I've been frustrated with you. Yes, there have been moments of tired, but you are an infant (Mommy says you're actually a toddler, but I refuse to believe it). You cry, spit up, blow out of your diapers, and absolutely do not do what I want you to... but babies are, well, babies. So I deal with it.

You smile when we make eye contact, and I always smile in return. You are a sponge, absorbing everything around you in wonder. If I am tense, unloving, or volatile, you will absorb that, and it will be reflected as you develop into a person. At your very young age, I make it a point to reinforce that you are loved. Even when you are at your worst.

(Naturally, this will shift as you grow. A six-year-old being coddled as they throw a tantrum grows into a selfish twat of a person, but at one year I think a calm voice is more effective than a stern one.)

One year and one month ago I had resigned to becoming a father. Now, forgive the cliché, I rejoice in my role as "Da-da." It's what my wife wanted, and since I wanted her, "In for a penny, in for the rest of your long, miserable life." Or something like that, I forget the exact phrasing.

Still, everything I've said aside, I could never bring myself to recommend or push having kids on anyone.

All too often there seems to be an "I'm right/you're wrong" mentality in life. Coke vs. Pepsi, Connery vs. Moore/Dalton/Bronson/Craig, Original Trilogy vs. The-Worst-Three-Goddamn-Movies-Ever-Made, Relationship vs. Single, and of course, Parenthood vs. DINK. Just because I was tricked into the best thing that ever happened to me doesn't mean it's for everyone. I got lucky, and I know that. Thing is, I know people who passionately claim to dislike things they have never tried, and are emphatic in their opinion. They firmly believe they know what's right without ever having experienced whatever it is they are adamantly against. Parenthood is a bit too big a leap of faith to try simply for the sake of trying. Skydiving, watching football, exercising... these are little events you can try once and never do again should you not have fun, or if your parachute doesn't open.

But to enter the role of parent—that should give one pause. You have to go in eyes open and fully aware. I went in knowing that even if every little thing was anything but magic, I had committed myself to the experience. Therefore, when I see parents angry with their child for doing nothing more than acting like a child, it angers me. And, of course, makes me feel sorry for the child. Did the parent think the baby was a programmable robot with an off switch?

Either way, make sure to remind me of everything I've written when you are sixteen, pregnant, and just wrecked my car while getting your first DUI.

"How do you like being a dad now, smart guy?"

sigh

Love,
Dad

September 13, 2013

Dear Hillary,

I am in Chattanooga, Tennessee, and missing you dearly. Though I promise to never pressure you, I am already hoping that one day you will give me grandchildren. Or in the least, a grandchild.

A bit much, I realize, given that you are less than two years old. But as I watch you grow my thoughts turn to you someday feeling the joy in watching your own child develop.

When I am home, you and I share "Morning Snuggles," a routine performed first thing upon your waking. You begin to sniffle, so I enter your room. You see me and hold your arms up; *get me out of this crib!*

As I lift you, you lay your head on my shoulder and pop a thumb into your mouth. On occasion, you alternate your thumbs, left and right, left and right, seeing which one feels better that particular morning. Once or twice, you've actually put both thumbs in for a moment, only to become disoriented and remove one.

We walk to the kitchen, and more often than not I've already poured your milk into a coffee mug and placed it into the microwave. It gets nuked for 35 seconds, and then the milk is transferred into a sippy cup. You take the warmed liquid eagerly; it's probably your most favorite thing ever.

I carry you to the couch and lie down. You are in my left arm, and when I lay back you are nestled in tight, half on me, half in the crook of my arm.

Ninety percent of the time I pull the fleece blanket off the back of the couch and cover us with it... but this past week I felt a little warm and declined to complete the ritualistic action.

And you know what? You, dear one, noticed.

As you lay back, happily sipping away at your milk, you realized something was different. Your eyes wandered up and to the left, and once you spied the lime green fleece you released one hand from your precious, plastic chalice, and started flailing haphazardly at the blanket. Your limited dexterity made it near impossible to pull the thing down, but damn if it wasn't important to you to be covered by it.

So, up I reached and covered the two of us, and you immediately resumed two-handing your sippy cup. All was well, and everything was as it was supposed to be. Dad, milk, and blanket, check, check, check.

It was a very small moment, but any parent would understand why it meant so much to me. It was a call to understanding. You realized something was different, and though you are incapable of expressing verbally, "Dad, you forgot the blanket," you knew that's what had changed. And dammit, you wanted to make things right.

That's the thing with parenting. Going in, you might think the big moments are what's important—first step, first word, graduating high school/college—but you're wrong. Those things are nice, yes, but it's all the little things that explode your heart. The looks, glances, giggles... little nothings that mean oh-so-much. Little nothings like how you respond to stimulus with curiosity.

I made cookies this week, and given how you respond to the blender and bread maker, I actually wish I had clued Mommy in and we had recorded you. I was in the kitchen. You and Mommy were in the living room, and Mommy was actually trying to procure something from you. I don't remember exactly what you had in your hand, but it was something you weren't supposed to carry around.

Mommy was cajoling, and you were ignoring.

I called out, "Don't worry, I'll get her attention."

And I did.

I turned on the mixer, and it stopped you in your tracks.

Immediately you dropped whatever items you had and beelined it to the kitchen.

The look on your face was so full of determination; your eyes were set in focused concentration. "Something is happening in there! I can hear it! I must see what is going on!"

You raced to my side and grabbed hold of my legs, not so subtle in your "suggestion" I should pick you up. Mommy joined us, and she did all the Hilly-holding while I turned flour, sugar, butter, and eggs into the deliciousness known as "cookie dough," which oddly enough you rejected when presented with a sample.

(Mommy and I are currently looking into DNA testing to make sure you are ours. Given how we take to beaters after a batch is mixed, that you rejected such a sugary treat gives us pause.)

Anyway, though they may sound insignificant, these are the moments that make me so happy you are in my life.

And they are why I hope you choose to be a mother someday yourself. Not only so you can experience them, but also so I can selfishly enjoy the memories...

...and hopefully see you in your little ones.

Love,
Dad

September 20, 2013

Dear Hillary,

I am in Pittsburgh, Pennsylvania, and missing you dearly. Monday was a landmark morning for you. That day was the first time you woke up without Mommy or me in the house you knew as home. It was, in fact, the first time you woke up without one of us around, period.

I had been in Chattanooga the night before and was doing my best to return to your side. Driving all night, I would achieve my goal slightly after 8am. Mommy was flying back from New York, a destination she had left for early Sunday morning.

With both parents working, "Grandparents to the rescue!" was the battle cry that sounded forth. Mommy's mom, Grandma Diane, arrived on Saturday and watched over you during the daylight hours Sunday; Grandma Janet and Grandpa Joe—from my side of the family—had the scourge of bedtime to deal with.

Everyone says you were fine while the sun was shining; the problems started come evening. You went down for bed mostly OK, but slept very fitfully, waking numerous times beginning around 3am.

When you finally woke for good, you were sad. Not "howling your howl of disapproval sad," something that alerts the entire neighborhood you're truly upset, but more a "confused sad." It consisted of whimpering and silent crying, with tears running down your face yet lacking their usual vocal accompaniment.

I walked in the door that morning to hear my mother exclaim, "Look who's home!" The words were pronounced in the most upbeat manner possible, as Grandma was trying to excite you out of your sorrow. In the living room, Grandpa Joe was doing his best to comfort you, but his efforts were being met with resistance. You were tolerating, but not appreciating, your babysitters. The moment I entered your eyesight, you near-lunged out of Grandpa Joe's arms for me. I reached back, and you took hold of me as if I were the final lifeboat off the Titanic.

If I have been away for several days, upon my return our mini-Schnauzer Kitty is so excited to see me he begins crying. He cannot get close enough to me in those moments, trying ever-harder to press his body against mine, as if he is attempting to meld our two physical beings, that we never part ways again. That is what you attempted when I took hold of you that Monday morning; you not only wanted to be held by me, you wanted to be absorbed into me. You put your head on my shoulder and collapsed into me, your body releasing all the tension that had been building since the night before.

Your tears stopped immediately.

I told Grandma I needed to relieve myself—long drive and all—and wondered if she could hold you for just one more quick second.

That was not to be.

My mother held out her arms and smiled, "Want to come to Grandma?" but you enacted what Mommy and I call your "Death Grip." If we try and put you down when you want to be held, your little legs lock tightly around our waist and your fingers claw into our flesh, signifying a battle is about to take place. Now, with me home, you had your walking and talking security blanket in a deep embrace. The hell if you were giving up such valuable real estate for Grandma.

I ended up holding you with one hand while steadying my stream with the other.

Having driven all night and awake roughly twenty-five hours solid, I needed a nap. Considering you had slept poorly and were refusing to leave my side, I figured co-sleeping was in order.

We lay down on the master bed and within seconds you were laughing. Laughing and smiling. Your bad mood ended, you were your usual festive self.

You began standing and falling down on me, an action repeated a half-dozen times through a flurry of giggles. So happy were you to have your favorite toy once again. Dad accepts all abuse with a resigned smile, because that's what a parent does.

After a generous series of love-flops performed upon my battered body, you looked lovingly into my eyes, popped a thumb into your mouth, and proceeded to roll into the crook of my arm and fall asleep instantly. You were zonked before I had a chance to expire my own weary eyes. It was if you had been waiting for the opportunity to sleep without worry.

As I was still (somewhat) awake, I stared at you a bit, and wondered what it must have been like for you to not know where your mom and dad were. At thirteen-months old, you haven't found your words yet, and you don't understand ours fully. Yes, you know simple commands—"Arms up!" works fantastically when trying to dress you, and you turn when called because you know your name—but the complexities of language escape you. This means as many times as Mommy told you (through kisses of sorrow), "I'm only going away overnight. I'll be back tomorrow, and so will Daddy," no actual content got through. All you knew was, *Mom and Dad are gone, and people I'm only sort of familiar with are in the house.*

Thus, when bedtime came on Sunday night, and neither Mom nor Dad tucked you in, a mild form of anxious "trauma" set in. It kept you fitful and restless, awaking constantly and needing constant reassurance all was well—Grandma said you would sleep if a hand was rested upon you, but the instant that hand was removed the fussing would return.

Children forget all, so in the morning, though you would never use such a detailed analysis, the thought "Mom and Dad being gone was probably just a bad dream! It's a new day!" was probably running through your brain.

But once again, instead of us, the semi-familiar strangers were there. What happened next? Did a small form of panic set in? Did you wonder if you would ever see us again?

The reason these questions pounded inside my brain is while I knew Mommy and I had only been away one night, it made me wonder what becomes of children involved in custody battles, or those who lose their parents for other tragic reasons. When all you know or understand is the love of two people, and suddenly they go missing, what kind of permanent damage does that do to a child?

I eventually nodded off and slept peacefully. Because of your disrupted night, Grandma also decided to nap, while Grandpa Joe wandered off on a shopping run. This meant Mommy arrived home to a quiet house.

Investigating the silence, Mommy made her way back to our room and gingerly opened the door, waking me in the process. Seeing you sound asleep, still napping in the crook of my arm, Mommy smiled and motioned that she would back away. If there is one thing you never want to do in life, it's to wake a sleeping baby.

Unfortunately, the return of Mommy was too much for Kitty, who was as excited as all get-out to have both Mom *and* Dad back under the same roof. He bounded up onto the bed, excitedly pouncing on me as if to say, "Look who's home! Look who's home!"

Naturally, this woke you quite abruptly. Waking a baby from her slumber is usually an invitation to disaster, but not this time. No, not this time... This time you awoke to find not only was Daddy still there, but now Mommy was in the room, too!

The bliss that began radiating from you was palpable. Your two favorite people, right there in front of you again. Christmas morn in September. A memory of you I will forever cherish.

Love,
Dad

September 22, 2013

Dear Hillary,

Why do I love Mommy? There are many reasons, but one is because she's outside right now jumping on the neighbor's trampoline with their kids.

I don't know many adults who do that.

Love,
Dad

September 27, 2013

Dear Hillary,

In the early 1990s, while attending the Berklee College of Music, I had an outgoing message on my answering machine that people seemed to enjoy.

(Before voicemail, where people could leave messages directly on your phone, you needed to own a separate machine that would record incoming messages.)

If I didn't answer, you heard the following: "Hello, you have called Boston's hottest phone sex line. To hear the sounds of a man and woman making love, press one, now. To hear the sounds of two women making love, press two, now. To hear the sounds of a man making love to a small household appliance, press three, now."

Immediately after the final "now," I turned on a vacuum cleaner and shouted a scream of pain.

Following that came the beep.

On any given day I'd return home to have anywhere from five to fifteen hang-ups, because people would call just to listen to the message and/or to play it for their friends. New callers would be laughing as they tried to leave their message.

It was, as the kids say, "silly."

(Those kids and their wacky vernacular.)

After hearing it, a casual acquaintance once asked me, "Dude, what if your mom calls you?"

I thought the question odd, and answered, "Um, she hears the message."

It took me a while to realize what the person was really getting at, because I had to remember a simple truth: most people lie to their parents about who they are. Not because they're bad people, but because the parents usually appreciate and participate in the lie. It's a give and take; the parents conveniently forget what it's like to be a teenager or young adult, and the teenagers/young adults pretend they're the little angels their parents always wanted.

Self-inflicted adult amnesia is a harmful thing, as it allows for the creation of nonsense like The Parents Music Resource Center. The PMRC was a product of the 1980s, and was founded by Senate housewives with apparently enough time on their hands to legislate, but too little time to be decent mothers. (Wrap your head around that for a moment.) They railed against the moral depravity in music, using songs like *We're Not Gonna Take It* by Twisted Sister and *She Bop* by Cyndi Lauper as examples of all that was wrong in the world.

What these women (and anyone who listened to their harpy-like accusations) failed to realize is that in their time, Elvis, The Beatles, and Woodstock were cited as examples of societal demise. Such has it always been, and most likely always will be. Adults lob accusations and incriminations at the youth of the day, and whatever is popular at the moment is full of "moral depravity."

As time passes, the teenagers become adults, what they listened to becomes innocuous, and whatever the kids of the day are listening to is contributing to the downfall of society. I cite one of the songs I listed as a perfect example of this cycle, *We're Not Gonna Take It*. The song was on a list called "The Filthy Fifteen," songs the PMRC found to be the worst of the worst offenders when it came to a lack of decency.

The fifteen songs were brought before the United States Senate, and *We're Not Gonna Take It* was played as an example of violence in music. The women of the PMRC said children everywhere needed protection from its lyrics and the accompanying music video.

That was in 1985.

Since 1985, the song has been used in more commercials than I can count. Two of the most notable examples being Weight Watchers ("We're not gonna take being fat, ladies! Come on and lose those pounds!"), and a carpet store advertisement ("We're not gonna take high prices!"). So, a song that is currently on the Senate record as having been a sign of ethical decay among the youth of the 1980s, was in the 2000s used to sell carpet and inspire women to get into bikini-shape.

It is almost too absurd to wrap one's head around.

Sadly, paranoia crosses all borders when it flies under the banner of "Protect the Children!" In the world of television, both *The Simpsons* and *South Park* were, upon their introduction to the world, decried as horrible programs that would lead the youth of America astray. Today both are Emmy-winning and celebrated. Following them, a program called *Family Guy* was a target of the cultural police. Even though neither *The Simpsons* nor *South Park* caused society to collapse, the cry against *Family Guy* offered the same refrain, "What about the children?" Those who trade in fear are always unoriginal in their paranoia.

Overall, the problem has never been the content of art (be it music or television), but the inability of parents to trust their kids. When I was a teen, my parents knew every single thing I did. Maybe I told them because I was lashing out and looking for a reaction, maybe I just didn't care what their opinion was. Either way, they knew I listened to "satanic" heavy metal, when I smoked cigarettes, drank, or went through my chewing tobacco phase. And you know what? They were mostly bored by it all.

"Oh, you're chewing tobacco? Great. Not in the house, that's disgusting and dumb, but whatever."

"You're going out drinking? Is someone staying sober to drive? OK, then fine."

One night after breaking into my bedroom because I was too intoxicated to find my keys, my mom rolled her eyes and chastised me for not checking the front door; she had left it unlocked for me because she knew I'd be returning from an AC/DC concert in no condition to operate a simple deadbolt lock.

My parents had gone through the exact same teenage "rebellion," and knew it was something I would do regardless of whether or not they yelled about my actions. They also, I believe, understood that if they reacted wildly it would only encourage me. An angry "You're chewing tobacco?! How dare you? You're grounded!" would have only elicited a sullen response of continuing to partake in hobbies detrimental to my overall heath. As is, I probably stopped the nasty habit within a couple weeks, because it was disgusting. If I had taken it up to be a rebel, and the authorities weren't buying into my nonsense, what was the point in continuing?

I knew my home life was an anomaly. Few of my friends were open with their parents about drinking, smoking, or whatever other dumb things they were doing. Most played the stereotypical "preacher's daughter" game, where they were prim and proper at home, and wildcats when given freedom. To me, the lie looked like a house of cards, where the nuclear family would implode if anyone broke the fourth wall and everyone started being honest with one another.

As I age, I try to remember that certain aspects of society are not meant for me. I watched the MTV Movie Awards in 2011 and had no clue who half the people were. And that's OK, *I'm not supposed to.* America chugged on before I got here, and the world will exist just fine after I leave it; I don't have to relate to everyone or every trend while here. It's better to be happily ignorant than to be middle age and trying to fit in with what the kids are up to. If you want to see a walking, talking example of "pathetic," just find any woman above thirty with a Twilight obsession.

(I know that reference won't be relevant by the time you read this, but it makes me giggle to write it anyway.)

All that said, I do think that children who lie to their parents may be more ready for the "real world" than those who grew up honest, especially in today's day and age. In 2011, a company called "Social Intelligence" received approval from the Federal Trade Commission to act as a Big Brother watchful eye for businesses. How Social "Intelligence" works is: a potential employer receives an application, which it hands off to SI. The investigation company, in turn, does a thorough search of the Internet for any photos, Tweets, or blogs by the applicant and discovers what they were up to in their free time. It then presents the results to the hiring business, which can then make a "sound decision" about the person.

"Sound decision" is in quotes, because it seems nonsensical that the hiring process involves what a person does in the privacy of their own home. While I can see the benefits of this—avoiding people who post pictures of themselves giving a "thumbs up" at a Klan rally or blog their pedophiliac sexual fantasies would be a good thing—the problem seems to be that it is more often innocuous acts that raise red flags. I know a teacher who asked a friend to remove a Facebook picture because she had a beer in her hand at a picnic. The teacher wasn't drunk, acting wild, or doing anything inappropriate, just hanging out in a park having a beer. But the teacher was worried what the school board might think of such a photo, the influence it might have on the children (the children!). Because of fear, the picture was removed.

As a site called Facebook gained in popularity, it was celebrated as a means of sharing your personal fun. Within a few years it was used as an incrimination of character. Because of this ugly trend, people began deleting photos and leaving social networking sites behind; Facebook lost 6 million users in two months in 2011.

People used to lying might have no problem with Big Brother keeping tabs on them, but the practice irks me. Even though I work in the field of comedy, it's just like any other business; at the end of the day, there are both intelligent and unwise people out there. Some will get the difference between your stage act and who you are as a person, others will see a post on Facebook or a random Tweet and think, "Boy, I could never hire him... he's talking politics, and audiences don't always like that." This despite the fact politics isn't a part of my stage act. Sadly, people don't always have the capacity to understand separation between professional and personal.

Where will it end? With a society so afraid of making a youthful mistake that even young children act like Stepford Wives? With people wearing constant masks, trying to sugarcoat every aspect of their life so they look like the most beneficial member of society possible? Personally, I'd love for everyone to remember their own failings, that they may respect mistakes made by others. Unfortunately, self-reflection, memory of one's own mistakes, and empathy seem to be too difficult for many people to deal with, and the cycle of lies will continue from generation to generation, handed down like the genetics of eye color.

All I can do is be responsible for you. I will teach you that you can always be honest with me. No matter what your sense of humor, no matter what your experimentation with illicit substances, no matter what your youthful confusions are, I have to remember that I was there once and not judge you or your growing pains. I must remember what it is like to be young and confused. As you make bad decisions, I have to remember all the bad decisions I made and not judge you for yours. I will do my best to guide you, but part of living is making mistakes. I cannot prevent you from that, nor would I want to.

I must also remember that whatever art your generation takes an interest in is probably not meant for my sensibilities. There are certain things I won't tolerate—with all my might, I will prevent you from idolizing whoever the Kim Kardashian or Paris Hilton of your generation is—but when it comes to art? Unfortunately, I will have to back off. No matter how unlistenable and awful the music (Backstreet Boys), or how anti-intellectual and God-awful the writing (Twilight), if you like it, you're going to like it no matter what I say.

It will try my patience, but it's part of the package called "parenthood."

God help me.

Love,
Dad

October 4, 2013

Dear Hillary,

When Mommy and I moved into our house, we had the only dwelling on the block. It was a new development, and while there were several structures to the west, behind our home, all else surrounding us was open field. We used to be able to tell visitors "Turn into the subdivision, take the first left, then right at the T..." because after that, there was only us. Now we have to be more specific.

From the office (eventually your bedroom) window, you could see the sunrise over trees in the distance. Now, house after house blocks that view. Deer used to frolic everywhere, and once 200 Canadian geese took refuge in the field across the street from us. Because I am a bit of a stinker, I had Mommy grab my video camera and record as I snuck over to them, and then charged into the flock as quickly as possible. They squawked their disapproval loudly and for quite a while as they flew away. It was most amusing.

The arrival of more houses and the people that go with them is a mixed blessing; there is good and bad in everything. Because we have neighbors, you have friends. You might not realize this yet, but a couple families have a Goldilocks-range of girls for you to play with: a little older, a little younger, and the same age.

(Just right.)

When you play at their house, everything is new and exciting to you. They have a kitchen play set just like you have a kitchen play set, and to my untrained Daddy eyes they look oh-so-similar. You see the differences; their spatula is different from your spatula. Their pots and pans are different from your pots and pans. And variety, as the ever elusive "they" say, is the spice of life. Whenever you are bored with the walls of our home, having an escape is a wonderful option.

You—via Mommy and Daddy—have one friend that lives a little isolated from others. His parents own a plot of land that is beautiful, but lonely. To interact with a neighbor takes a five-minute drive, minimum. And that's assuming the closest neighbor has children he can play with. If not, then it's more like fifteen minutes in the car.

I can see both sides to each living situation; I wouldn't mind being a little more inaccessible, and I do miss the days when we were the only game on the block... but I also am happy you'll be well socialized as you grow. Not that your friend won't, but it will probably just be a little easier for you. Everywhere we look we see families, people like us just starting down the path of child rearing. Similar experiences create conversation, which creates community, which is oddly relaxing.

We have run into a plethora of neighbors who are more than generous with their yards and play areas. While out on a walk with Kitty, you spied a swing set in a backyard. Several adults and their respective children were gathered around it, and without a thought or care in the world you darted in its direction upon first sight. Mommy tried to call you back to us, but I told her to let you go. Anyone with children of their own would more than understand the excitement of a toddler.

Mommy and I followed you, and as you ignored everyone and made straight for the climbing wall the play set had, I stuck out my hand toward one of the adults. My assessment of their nature was correct, and they were more than welcoming and understanding.

"This was built for use," the man smiled. "You're welcome to use it anytime you want, whether you see us out here or not."

We all chatted a bit as you played, and I thought to myself how nice it was that Mommy and I were hearing that same invitation so often. Many of our neighbors had the same standing offer—our yard is your yard, come play whenever you want.

I don't know when exactly it was—the 1980s, maybe the 1990s—but there was a shift in the American psyche. When I was a child, "Play wherever you want" was a way of life. Somewhere along the way, unfortunately, a child was injured doing just that, and lawyers got involved. America went lawsuit crazy, with people trying to sue other people for whatever they could get. Personal responsibility and the idea "accidents happen" seemed to become a thing of the past.

As the paranoia of being sued took hold, invitations to use others' play sets faded. If a child got hurt falling off a slide in your backyard, their parents could sue you and take everything you had. You protected what you had by being less welcoming than you might have desired. I don't know when the re-emergence of kindness arose, possibly the late 2000s, but it is quite nice. Or maybe it's just a Midwest thing.

Not that the threat of a petty lawsuit has gone entirely away, and not that there still aren't less-than-kind people out there. No, unkind people never go away entirely, it's just that sometimes you don't notice them until something doesn't go their way. When they are upset, however? Oh, they let you know.

We have a couple bad eggs surrounding us, but that's to be expected. And the nice thing about life is, sometimes bad things do happen to bad people.

I shall explain.

As our neighborhood expanded, and new houses arose, Mommy and I discovered a tacit form of leeching taking place among neighbors. The first home up would put in a fence, and then the next resident would take advantage of that by hooking on to the existing fence when putting in their own. This saved the later-arriving people money.

When Aunt Shelby and Kevin moved in next door to us, we didn't have a fence, but Mommy wanted one. She asked them if they were going to erect a fence, and they affirmed it was part of their plan. Mommy thought about it a while, and then offered them a little money to defray the cost.

"We're going to be attaching to it," she explained. "So you're technically saving us money."

That opening gesture was not only the right thing to do, but it got things off on such a good first foot that today—obviously—you call Aunt Shelby "Aunt Shelby," even though she is not biologically related to you.

Not everyone is as nice as Mommy, however. A few months before you were born, one of the few remaining lots in our area was sold. As the builder started erecting the new house, he noticed something odd: the family next to the lot had accidentally placed their fence 12" across the property line, and were therefore encroaching into the new home's lot. The builder informed the future homeowner—we'll call him "Mr. Jones"—of this discovery.

For reasons I don't understand, this infuriated Mr. Jones, and he immediately contacted his soon-to-be neighbor—"Ms. Smith"—and cried, "Get your fence off my property!"

Embarrassed, Ms. Smith contacted the fence company and explained, "When you put the fence in, you put it in the wrong place."

The fence company, for reasons that defy all logic, said, "Well, it's going to cost you $900 for us to move it."

I shall repeat that. The fence company that put the fence in the *wrong* place the first time, said they were going to charge $900 to correct *their mistake*.

Ms. Smith was unhappy with this arrangement, and tried to work things out with Mr. Jones; "Does a foot really matter?" After all, it was an accident.

Mr. Jones was adamant: Move. The. Fence.

Through diligent searching, Ms. Smith found someone willing to move the fence for $400. Why she paid at all and didn't take the fence company to court is unknown to me, but that's not the point of this story. The point of the story is what Ms. Smith did, something that made me smile muchly. Mrs.

Smith not only moved the fence, she had it placed 10" inside *her own* property line.

This did not go unnoticed by Mr. Jones, who quickly contacted Ms. Smith, "Hey, you put your fence too far from the property line. The fence company I'm using needs your permission to attach to it."

Mrs. Smith politely declined Mr. Jones' request.

"It's going to cost me $900 to build a section of fence down the property line!!" he complained.

Ms. Smith explained, "Yes, that was the point."

Now there are two fences, side-by-side, separated by only a few inches. All because Mr. Jones couldn't allow for the loss of a little yard of his own due to a mistake.

Karma exists, the middle finger isn't just for driving, and people should always remember what a best-selling book says, *Don't Sweat the Small Stuff.*

The point to this silliness is: as you grow and develop, little one, I hope you learn from Mommy and how she makes excellent first impressions. You can create a lasting friendship or animosity from your very first interaction with someone. As a fictional knight once told a man named Indiana Jones, "Choose wisely."

Love,
Dad

October 11, 2013

Dear Hillary,

I am home this week, and thought I'd take a moment to tell you about Mommy's sister, your Aunt Kayla.

Last year, Aunt Kayla was at a grocery store she wouldn't have normally entered. For her city, it was the "ghetto location."

(The title amuses me, personally, because having lived in Milwaukee, Boston, and Los Angeles, I always smile when people in Iowa discuss their version of "the bad part of town." But, perception being subjective, given the relative city-surroundings, the particular grocery store in question was indeed "ghetto" when compared to its peers.)

It was nearing the Fourth of July and two of Aunt Kayla's children were insistent on celebrating the occasion with sparklers—Aunt Kayla's third child, being an infant, had no say in the matter. His vocal cords were limited in expression to "Waaah," which meant either "I'm hungry" or "I'm tired," depending on the tone.

Aunt Kayla had two options: quickly pull in to the store she happened to be closest to and buy the sulfur and charcoal sticks, or go out of her way to find a more "appropriate" site for the purchase. When three children are in tow, ease usually supersedes all other options, so the "ghetto location" became her go-to shopping experience for the day.

While wandering the store—why stop for just one item when you can get all of your shopping out of the way—Aunt Kayla noticed a downtrodden woman carrying an impossibly tiny baby in her arms. The woman looked, for lack of better description, like she belonged there. Where someone might see

Aunt Kayla and wonder, "What's she doing shopping here?" no second glance would be given to the woman wearing less-than-stellar apparel. She was pushing a shopping cart with one hand, holding her baby to her chest with the other.

Aunt Kayla's heart sank.

The child was the smallest baby Aunt Kayla had ever seen outside of a NICU; it couldn't have weighed more than five pounds at best.

There are bonds in life, such as that between members in the military or those that tie a family together, and one such connection exists between mothers. Creating and giving birth to life generates empathy among those who have shared the experience. Without being exactly able to put a finger on *why*—maybe it was the mother's shyness in body language, maybe it was the way she gingerly held her infant in one hand, having no carrier for the child—Aunt Kayla's emotions demanded she speak with the woman. There are moments in life where you know you have to act, or forever regret your decision should you not. Aunt Kayla decided to go with her gut instinct and approached the woman.

After a quick introduction and name exchange—Kayla/Carrie, Carrie/Kayla, nice to meet you—Aunt Kayla began lightly probing.

"If it's not too forward of me," Aunt Kayla began, "is this your first child?"

Carrie beamed; this was a topic that held much pride for her. "Yes, it is!"

"He's very small..." Aunt Kayla offered, pausing to allow Carrie to finish the thought.

"He's only twelve days old," Carrie explained. "He was very premature, but he's out of the hospital and healthy now."

She beamed again, proud of her child, the survivor.

Aunt Kayla did not ask for specifics regarding exactly *how* premature the child was. Instead, she began realizing why she had been drawn to Carrie; Aunt Kayla's soul was informing her why she felt the need to talk to a stranger in the grocery store.

"Well," Aunt Kayla offered, "as you can see, I have three kids, and am done having babies... I'm moving and I have a ton of baby stuff that I was going to put on Craigslist and sell... but I'd rather give them away to someone who needs them. Do you need anything I could just... give you?"

Aunt Kayla was slightly nervous, and hoped she was treading lightly enough upon the eggshells she was walking. To approach a complete stranger and offer charity could easily be deemed offensive.

"I do..." Carried answered, growing meek.

She looked embarrassed, and Aunt Kayla wondered if she had overstepped her bounds.

"I do..." Carrie repeated, "but I wouldn't have any way of getting anything from you. I don't have a car."

"That's no problem. I'm a teacher, and have my days free for the summer. I could bring everything to you."

"Oh..." Carrie said in an apologetic tone. "You don't want to be coming down in my neighborhood. You *shouldn't* be coming to my neighborhood..."

Aunt Kayla was determined, and pressed on; "It'll be fine. My husband will come with me."

There is a look you see in certain people, that of someone cautiously hopeful. They want to believe something good is happening to them, but have been let down so often in life uncertainty casts a long shadow across their thoughts.

Aunt Kayla received an address and a phone number. If she thought the grocery store was in a sketchy neighborhood, she knew she was about to see worse. A quick, mental calculation told her that if she knew her city, the address Carrie offered was a stone's throw from where a stabbing had just taken place. The stabbing had received widespread local news attention.

They parted ways, and though it is impossible to know what went through Carrie's mind, it would be safe to assume she believed she'd never see Aunt Kayla again. Blanche DuBois may have always depended on the kindness of strangers, but many people view the world through suspicious eyes and with guarded emotions.

Aunt Kayla returned to her home and, despite her promise to Carrie, did not wait for her husband to return before loading her car. Aunt Kayla was now on a mission. If seeing Carrie in the store with her infant had been emotionally jarring, knowing she owned no car, lived in a poor neighborhood, and had few (if any) of the necessary items to care for her child hurt Aunt Kayla's heart.

Aunt Kayla searched through plastic storage bins of baby clothes, pulling out a wide assortment the child could grow into. She grabbed a baby swing, and at the last moment, a $150 Pack-n-Play—a portable crib the child could to sleep in for years to come.

All three of your cousins in the car once again, Aunt Kayla drove to the address Carrie had provided and quickly discovered it was not the location of a house or apartment.

Carrie was living at a homeless shelter for women.

Though the surrounding neighborhood was a study in decay, the Women's Shelter looked clean, new, and secure. It was a beacon of hope amid the rotting facades and crumbling edifices.

Though it was the middle of the day, the front door was locked. Not surprising, given the neighborhood and the nature of the place. A two-way speaker system was present, so Aunt Kayla buzzed and was allowed into the lobby.

A woman greeted her—possibly expecting Aunt Kayla and her three children to be in need of assistance—when Aunt Kayla explained she had some items, "For Carrie."

"I cannot confirm whether or not Carrie is staying here," the woman intoned.

This was to be expected. Women-specific shelters are for those who have suffered the worst of abuse at the hands of those who are supposed to love and protect them. When boyfriends, husbands, or fathers have problems with anger, alcohol, or both, the shelter offers a harbor from the tempest known as domestic abuse. Often times these pathetic men are possessive as well as violent, and do anything they can to keep women under their control. When one escapes the bonds of abuse, the men hunt them down, enlisting the help of family or friends to aid in their cause.

Aunt Kayla, understanding the situation Carrie might be in, asked if she could leave everything in the lobby, allowing Carrie to retrieve the items later.

The woman softened, and said that would be fine.

"By the way," Aunt Kayla began. "I have a Pack-n-Play in the car. Does the baby need one here or..."

Aunt Kayla trailed off, allowing the woman to pick up the slack.

"Here, the baby has a place to sleep. But if Carrie leaves, the baby will not have a crib or bassinet, no."

Aunt Kayla nodded. That meant Carrie would be co-sleeping with her child, which could be a dicey proposition.

"I'll be right back," Aunt Kayla said, leaving with her children for the car.

When she returned Carrie was waiting for her, surprised and pleased to see the woman who had offered her assistance in the grocery store.

After giving Carrie everything from her car, Aunt Kayla made a few inquires with the headmistress; she still had plenty she could donate, would the shelter take the items?

"You can give to specific people," it was explained, "but we don't take donations outright."

A center existed next door, however, that was affiliated with the shelter. Women seeking protection were allowed to "shop" there for free. If Aunt Kayla donated anything, women in need could pick it up at no cost.

Perfect. Now Aunt Kayla had an outlet for everything her children had outgrown.

Aunt Kayla went home, and a little while later texted Carrie, asking if, even though she had no use for a car seat per sé, would she be interested in one as a hand-held carrier?

Carrie texted back that she already found one, and thanked her.

And then Carrie sent one more note. Her son was happily sleeping in the swing Aunt Kayla had given her. Gently rocking back and forth, knowing only the love of his mother and none of the awful that surrounded his life at the moment.

A smile crossed Aunt Kayla's face, and her eyes watered just a tinge.

Hope.

The next time you see Aunt Kayla after reading this? Maybe give her an extra hug.

When she asks, "What was that for?" answer, "Just because."

Love,
Dad

October 15, 2013

Dear Hillary,

You and I bumped into my friend Richard at the grocery store today. Richard is an African-American fellow, which isn't overly important other than it plays into what I did at the checkout.

We walked around the store visiting, and then eventually made our way to the registers. I had you in one arm, and was emptying our cart as Richard started looking over junk food muffins.

I started giving him flack regarding the fat and sugar content, picking on him regarding his diet and how he should eat healthier. He returned my volley, and our fake bickering caused him, the checkout girl, and the bag boy to enter into a fit of giggling.

Noting this, I asked the clerk in complete seriousness, "Is it obvious we're an interracial homosexual couple?"

Richard kept laughing; the checkers did not.

Small-town folk are very easy to confuse. Always remember that, and use it to your advantage when attempting to amuse yourself.

Love,
Dad

October 18, 2013

Dear Hillary,

I am in Chicago, Illinois, and missing you dearly. I enjoy Chicago, if only because it is the setting of some of my favorite movies. *The Blues Brothers*, for example. It was the first R-rated movie I saw, and since I have played snippets of it for you—the musical numbers—already, it will be the first one you'll see, too. More importantly, Chicago was the setting for many a John Hughes movie.

John Hughes was a writer/director who was of major importance to anyone coming of age in the 1980s. When I introduce his movies to you, my hope is the themes will be timeless enough to translate to the 2020s and be of meaning to you. I also hope that watching and re-watching them will remind me how confusing it is to be a teenager, and allow me to relate better to the emotions you will go through as you grow.

(Yes, I'm re-treading some ground I covered a few weeks back, but I feel there's more to say on the subject. Forgive my repetition.)

One constant in many John Hughes movies is the out-of-touch parent or adult. Authority figures are often presented as being clueless to the world around them, either blissfully unaware of what it's like to be a teenager or outright hostile towards the situation. Think of Ferris Bueller's cheerful yet dim parents. Think of the scolding or neglectful parents at the outset of *The Breakfast Club*, or the principal in the same movie.

Watching John Hughes films, I always wondered, "At what point does someone go from being an emotional, confused, and hormonal teen to an apathetic, boring adult with no memory of their own past?" Now that I am (technically) an adult I see it happening among some of my peers, but am still confused as to what process they go through that allows it to occur.

I received a text from a friend, "I'm looking for a place to unload my used heavy metal albums."

I was a little confused, and responded, "Unload? Your kids get those."

My friend not only has kids, but sons. As I have boy parts between my legs and lived a boy's life, I was fairly certain that *they* of all people would be especially interested in the albums he was trying to do away with.

I think my friend agreed with that scenario, because his response was, "You want them for *your* kid? Slayer, Overkill, Venom... lots of offensive and satanic stuff."

That pretty much ended it for me. I stared at my phone in utter confusion, my head tilted like a dog.

In high school, this was the music my friend and I listened to. It got us through the silly moments of teen angst every youth feels at some point or another. We attended numerous Slayer concerts—saw upside down crosses and pentagrams aplenty—and turned out just fine. Neither of us ever worshipped the devil and the music didn't cause us to fail as adults; my friend exists in an upper middle class world, owns his own home, has a wife and (obviously) kids... So why did he suddenly feel the need to protect his kids from music that did no damage to him?

Adult self-created amnesia bothers me, and I'm offended it's still so prevalent. You would think teenagers would become adults with empathy and understanding for what it's like to be a young adult, but that rarely happens. Instead, adults look at the youth of the day and wonder why they're so surly.

I remember when director Steven Spielberg revamped his biggest movie, *E.T.*, editing it to be more politically correct and changing the word "terrorist" to "hippie" and digitally removing shotguns and replacing them with walkie-talkies. I also think of George Lucas feeling remorseful he made Han

Solo so very violent and going back and having Greedo shoot first.

Their press releases said silly things, like "It's a different world we live in today" and other such meaningless noise; Spielberg believed that a child hearing the word "terrorist" post-9/11 would curl into the fetal position and weep for days on end, unable to leave the house and (possibly) support his newer movies like *War Horse* or *Tintin*.

Personally, and I could be wrong, but I believe these are the situations that create disenfranchised, angry teens. It's because we lie to and coddle them as children that when they get old enough to realize they've been spoon-fed a pile of nonsense, they lash out in response. I cite Jenna and Barbara Bush as examples.

Right before Election 2000, it was uncovered that G.W. Bush had a drinking and driving violation in his past. When asked about it, he said he "didn't want his kids to see their father in such a poor light." Instead of being honest with his family, he tried to place himself on a pedestal to be idolized and emulated. Unfortunately, the example he presented was a lie, and the Bush twins were—because they weren't exposed to honesty involving their father's imbibing—notorious party girls themselves. Tales of the Secret Service monitoring their drinking and pot-smoking ways were legendary during his presidency. If leading by example was supposed to work, it damn well didn't.

But here's the thing: after getting it out of their system, the twins both turned out OK. They became mature women, Barbara working with AIDS patients in Africa and for LBGT equality in New York, and Jenna spending time with UNICEF. Yes, they had powerful family connections handing them whatever they needed, but the point is they both turned out fine, even after *OMG, drinking* (a lot) in their early twenties.

The attempt at a point rolling around my empty head is that life is about mistakes. You make them, and then learn from them.

If you want to lead by example, you must do so with

unmasked honesty: "This is my life, these are the places I stumbled, and these are the consequences I faced. If you want, I can help you avoid certain pitfalls, but I'll be here with a non-judgmental helping hand should you become mired along the way."

This brings me full circle to my friend. If people attempt to cover their "actual" mistakes from family, what chance do kids have when non-mistakes (like musical choices) are hidden away? The idea "This was OK for me, but I must protect my children from it" probably causes a larger disconnect between child and parent than anything else. Kids are not stupid; they can sense a cover up or half-truth. They may not be able to articulate their feelings well, but they do know sullen resentment, and they damn well know how to carry a chip on their shoulder.

As I continually walk my own path of parenthood with you, my hope is to remain as indifferent to the stupidity of my own youth as I always have. John Hughes remembered what it was like to be a confused teenager, and I appreciated the help his movies offered me when navigating the minefield of teen life. As I look back from this vantage point, I realize that anything I did—mistakes and all—got me here. I'm happily married, a homeowner, someone with a kitty and one doggy (named Kitty)... and guess what? I still own the Slayer records from my youth. They're in a milk crate in the basement, and when you are old enough? Oh, I am absolutely going to introduce you to them. And you will scrunch up your face and say, "Daddy, that's awful."

But it will always be better than Justin Bieber, or whatever feminine boy is being pushed on tween girls in the future.

Oh, yes indeed it will.

Love,
Dad

October 25, 2013

Dear Hillary,

At 6½ weeks old, you made the big-step transfer from a bassinet in the master bedroom to the crib in your own nursery. Mommy said the move needed to be made, but I was having none of it. I asked if one of us should sleep in the spare bed we put in the nursery, just for the first few, say, seventy-some nights. Mommy thought me silly and started climbing into our bed, and was genuinely surprised when I headed over to the tiny, nursery-room bed.

I cannot explain it, but I just *had* to be near you, my little button of a baby. For all nine months of Mommy's pregnancy, people informed me of every awfulness and joy that would arrive with the birth. From poopy diapers and sleepless nights to smiles and limitless love, I thought everything under the sun had been covered. I was wrong. One important emotion had gone unexplained: *fear.* No one told me about the crippling fear that overcomes you randomly when you aren't near your child.

For almost every year of my life I'd heard mention of a parent checking on their child as it slept. I understood the concept, but couldn't grasp the importance.

"OK," I would think. "So, you check on your kid. Big whoop."

Big whoop, indeed.

The cliché says "Silence is golden," but not when a baby is sleeping. The little buggers are so motionless, that sometimes staring isn't enough; you have to actually place a hand on them to make sure they are breathing. The reality of "checking on your baby" slammed home to me immediately upon bringing you home.

At the hospital, I woke a couple times during the night, but that was different. We were, as stated, in a hospital. Should anything be abnormal, a crack team of nurses and doctors were seconds away, 24/7.

Being under our own roof, however, felt very, very alone. Isolated from help and knowledge.

Here we were, two first-time parents, people who nine months earlier could have done whatever we wanted, whenever we wanted, being told, "This little mewling creature is now 100% dependent upon you." Off they sent us into the abyss with a slap on the back and a "Good luck!"

Should anyone allow it, the abject terror of the weight of that statement, the reality/magnitude of what was happening, could be crippling.

This all stemmed from the very natural fear of the unknown. In "Baby Safety" classes, SIDS was mentioned in serious tones: "No one knows exactly why some babies die in their sleep, but it happens, so be vigilant!" It was fine to hear and attempt to absorb when you were still baking in the oven of Mommy's belly, but the weight of it all wasn't fully on my shoulders until after holding you in my arms. The knowledge that such a little, fragile being was entirely dependent on me for survival... The pressure could have been overwhelming, if I allowed it to be. The idea something unexpected might happen to you before the morning sun was, and still is, the most panic-inducing thought I've ever had.

During your stay in our room, I would lie awake, listening to your little "pig noises" as you snorted and shuffled in your sleep. This kept me calm. Wide awake, but calm. When you finally settled into a deep sleep, I would stare at the ceiling, near-paralyzed by the silence. My panic forced me to get up and check on you multiple times in a row. Once, I literally checked to make sure you were breathing, started to get back into bed, and immediately got back up to double- and triple-check, *just to be sure.* My butt touched down on the mattress, and before I could even swing my legs into a sleeping position, the thought, "Better check again" ran through my mind. The rational, logical side of my mind may have whispered, "It's been three seconds since you checked. You walked five feet from the bassinet to the bed, nothing has happened in those three seconds," but the emotional side of me was shouting, "GO CHECK! JUST IN CASE! WHAT IF THIS IS THE MOMENT SHE NEEDS YOU TO PICK HER UP AND HOLD HER?!"

Only after sharing this midnight panic with other parents did the normalcy of my reaction become clear. Every new parent is afraid when their child goes silent, and every new parent checks on their baby multiple times.

There are negative emotions in life such as anger, sorrow, and fear, but the most awful is helplessness, the idea something that could happen outside your ability to provide assistance. So when you moved from our room to your crib that first night, I was uncomfortable, and needed to be near your side. Logically, I knew that were something to happen while I slept, it wouldn't make a damn bit of difference if I were inches or miles from you. But the comfort of closeness was important to me; I wanted to *feel* that my location mattered.

That first night, you had gas. Truck-driver-after-a-Mexican-dinner gas. You were having problems sleeping, and were doing little but fussing and becoming red-faced as you scrunched up your furrowed brow and pushed the farts out. Had I been in my own room, I might not have heard you squeaking and shuffling, but as I was next to you it was all too noisy to sleep. Instead of trying, I got up and bounced you. I discovered that when laid down, you would cough, spit, and begin to cry. If I placed you on my chest and laid down myself, with you atop me, it was a different story. When you squirmed, I could rub your back, causing you to burp, fart, and return to peaceful slumber. Had I not been there, I'm sure you could have worked it out on your own, crying until you burped and farted, but why would I want to subject you to that? That night I was awake with you from 1:30am to 6:30am, and this was after having gone to bed only around midnight. But, it's what I signed up for. If exhaustion was the sacrifice I had to make so you could sleep better, it was worth it. I cannot explain why, but it made internal sense.

Not a single person said, "Parenting is easy." In fact, everyone said the exact opposite.

The best knowledge Mommy and I received during the first few months of your life is that all the little squeaks and bursts you made in your sleep were natural. "Babies transition noisily between sleep stages, and are confused by the world they've been thrust into," we were told. "If she really wants your attention, you'll know. Until then, if she's silent, be happy."

Sage words, indeed. But as I wrote this, I still checked on you several times.

How could I not?

You're my little Peanut.

And I love you.

Dad

November 1, 2013

Dear Hillary,

I am in Indianapolis, Indiana, and missing you dearly. Because of my job—comedian—I drive a lot. Last year, I put over 12,000 miles on my car in a four-month period. Sometimes I get two oil changes in one month.

On occasion, my travels take me through Madison, Wisconsin, where the woman you call "Grandma" and I call "Mother"—said in a non-Norman Bates way—lives. When Mommy is interested in freedom for her weekend, or will be traveling herself, or whenever the stars align and I can rid her of our doggy for a few days, I up and away with him to Madison. I drop him off at Grandma's house—she calls him her "Grandpuppy"—and then I head to my gig.

It's about three hours, door-to-door, from our home to hers, and for that whole while, Kitty refuses to leave my lap. There is always a perfectly good, empty passenger seat for him to curl up on, but he spends approximately 90 minutes of the ride sitting and looking around at the scenery we are zooming through, and 90 minutes sprawled out and sleeping. All on my lap; never anywhere else in the car.

I'm not sure if it comes from anxiety or just an internal tic, but at some point in the drive he usually decides it's time to lick something obsessively. Sometimes it's his paw, but more often than not it's the seat next to us or a spot on my jeans. Lydia and I try to discourage the paw-licking, but according to most websites (and our vet), if it doesn't go on for hours and hours, it does no harm and probably sets his mind at ease. That being the case, we usually allow the cushion or knee to be turned into a slobbery spot we then have to deal with.

Oh, the joys of pet ownership.

On a recent drive, Kitty did something a little different from his norm. He was sitting up on my lap, looking around, looking at me, and looking around some more, when a spot on my leg at about mid-thigh captured his attention. The licking began, and I rolled my eyes and ignored it. Five minutes later, he stood up, stretched, spun, decided that my other leg had a spot on the jeans that needed cleaned, and away he went.

Again I ignored.

This continued for two more cycles, with him licking, spinning, and licking again... until I noticed a discolored dot in area in which he had just been parked. The more I paid attention, the more I realized that every time he stood and spun his 180 to the other direction, he left behind a blotch. This blotch, then, is what he was discovering and attacking with his tongue.

While I may not be a Sherlock Holmes by any measure of the imagination, I am bright enough to figure out certain things in life. My simple understandings include: never vote for a candidate the Tea Party supports, 2 + 2 = 4, and cause and effect is a reality. I soon comprehended quite easily that every time my doggy-named-Kitty sat, his little starfish was leaving behind a stain, one he would then see (or smell) when re-positioning himself. Upon each discovery, he would look at me apologetically—"Oh, hey, let me take care of that for you"—and do his best to remove it as if his tongue were a bottle of Tide.

Once I discovered the pattern, I decided to put an end to the nonsense and opened my glove box. Like many an American, I keep a handy supply of napkins in there. With one in hand, as the dog licked, I lifted him to a standing position. Then, as he stood and took care of a stain, I did my best to prevent another. While his anus was in the air and not rested upon my thigh, I pressed a napkin to said pucker and held it for a few moments. When I pulled it away, aye, it was indeed wet. So I folded it over and on I drove, 70 mph down a Wisconsin highway, one hand on the wheel, one hand pressed against my puppy's pooper.

It took about four folds for the napkin to come away dry.

Good times.

Well.

I hope you have enjoyed this tale involving your favorite playmate. You love Kitty, and in fact your first (and favorite) word was "Doggie!" For a span of several months, everything was "Doggie!" You'd look at breakfast and proclaim, "Doggie!" You'd look at a chair and shout, "Doggie!"

But as much as you got many things called "Doggie!" wrong, you grew especially animated and happy when actually pointing and yelling "Doggie!" at Kitty, your actual puppy-brother.

You may have been describing a chair as "Doggie!," but you *knew* Kitty was indeed "Doggie!"

And he always made you smile.

Love,
Dad

November 8, 2013

Dear Hillary,

"Hey, are you OK?"

I get asked the question more often than I think I should, and it used to bother me.

The question was from a hostess at a show going back many years now. She wasn't too wrong in wondering; my performances in the small Texas town had been fine, but not fantastic. The problem was, I was following a local Hispanic comic who was doing local references and Hispanic humor to 85% Hispanic audiences. Guess what the masses thought of a white guy from Iowa after sitting through "Taco Bell makes you poop!" and "Drinking, woooooo!" humor?

While he was on stage, I would stroll around the restaurant, re-arranging my set repeatedly to try and overcome the challenge of getting people to engage their brains and think a little after hearing lowbrow material they could relate to. That's when the hostess interjected.

So while I wasn't moody, I was of blank expression, which has gotten me sideways wonderings more often than not.

The thing is, my eyes droop. At the outer edges, they slope downward rather than resting centered on my face. My mouth has small, south curves at its sides, suggesting a slight frown. It's not exactly a scowl, but a placid expression resting on my face often emits a lack of approachability.

My hair is dark, which lends itself to a more forlorn appearance than that of a sunny blond, and between my eyebrows rest two small crests that give the impression I am of furrowed brow, even when not.

Sadly, if actually relaxed while reading, writing, or wandering around a comedy club, I still project agitation or sorrow. In reality, my mind is probably quite serene, and most likely I am singing an internal song about our doggy, Kitty. You know the type, because I sing them to you constantly.

Maybe my mood has been questioned my whole life, but I remember the interest (or concern) growing in frequency around college. Had I been a smarter, more self-aware person back then, I might have realized that some of the women asking me if I was "all right" were opening a door for conversation. They thought I was a brooding loner, and they were probably the type of woman attracted to silly misanthropes.

Understanding this, I will absolutely be raising you to have more self-esteem than any one of them, dear one.

Anyway, as I am continually asked if I am unhappy, I've always wondered what my aura looks like, or if it has changed over the years. Is there an aura you are born with, or one you become? Does your projection change with mood, or is it a constant, something showing your inner you through whatever you are experiencing? I mean, I've been both insanely joyous and abjectly unhappy at different points in my life. Did my aura look the same on both ends of the pendulum's arc?

Even though I am quite happy now that you're in my life, I'm still sometimes asked if I'm upset.

At the comedy club in Texas, there may have been something to the hostess' words, but more often than not, if you wonder if I'm upset, you needn't worry. All is well in my world, even if my expression doesn't show it.

Now I consciously smile more.

In part because I understand the contours of my face, but mostly because of you, dear one. I make sure I am always smiling at you.

Whenever you steal a sideways glance at me, to look to see where I am or if I'm wasting time on my phone when I should be paying attention to you, I make sure I am smiling.

Right or wrong, I believe atmosphere influences development. If you see me bored, indifferent, or agitated, you will internalize that, and probably believe in some part that it is your doing. Which would be completely untrue. Nothing you do makes me bored, indifferent, or agitated. I also believe the reverse is true, that if you see me happy, then you will believe you make me happy.

But in that case, you will be right, because you do make me happy. Just your existence makes me smile. And I figure it is important to let you know that.

The small-town Texas audiences, however, did upset me, which showed on my already questionable face. To win them over I had to sell my soul and stoop to lowest common denominator jokes. Sometimes people just aren't capable of enjoying anything above their groin.

Sad, but unfortunately part of my job description.

It is, dear one, what it is.

Love,
Dad

November 15, 2013

Dear Hillary,

I am in Moorhead, Minnesota, and missing you dearly. On Monday, January 9th, 2012, I saw my first ultrasound. Not just my first ultrasound, but the heartbeat of my very own first baby-to-be, you. The heartbeat was a little white mass, floating inside a gray mass, floating inside a black mass, throbbing furiously on a screen. Though the ultrasound tech pointed out a supposed head and limb, I couldn't make out anything; it all looked like a blob to me. But the white, pulsating mass inside? That eclipsed all else. It was distinguishable to an eye of any caliber.

I started fielding texts and emails alternately telling me how excited I must be and asking how I feel. Which I appreciated; the support of friends was overwhelming and wonderful. The thing is, I was somewhat emotionally neutral during most of Mommy's pregnancy.

In his book *Home Game: An Accidental Guide to Fatherhood*, author Michael Lewis discussed something I talk about on stage, the idea there is no such thing as "paternal instinct." It is easier for a woman to have an immediate connection to a baby, because it is literally a part of them. The child has gestated within their body, creating sensations no male could ever fully understand. Men, on the other hand, have to form a bond with the child, and that union can take months to develop.

Watching your heartbeat had one thought flash across my mind—"*What will you be, little pea?*" It was an all-encompassing query as to whether you would be a boy or girl, colicky or quiet, athletic or musical, and every other question under the sun regarding impending parenthood.

After that instant? Well, it's not that I felt nothing, it's that seeing the heartbeat wasn't an abrupt, life-altering event. I didn't feel the need to suddenly paint ducks on a bedroom wall, research high-chair safety ratings on the interwebs, or call everyone I knew and shout joy at them. I had a neat little moment that made me smile, and then went on with my day.

I don't believe I was in denial about anything, nor do I think I was being emotionally distant. I knew you were on the way, that preparations were being made, and that my life was about to ~~come to an end~~ change. It's just that there is a vast difference between knowing and feeling. I *understood* change was afoot, but I *felt* like I always had for the most part.

And therein lies the rub. You see, this is nothing I ever actively pursued; fatherhood was something agreed to when I married Mommy. I half-jokingly say we arrived at it through lies and manipulation by her, but Mommy doesn't call what happened lying. She states, "My feelings changed."

When we started dating, there eventually came that point where conversation became a little more serious and we examined how devoted to the relationship we were going to be. The issue of children came up, and I stated my absolute disinterest in the little parasites. Fortunately, Mommy agreed. Kids were not on her agenda.

But when we got to that next stage of the relationship, where we had invested in one another and deep roots had anchored, something had shifted. As we spoke again about the future—the probability of wearing rings upon fingers and spending a lifetime together—a child became what is known as a "deal breaker." She wanted one, and it was non-negotiable.

So what had changed?

Mommy says that when we met, she had never been in a stable relationship, and therefore never found herself in a situation where she'd want to raise a family. It is against all logic and just dumb effing luck that somehow I opened her eyes to the joys of solid emotional footing and an arena in which a baby would make sense.

(To quote Archer, "Hooray.")

By this point I was in over my head, and my choices were: attempt to find someone as perfect for me as Mommy (not gonna happen), or go back on everything I had stood for as a single man and actually have a child.

There were, to a point, negotiations. Mommy wanted two kids, I wanted zero. We "compromised" on one. Which in essence means she won. While one is less than two, when it comes to babies one is a billion more than zero.

Before you were born, I viewed parenting as "Giving up everything you live for in order to cater to the whims of something that in the beginning only exists to cry and poop, and then later wants to wreck your car and spend your money." But as soon as Mommy became pregnant with you, I started to change in little ways I hadn't expected. I started having irrationally silly and stupid thoughts rattle around my noggin. For example, Mommy and I went to the gym, and an idiotic-as-can-be paranoia kicked in. I didn't want her doing any sit-ups and smooshing you in the process.

Again, the difference was between *knowing,* and *feeling.* Intellectually, I am of sound mind and knew a sit-up wasn't going to cause a miscarriage. Emotionally, I was suddenly as irrational as a member of the Teabag Party, my saving grace being I was at least aware I was being stupid.

If I was being stupid, however, Mommy went near-insane. Mommy joyfully approached being pregnant to the point of obsession. She constantly checked websites to determine what she was supposed to feel or do at any moment during the day, and with her iPhone discovered "There's an app for that." And by "that" I mean "*everything.*"

If there was a symptom of pregnancy, Lydia wanted to make sure she was experiencing it. While at the hospital, a nurse casually mentioned Mommy might be more thirsty than normal, to which Mommy immediately responded, "You know, I *have* been thirstier lately. May I have some water?" Before that instant, she had never mentioned being parched; the nurse made it OK for her to feel that way. I swear, had Mommy read, "During pregnancy, it is sometimes possible to become ambidextrous," she would have attempted to write using her left hand. Mommy, as you will learn, is a big fan of validation.

Where our emotional paths converged was in crossed fingers. Given what it took to get to the first ultrasound, another setback would be frustrating beyond words. Two years of infertility treatments, a failed in vitro attempt, low HGC numbers for the first few tests and a nurse who casually emailed, "This one probably won't take" regarding you... we were ready to stop walking on eggshells and move forward full force. We crossed our fingers and hoped you would continue to be compared to ever-growing sizes of fruit—apple seed, pea, blueberry, raspberry, grape, orange, grapefruit, and so on.

(I'm not sure why a fetus is size-compared to food, much less fruit. Maybe it's because both grow from seeds and there's a food/belly relation to where the baby is growing?)

We monitored the present, and kept a cautious eye on the future. Because from that point forward, all we had were questions.

Or, in reality, one question. *What will you be, little pea?*

The answer? A bundle of joy better than anything we could have ever imagined, you.

Everything I once thought about child rearing has been thrown out the window, because you are anything but a burden. You, my dear, are an externalized version of my heart. And I am absolutely happy Mommy made me experience fatherhood.

Love,
Dad

November 23, 2013

Dear Hillary,

I am in Chicago, Illinois, and missing you dearly. This past week contained quite a few wonderful moments, which you didn't notice as you are a delightfully unaware fifteen-month-old.

Monday was my birthday, and it's the first time I've ever felt old. My whole life I'd looked at being an adult as something more interesting than being a teenager or dumb punk in my twenties, but now reality is sinking in. I lament the thought I had you too late in life, and that had you been born when I was thirty I'd have another whole decade to spend with you.

I worry about being an "old dad," someone you will be embarrassed by in your teen years. I know kids are naturally embarrassed by their parents, but I'm talking about the "Is that your grandpa?" situation.

Well.

Also on Monday, I posted a meme of a joke of mine online. It soon went viral, with people sharing it around the world. It hit the front page of two very popular websites—reddit and The Chive—and within a day several hundred thousand people had viewed it.

That was pretty nifty.

Because of this success, I posted a video of the joke online Tuesday night. When I woke up Wednesday morning, the video had received more views by far than most of my offerings do. I soon found out that some unknown kind person posted it on Huffington Post, which is a goulash of entertainment and news. 17,000 people watched me (and hopefully giggled) within 24 hours.

Finally in the Wednesday world of Dad's career: my latest CD was approved to stream on a service called Pandora. With millions of subscribers, this will hopefully expose my comedy to many new people.

All this attention could be nice for my career; whether or not the Comedy Gods take notice remains to be seen.

I remain ever hopeful.

Thursday follows Wednesday, and Thursday, November 21st may become a milestone... or perhaps it will fade into obscurity. Mom and I will soon learn how the day will be defined.

On Thursday, Mom and I went to the hospital and she had a microscopic embryo implanted in her uterus. In vitro fertilization, it's called, and it's how we were able to bring you into our life. The procedure is too much to go into at the moment, but suffice to say we are trying to bring another child into the family.

You, dear one, were such a wonderful addition that we are trying to give you a brother or sister you can befriend and mentor. Someone you can grow up with, someone you can play with night and day, a secret-keeper, someone you will watch learn to crawl and walk, just like your Mom and I watched you learn to crawl and walk.

From the moment you were born, your Mom has been resolute in the concept that when she and I are gone you will need someone to share memories with. Personal memories, like she shares with her sisters. Someone you can always call upon to wax philosophic about childhood.

We named the embryo Squeak, just as we named you Peanut, because Mom feels it's good luck to add a little flavor and personality to the proceedings. When Squeak was injected into what is (hopefully) a nice warm home in Mommy, a small amount of air was released. This air made the embryo appear white on the ultrasound monitor. Amidst the gray and black hues on the screen, the embryo looked like a star in the twilighted sky, a tiny white dot living inside your mother.

You, Hilly, were once a tiny white dot living inside your mother, and look how perfect you turned out.

Because of all the struggles to get pregnant with you, all of our friends and family were told the instant you were placed into Mommy. After two years of struggling with infertility issues, everyone was with us every step of the process used to create your life.

But we're keeping Squeak a secret until the time is right.

Because sometimes... well, it's just nice to surprise people.

Love,
Dad

November 28, 2013

Dear Hillary,

I am in Sault St. Marie, Michigan, and missing you dearly.

Today, a good friend of mine who is a firefighter said the following: "The only good part about a dead five-year-old kid being your first call is that your day can literally not get any worse."

Today I am thankful for him, and anyone that has a job that I do not have the fortitude to handle.

I see people who get angry with their waiter because their food arrived a little cold, or their order incorrect. I see people frustrated with the fact a grocery store line is longer than they'd like it to be. I see people get irate over the smallest little nothings, and I wonder if they realize that as they rant over their petty problems, somewhere out there a person is having the worst day of their life.

Perspective is one of the most important characteristics a person can have. Maintain yours well.

Love,
Dad

November 29, 2013

Dear Hillary,

I am in Duluth, Minnesota, and missing you dearly. I missed Thanksgiving this year because of work, and I am working because I am not always the brightest bulb.

When I accepted this gig, I looked at the calendar and said, "Well, that's the final week of November, just a couple days before December. Thanksgiving is probably the week before."

No.

Booked the gig squarely on Thanksgiving Day.

(Like I said, not too smart.)

You probably didn't notice my absence—you were surrounded by too many aunts, uncles, cousins, and even a great-grandmother—and that gives me solace. But I wonder what it will be like when you do notice I am away, and when you start to care.

Because of work, I wasn't around for your first steps, and possibly your first word. I didn't see you learn to cruise, where you take hold of a surface and shuffle back and forth as you find your walking feet.

Missing these milestones didn't upset me; that's more a Mom thing. Even if I wasn't around for your first wobbly steps, I knew I would be able to watch you learn to walk. Even if I missed the first time you said "Mama," I'd still be around as you learned sentence structure and language.

But I wonder what it's going to be like when you have your first dance recital, or you test for a new belt in martial arts, and I cannot be there. I especially wonder what it will be like after you find your words and can say, "Daddy, where are you going?" as I pack my bags.

I fear you someday saying, "I don't like your job..."

When I was younger, I saw comedians get married, have kids, and leave the road behind. I never understood it.

Now I do.

I'm nowhere near ready to stop touring, but I get it. Right now the best moment of my week is coming home and watching your face light up when I come in the door. You pause, as if seeing me isn't really happening, and then you let forth a blast of joy from your vocal cords. It's part laugh, part squeal, and all affection. Then you charge me, as if getting into my arms is the most important thing in the world. I sit down on the floor so I am your height when you arrive, and you collapse into me.

And I am overwhelmed with love.

The only good part about leaving is returning home once more.

Love,
Dad

December 8, 2013

Dear Hillary,

I got to stay home this week, which was nice. On Friday I drove a couple hours to a corporate gig, a Christmas party that paid handsomely; some money for your college education.

Tomorrow I have my annual "Comedy for Charity" show, where I try to combat all the negative karma I've accrued in my life by doing good. In five years, I've been able to raise over $12,000 and give it to causes ranging from pediatric cancer to Iowa veterans returning home from combat. It's not a lot, but every little bit helps.

The nice thing about being home is our ritual, "Morning Snuggles." I'm not the sleeper Mom is. I'm generally easy to wake, and I don't tend to need much sleep overall. So when you give your first morning whimper, I get out of bed, warm your milk, and then collect you. I warm the milk first, because every so often you grunt and fall back asleep. When that happens, I piddle-fart around on my computer until you're *really* awake.

When you do rise, I gather you up and we share time on the sofa. I put you in the crook of my arm, and you guzzle your milk as if manna from heaven.

After finishing, you toss the cup aside and pop a thumb into your mouth.

Sometimes you fall asleep in my arm; sometimes you just lay there contemplating your day, organizing your thoughts.

When it's time to start wandering the house, you lift your body up and look at me. You smile, and occasionally sneeze in my face, which makes you giggle.

I know these moments won't last forever. You are a very independent girl, and enjoy more than anything attempting to do things on your own. You've already left the high chair behind, because you like having a table and chair your size; you like sitting at a table like Mom and Dad do. And when we tell you not to do something, you double down and want to do it all the more.

Earlier this week you were especially silly. When Mom was ready to take you out and about with her, you were in the living room playing with a toy. Mom was a few feet away from you, and reached down and called you to her.

You looked at her, irritated, and walked over specifically to bat her hands away: *No Mommy, I'm busy.* You then went right back to playing with your toy. Mom had to fetch you, which you protested quite vocally. It was funny, but as you grow ever more strong-willed I fear the end of such things as Morning Snuggles. I hope for the best, but emotionally prepare for the worst.

I think I enjoy Morning Snuggles because I believe, in my own way, that I'm warming you up after a long, cold night. Because babies cannot regulate their body temperature all too well, we've had a sensor in your room since, well, probably your birth. This winter your room has been coming in one to two degrees cooler than the house temperature, meaning when the living room was 70, your room was 68.

To combat the temperature discrepancy I put plastic film over your windows, and we placed a warm mist humidifier next to the dresser. It worked, too. Your room bumped up a degree or two nightly.

But it wasn't enough. We felt we shouldn't have to play these tricks to keep your space as warm as it should be, so we tried one more thing, rearranging the furniture.

Mommy and I realized if we moved the spare bed, we could create a wide-open space in the center of your room, one that allowed the heating vent to push warm air everywhere. In doing this, we moved your crib from the corner to flat along the wall right next to the door.

And, as fate would have it, right under the light switch.

So, whereas a week ago you would wake and sniffle, now you apparently wake and look for amusement.

Ever since your crib has been in its new home, you have barely sniffled. You wake up, squeak ever so slightly, and then there's silence... until you start babbling to yourself delightfully.

Every time I have investigated this joyous babbling, I have watched from the hallway as your light flicks on and off, on and off. When I open your door, there you stand, experimenting. Flick the switch up, let there be light! Flick the switch down, darkness. Flick the other switch and ooh, your favorite thing happens! The ceiling fan begins rotating! You are enraptured every time the five blades begin their spinning. I do not know how long this simple pleasure will keep you distracted, but it is very nice to retrieve a happy Hilly over a disoriented and sad one. Not that a disoriented and sad Hilly is problematic, it's just that I always want you to be as happy as possible.

No matter what your mood, when I pick you up you nuzzle into my shoulder, and then we retrieve and warm your milk together. Following that is my favorite part of the day, Morning Snuggles. Some people drink coffee in the morning, I get to snuzzle with you on the sofa as you gulp from your sippy cup. When I travel, I miss Morning Snuggles above all else.

Anyway, big news for you: Mommy's first blood test was Monday, and it came back positive. Her second was Wednesday, and it came back positive, too. This means Squeak is growing in her belly as I type. Your birthday is August 8th; Squeak's estimated arrival date is August 9th. If somehow you two came out on the same day two years apart? Well, that would be something.

We shall see.

Love,
Dad

Post Script: It appears our furniture rearrangement may have backfired. I wrote the above somewhere around the midnight hour, before retiring to bed. This morning at 5am I heard you squeaking, so I got up to check on you and, like described, you were happily flicking the light on and off. Normally you might have woken up, squeaked, and gone back to sleep. But when you can turn the light on and stimulate your eyes into an awakened state? Yeah... oops.

It looks like Mommy and I will be taking your new toy away, and turning the light off at the source so flicking the switch does nothing. Maybe that way when you wake up at 5am you'll bore yourself back to sleep instead of beginning playtime.

December 14, 2013

Dear Hillary,

I am in St. Cloud, Minnesota, and missing you dearly.

This week was a rollercoaster. Even though all is stable at the moment, I still feel as if I am on the edge of a cliff, waiting for the ground beneath me to crumble.

On Sunday, Mommy started spotting.

This means she found blood in her underpants. It was brown, denoting old blood, and Mommy felt fine, which were both good signs. We were cautious, and a little worried, but not yet in panic mode.

On Monday, bright red blood arrived, and Mommy began cramping. Now we were frightened. Bright red blood and severe cramping are two signs of a miscarriage, where a pregnant woman loses her child for sometimes-unexplainable reasons.

When the cramping started, Mommy called the doctor. He advised her to leave work, so Mommy came home crying and snuck into the bedroom so you wouldn't see her. Not because she didn't want to spend time with you, but we knew you would want Mommy to pick you up and Mommy was under orders to lie in bed and exert no effort upon her body.

You and I played in the basement, one of your favorite places in the house. We keep your kitchen set down there, and the room is less cluttered with furniture than other areas of the house. You have ample space to scamper and explore, more so than upstairs where you are forever banging your head into the sofa or a chair.

After a spell, we made our way back to the living room and you wandered to and fro, hither and dither, until you finally made your way into the master bedroom and discovered Mommy in bed. You were overjoyed. Mommy is never home before 5pm! What a treat!

Mommy picked you up, which had me arch an eyebrow; should she be doing such a thing?

She explained that while you and I were in the basement, she had gone to the bathroom. When she was finished, there were clumps of clotted blood in the toilet.

Regular blood is a bad enough sign while pregnant, but for it to be clots? All signs pointed to miscarriage.

Squeak was gone, so it didn't matter whether or not Mommy picked you up or exerted herself. The band of cells that had taken to Mommy's uterus seemingly so well had lasted exactly one week.

She was sad; I was disappointed.

The reality of life is that there are setbacks, but everything happens for a reason, and more importantly, everything happens when it is supposed to. Your mother and I each went through a series of failed relationships before finding one another. We also went through a series of failed attempts at creating a child before we struck gold with you.

So though this was unexpected, it is part of life. If I may quote a great movie I will introduce you to someday, "Why do we fall down? So we can get back up."

On Wednesday, we went to the doctor to receive confirmation the embryo had indeed departed, when our expectations were slammed in a very good way.

When implantation took place, part of the uterine wall was damaged. Blood had been pooling, and was now being expelled.

Squeak, on the other hand? Against all expectations, it turns out Squeak is fine and dandy, and meeting all projected milestones. Your mother and I were stunned. We had steeled ourselves for the worst possible news, had even expected it, and yet as the ultrasound began the tech opened with, "OK, there's the gestational sac, and there's the embryo..." We were speechless and overjoyed.

Right now, Squeak is only the size of a sesame seed, if even that. But before we all know it, Mommy's belly will bulge and he (or she) will be here.

And naturally, I'm already booked on the due date.

It begins again...

Love,
Dad

December 18, 2013

Dear Hillary,

I posted this blurb about you on Facebook at 3am.

Hilly just woke up.

Cried a little, so I waited a minute to see if she'd fuss herself back to sleep, or actually wake-wake up.

The cry began increasing in volume, so I went in and picked her up. She immediately began struggling: "Want down, Dad!"

I set her on her feet and she bolted out of the room, across the living room, and into the dining room where she plopped down in her chair and began looking at me expectantly.

Knowing this look, I prepared some milk and handed it over, then sat down beside her (like a fairy tale spider) and gently stroked her hair as she gulped happily.

Two minutes later, her eyes drooped as she struggled to maintain consciousness. The cup left her mouth and a thumb was inserted in its place.

Picking her up out of the chair, I carried her back to her room, her head now upon my shoulder; no struggling to get down and explore anymore.

Gently set to rest in her crib once again, she is blissfully asleep once more.

I think I will try to do alike, and with that bid Facebook goodnight.

And now you know why I'm not a poet.

Love,
Dad

December 20, 2013

Dear Hillary,

I am in Logansport, Indiana, and missing you dearly.

You and Mommy are at your great-grandmother Joan's house, celebrating early-Christmas. As rude as it sounds, I am mostly fine when missing a trip to southern Iowa. I don't dislike your mother's extended family, but at times some of them can be... oh, what's the best way to explain it? Racist and homophobic. Fortunately, at sixteen months you are too young to catch everything that is said and/or the political undertones when something not-very-wise is offered. This is a horrible thing to say, but by the time you are old enough to grasp sideways remarks we will no longer need to visit them. Once your great-grandmother departs this world, the need for seeing that section of your extended family will be reduced mightily. Those points of view are nothing I wish to expose you to as you grow and develop as a person.

Though I am not a part of today's celebration, I will be around for Christmas-proper. For the actual holiday, we meet up with the more immediate side to Mommy's family, your maternal grandma, grandpa, and all your cousins and aunts and uncle. They are wonderful family to have, and somehow escaped the narrow-minded views they were raised among. A large part of that is because of your grandfather, but that is not a story for now. Right now, the worry has returned.

Last week, after the miscarriage scare and relief, we thought we had entered smooth sailing. Unfortunately, the ongoing drama involving Squeak rests heavy in my gut like a brick.

On Thursday we went to the hospital for an ultrasound. Last week, we were told all was well; this week they discovered the pool of blood is still surrounding Squeak.

This complicates things.

Everything else was normal. Good heart rate, good size—that of a blueberry—good measurements. But the pooled blood is troubling.

A doctor said, "It's most likely nothing. Many women bleed start-to-finish throughout their pregnancies with no complications." Which is nice to hear, but it's not the absolute gold star you want. The words "*most likely nothing*" leave room for worry, and when dealing with a child's development you want two thumbs up and nothing more.

Right now there are more questions than answers bouncing around my exhausted noggin, and I haven't been sleeping much. Three, four hours a night tops. The rest of the time I stare at the ceiling, or fart around out in the living room. Writing, browsing the Interwebs, reading... anything and everything to keep my mind aside the thoughts that wish to inhabit my consciousness.

On December 26th we will receive another ultrasound and a Squeak progress update.

Generally ultrasounds aren't administered until week 12, but when dealing with in vitro fertilization they want to know early and often if something is wrong. When a red flag like bleeding is raised, it needs monitored, so away we will go to the hospital again, third week in a row.

My worry in the week going forward is wondering if Mommy is still bleeding internally. Will the pool of blood be larger next week? Why is it pooling in her uterus, Squeak's home, and not coming out? The answers we receive should help bolster the assurances already received... or, unfortunately, extend the worry. We could enter a holding pattern of "wait and see."

There is little more frightening than the unknown.

As I write, I realize that by the time you read this, all the mystery will have ended; you'll know the outcome before you even pick up this diary.

I hope you will have a sly smile across your face, safe in the knowledge that somewhere out there Squeak has turned into a wonderful sibling for you.

Love,
Dad

December 28, 2013

Dear Hillary,

I am in Prairie du Chien, Wisconsin, and missing you dearly.

First, the good news: another ultrasound, and things are still "thumbs up" for Squeak. Growth rate is normal, and the blood surrounding Squeak's sac is dwindling. This means we are on track for providing you with a playmate come summer. My hope is you love Squeak as much as you love Kitty and Simon, your furry brothers.

So.

I want to talk to you about my father, your paternal grandfather. I cannot predict what kind of relationship you will have with him, but as of today, with you being a year-and-a-half old, you have met him twice. I am hoping that as you grow you will know your grandfather well, but I fear the chaotic relationship he and I have may infect the one you share. As it stands, I will do my best to be non-judgmental and allow your relationship with him to grow and develop on its own without any interference from me. I say that, because my relationship with my Dad is... sometimes hit or miss.

To provide forty years of backstory would take too long, so I'm going to write up a little recent history. Hopefully this will explain why you see your grandpa and me interacting in ways you neither understand nor enjoy.

August 8th, 2010, was a day of celebration and slight introspection. On one hand, the date marked the one-year wedding anniversary of Mommy and me. On the other, it also marked one year since I had spoken to my father.

There was no fight, no big blow up between us. In fact, I wasn't entirely sure why we weren't speaking. We were in the middle of some bizarre Mexican Stand Off, neither of us willing to blink or show weakness. My silence came from patience, combined with an ability to shut down emotionally and wait a situation out to its finish. I did not attempt to second-guess my father's intentions or distance. Speculation usually leads to incorrect assessments, and I hoped to avoid that. I simply stuck to what I was witness to or told firsthand. Beyond that, all has been left to my imagination.

I should point out two important attributes regarding Grandpa's character: he is both generous, and pragmatic. For the wedding, his checkbook opened immediately, and his endowment was the largest Mommy and I received. That speaks volumes. Since every parent went above and beyond the call of charitable for our wedding expenses, the fact my father reached even deeper into his pockets shows he believes money is to be given, not squirreled away. Another example of his giving nature came a year before the wedding. In June, Mommy and I moved into a new house, our first. As the leaves turned and the chill called autumn crept into Iowa, my father called out of the blue and told me to go pick out a snow thrower, his treat. With me constantly traveling for work, he did not want Mommy stuck shoveling a snowed-in driveway alone. Price was no matter; Dad wanted us to pick something big and powerful. It was an unexpected and overly kind gesture.

On the subject of my father's no-nonsense side, I remember the first time I got drunk. I would have been fifteen or sixteen, the specific year escapes my ever-misfiring mental synapses. Regardless, as is usually the case with alcohol-fueled evenings, the following morning I was hung over beyond decent description. My head was throbbing, my body ached, and my tongue weighed more than an Olsen twin. My mother marched me downstairs to face a father's wrath, expecting him to tear into me for my behavior. Instead, he took one look at me and asked, "So, how do you feel right now?" I'm not sure what answer I was able to muster up, but my dad nodded, said,

"Well, that's what drinking does to you," and let it go. I didn't imbibe alcohol again for years.

Those positives on record, I should note that it could be speculated the reason his wedding endowment was larger than any other is because he inquired as to what others were contributing. After learning that Mommy's mother and father, and my mother and Grandpa Joe, had all reached an agreement to kick in equal amounts, Dad may have felt the need to better them, as if generosity were a competition. I think this only because he asked what the baseline was before contributing.

Mommy was a trooper when it came to planning everything. She took the lion's share of all responsibilities, and where possible went homemade over mass-produced in order to save money. Mommy created the wedding-day program, which provided the first inkling friction lay in the path ahead.

When trying to decide who to list on the front—typically the parents—Mommy asked me if I wanted just my biologicals listed, or my parents and their new spouses/girlfriends. Hoping to keep closed that can of worms, I responded, "Just my parents. Keep it simple." Unfortunately, Mommy thought Grandpa Joe would have hurt feelings if not mentioned. Instead of listening to my advice, she called my mother for input. Grandpa Joe wasn't home, but my mom agreed that not listing him would make Grandpa Joe a sad panda.

"Bullshit," I countered. "He's a man, men don't give a shit about that sort of thing."

Mommy was unswayed, and now in a tough position. If we honored Grandpa Joe, should we mention Alice, my dad's girlfriend of several years? Is there a fine line between listing a spouse vs. a partner, just because one wears a ring? Mommy thought it best to call my dad and ask for his wishes; would he like to see Alice included on the program? My dad appreciated the call, and got bizarrely cryptic.

"If *certain people*," he emphasized, meaning his ex-wife and my mother, "are uncomfortable seeing Alice's name there, you can leave it off. I appreciate the call, because it means a lot to me you're looking into such things, but I also understand if you have to cater to the emotions of *certain people.*"

My father's ability to accentuate the absurd is an interesting one. In his mind, his ex-wife, a woman who rarely spoke of him unless pressed, was somehow going to be offended by—fifteen years after the divorce she had asked for and ten years after her remarriage—seeing my father's girlfriend's name on my wedding program. In reality, my mother hadn't given any thought to Alice, my dad, or anything else on the program; such worries were all my father's invention.

Naturally, within seconds of that frustrating conversation, my mother called with an update: Grandpa Joe had returned home, voiced his opinion, and didn't care one way or another if he was listed. Just as I predicted, he had a penis, and therefore shrugged when presented with nonsense such as "Do you want to be listed on the wedding program?"

In Mommy's mind a quandary now existed, a self-invented mess. The cover looked untidy with all the names, but after all the phone calls she felt obligated to include everyone. Ever the caring fiancée, I washed my hands of it and walked away. Up front I had said to keep it simple, but the advice went unheeded. Neener, as they say, neener. Either way, the conversation gave us insight into my father's mindset. He seemed preoccupied with his ex, whereas my mother had moved on with her life.

The day before the wedding, my father told me he was opting out of that evening's rehearsal ceremony. I was fine with that, since the full scope of his duties involved walking down the aisle and sitting in the front row with family, then walking directly to the reception line after all vows had been exchanged. Pretty simple stuff. These weren't IKEA "Build-a-bookshelf" instructions; this was three bullet points easily memorized. I told Mommy, she rolled her eyes and agreed that it would be easier to let my father call his own shots than to argue about it.

He met up with everyone at the rehearsal dinner and looked to be on his best behavior, until he insulted the Matron of Honor, Jamie. She, a very politically unaware (and somewhat shallow) person, became involved in a discussion with my father involving her state legislators, and she got trounced. Like anyone on the losing end of a debate, Jamie was offended. Having grown up "the popular girl" meant being put in her place was something she would not soon forget, and ultimately was another notch on the frayed rope that bound her and Mommy in friendship.

(This friendship ended before you were born, which is a story for another letter.)

The next morning, go-day for our marriage, my father informed us he was now opting out of the wedding pictures. Mommy and I wanted our guests to have as much fun as possible, so we planned a back-to-back wedding/reception. Some weddings put several hours between the two events, which forces guests to twiddle their thumbs while the wedding party alternately takes post-ceremony pictures and/or piddle-farts around in a limousine.

Having our reception immediately follow our ceremony meant we had to take all our pictures early in the day. As said, much like the rehearsal, this was something my father was uninterested in. My father said he "Didn't want to be a part of those proceedings" and would arrive at the ceremony before we got to the altar. Had I pressed, he may have participated begrudgingly, but I wasn't going to make an issue of it. Pictures of family were important to Mommy, but as my father was not her immediate relation, she was fine allowing the incident to fade without becoming a battle of wills. The end result is that when you look through our wedding album, you will find only one picture of my father. It is not a photo of him standing next to or with arms around his son and/or new daughter-in-law, nor is it a posed capture. My father is in the background of a candid group shot, and it was an accidental capture. His jaw is square, his eyes are stern. He is watching a slideshow of my childhood play across a screen, and if the axiom "A picture is worth a thousand words" contains any truth, the fact my father is not wearing a celebratory face is evident to anyone with eyes.

Toward the end of the evening, I would learn what thoughts were happening inside his head as he watched the images flicker across the screen.

After our formal photos were taken, as the ceremony grew near, my father decided against sitting in the front row with family. When I walked down to take my position at the altar I noticed him several rows deep among the guests, not up front as one or both ushers had requested of him. Mommy and I didn't have preordained sides for bride or groom; people were free to sit where they wished. But the front rows were explicitly—as they are at any wedding—for family, and every family member was made aware of this arrangement. However, because of our non-traditional lack of bride/groom side seating, Mommy's therapist happened to end up directly behind my father. At their next session, she mentioned this to Mommy.

"When the couple sat down in front of me, the man said to his girlfriend, 'I know they want me to sit up front, but I'm not going to play that game.' I was shocked later when I found out it was Nathan's dad!"

It's an interesting statement any way you look at it, "I'm not going to play that game." As if reserving a section of importance for close family was somehow manipulative.

As the ceremony progressed, there was a point where our minister, one empowered by the state of Iowa and the Internet (but not Jebus or any other religious icon), began an introduction to the rose ceremony. During this portion of the service, Mommy and I were to present a flower to those who raised us. Sadly, as the minister waxed philosophic on the meaning of the rose, Mommy looked at me in wide-eyed fear and whispered, "Ohmygod... we left the roses up in the refrigerator!"

We were smart enough to not want the petals to wilt in the blazing August sun; we were not wise enough to remember how clever we were in storing the roses in a close-at-hand refrigerator. Our best laid plans laid to waste, when the words, "And now, Nathan and Lydia will hand out the roses" were spoken, I turned to everyone gathered and shouted, "We forgot 'em!"

Many people burst out giggling—making a joke at your own expense is generally the best way to deflect potential embarrassment. As everyone laughed, however, a voice rose above the din: "Maybe you'll get it right at your next wedding!"

My father let his wit get in front of his senses and had shouted it over the titters.

While many people gasped in horror, I rolled my eyes. My father comes to as many of my comedy shows as he can, and quite often heckles me. I bust his chops, and the audience usually gets a kick out of our back-and-forth harassment of one another. It's all done in good fun; no harm, no foul. So when he volleyed "Maybe you'll get it right at your next wedding," I returned, "Maybe I learned from your fuckups and won't get divorced!"

Everyone laughed again, but this time with a marked sense of discomfort.

The ceremony ended, and the wedding party walked down the aisle and up to the reception hall to participate in the receiving line. Everyone save for my father, that is. He never discussed not joining the receiving line, but at this point it was to be expected. In such a situation you can either make the decision to be angry, or let it go and enjoy your day. Mommy and I let it go. Too many generous friends and family members had made the trek to Iowa for us to be bothered by little things. I was meeting new people, and more importantly, saying hi to friends I didn't and don't see often enough.

Moving inside for the dinner, all was well. My father found a table to sit at away from my mother, and I didn't hear much about him until much later in the evening when the socializing began. At one point, the photographer said she was ready to leave, but that she still didn't have a professional shot of my father. Mommy and I made one last-ditch effort to corner him for a picture, but he ran away in search of leftover pizza for our security guard. I told the photographer not to worry about it, and that there was no need to wait around.

As the night wore on, I started hearing little stories about my father, coming first from an aunt on my mother's side.

"Your dad just said 'hi' to me," she began, laughingly. "He said, 'Well, I know you've been ignoring me since the divorce, so I thought I'd be the bigger person and come over here and say hello.' I said 'hi' back, but in my head couldn't stop laughing, thinking, 'Well of course I've been ignoring you! You're not married to my sister anymore, I don't *have* to talk to you!'"

I laughed, knowing full well my aunt could take care of herself.

Unfortunately, he didn't limit this approach to those he knew. Mommy's father, Grandpa John, got the same speech. Grandpa John was milling about, enjoying the evening, interacting with family and friends and watching his daughter smile and enjoy what is labeled one of the most important days of a woman's life, when a stranger walked up to him.

"Hello," the man started. "I know you've been ignoring me, so I wanted to be the bigger person and come over and introduce myself. I'm Nathan's father."

Grandpa John didn't know what to say and began to stammer out an introduction, but like a ghost, my father was gone before he could finish. This left Grandpa John stunned by the interaction.

My friend Keith, a professional videographer and editor putting together a tape as our wedding present, pulled me aside.

"What's up with your dad?" he asked, somewhat irritated.

I laughed, "You have to be more specific. So far today, he's just been acting normal for him."

Turns out Keith had been going around and asking people to record little confessionals for Mommy and me. People were allowed to speak from either their heart or funny bone, whichever they chose. Touching, lighthearted, serious, or silly, anything they wanted in order to express how they felt about the day. When approached, my dad met Keith's query with a terse response and quick departure. Instead of taking a couple seconds time to wish Mommy and me well, something else was evidently more important.

I told Keith not to worry about it, and my Uncle Tod stepped in with congratulatory words.

I should point out my father wasn't entirely off-putting that day; he was quite helpful behind the scenes. Toward the end of the night, he showed his amazing ability to sacrifice for the team. He asked if the rental company was going to collect the two hundred chairs from the wedding, or if they needed to be stacked and organized for return. Sadly, they needed to be stacked and organized, so without hesitation he went off to take care of it. I couldn't allow that to happen alone, so I went with, and your aunt's new boyfriend (now husband) joined us. In a miserable August heat, the hottest day of the summer which had turned into a sweltering night, we pulled and stacked chairs until entirely drenched in sweat, as if we had just jumped into water with our clothes on.

As we began piling up chairs, my father explained that his comment during the wedding was supposed to be a joke, and that he meant we'd get it right when Mommy and I renewed our vows as a happily married couple. I told him the quip didn't bother me, and it didn't. I mean, it had only made him look bad, and as said, I was used to our exchanges. Unfortunately, after that initial salvo the conversation turned to lecture, and he used the time not to talk of the wedding or any upbeat aspect of it, but instead used the alone time to inform me of the many different ways my mother was being controlling. He described how she was exuding her power over Mommy, meddling in the wedding just like the Scooby Gang at the scene of a murder. Considering I knew for a fact Mommy had planned the wedding almost entirely on her own, and actually stood her ground when my mother offered her opinion on several subjects, I recognized what my father was saying as entirely untrue.

Yet he persisted.

In his mind, my mother was in control of the invitations. She was allocating money for things that were supposed to be outside her realm of control, like the rehearsal dinner. There were many other accusations that are thankfully long gone from my memory. What could have been a nice moment became just another time to hear my father rail against his ex. Being used to these speeches, I shrugged and stacked the chairs. Just another day with Dad.

The reception took place in a large central room, with a wide-open kitchen along the back. When the dancing began, all lights in the hall were lowered to create atmosphere. This left the kitchen a bright eyesore, because its lights remained on so the caterers could work. At some point several hours into the celebration, I looked up to see my father and Grandpa Joe in front of the kitchen. Because this was the only area illuminated, they might as well have been under a streetlight. Grandpa Joe looked alternately exasperated, bored, frustrated, or a combination of all three. My father was rigid. His posture suggested anger, and he had one arm out with a finger pointed at Grandpa Joe, as if lecturing.

I rolled my eyes. At your aunt's first wedding, I was present when my father cornered my mom and demanded an apology from her. He asked her to "own up to everything" that went south through their marriage and divorce. He kept stating "All I want is an apology," which my mom gave in an exasperated "Just-leave-me-alone" manner. It was an awkward, silly moment, and it looked like it was being repeated. Only this time Grandpa Joe was in the hot seat.

Something had to be done, and I knew exactly what.

My whole life, I've sought out original, interesting people to befriend. Somewhere along my journey, a pudgy fella named Baxter and I bonded. Describing Baxter is difficult, so I'll do my best using an event from his life: Baxter once stunned a physician with his honesty.

The doctor was meeting Baxter for the first time and reading through a standard medical history form. He was asking questions lackadaisically, having done it a million times before, and pretty much filling in answers by rote. Out of the blue, something threw him for a loop.

"Have you ever been with a prostitute?" the doctor inquired, checking "No."

"Yes," Baxter responded.

The doctor paused.

"Excuse me?" he asked.

"Yes, I've been with a prostitute," Baxter shrugged.

The doctor was dumbfounded. In his fifteen years, he'd never had anyone answer "yes" before. He had to change the intake sheet, having already marred it by incorrectly pre-guessing the patient's answer.

"Doc," Baxter continued, "I have more tattoos on my body than women in my past."

The prostitute, for the record, was my idea.

Baxter takes an annual weekend getaway to Las Vegas, and unfortunately he—for the longest time—was the guy you've always heard about, but never believed existed. Baxter was the "I think the stripper really liked me" guy.

He would return from his sojourn and begin regaling our friend Bryan and me with tales of drunken revelry. These tales usually began with the stripper laughing at his jokes, and ended with her touching his penis. Nothing more sexual or outrageous, such as a hand job over the clothes (or even under them, for that matter), just a simple "She touched my penis."

Naturally, Bryan and I would counter with, "And how much had you given her at that point?"

One year, the answer was, "Around eight hundred dollars."

Bryan and I knew it was time for an intervention.

Before his next trip, we sat Baxter down and said, "Look, if you're going to blow that kind of money anyway, you should get something for it. This year, buy yourself a prostitute. Get laid instead of just the half-second brush of a hand."

Our words resonated truth, so on his next visit Baxter opened up the escort pages, negotiated a price, and split the cost with his buddy; they'd each get thirty minutes.

To satisfy his white male fetish, Baxter purchased an Asian—specific country of origin unknown—but he said the experience was both worthwhile, and hilarious.

"She answered her phone while we had sex," he explained. "She was on top of me, and her phone rang. She asked if she could answer it, and I didn't care, so she did. Spoke with her pimp for a second, looked at her watch, asked me how long I was going to take, then said 'I can be there in thirty minutes' into the phone and hung up."

The escort was already lining up her next client.

Either way, that year, Baxter returned from Vegas with a smile upon his face. It was a very good trip.

So when the doctor asked, "Have you ever been with a prostitute," Baxter felt compelled to be honest. Why lie? Bartering a for-hire liaison was nothing to be ashamed of.

That description of my friend in hand, we can return to my wedding day, where Baxter was an usher. He was wearing a kilt, because for as long as I've known him Baxter has never worn pants. Even in the coldest Wisconsin January, Baxter would wear shorts. He even turned down a job offer once, as the position required he wear slacks to look "professional." And this was a janitor position. So when it came time to dress formal for my special occasion he didn't mind having to wear a shirt and tie, but covering his legs was a concern.

Trying to find an end around, Baxter asked, "Can I wear a kilt?"

Mommy didn't mind, and I didn't care, so the answer was, "Sure."

"It's a dress kilt," Baxter assured us.

Now, under that kilt, on our wedding day, Baxter declined to wear underpants. As any a man can tell you, a little air movement up and around the twig and berries feels delightful, especially so in summer. So that's the path Baxter decided to walk. But he also wanted to go one step further. To make matters interesting, Baxter bought food dye, and before the blessed event took a sponge and gently dyed his penis and testicles a dark green hue. This, he explained, would allow him to lift his kilt and say "HULK SMASH" when he was sufficiently drunk.

As my dad lectured Grandpa Joe in the most visible location in the room, I decided action had to be taken. The word went out: find Baxter.

Once he was located, your aunt's boyfriend, a man carrying a very expensive camera, was rustled up and given instructions.

The situation was explained to Baxter, who shook his head at the stupidity of anyone creating drama at a wedding, and set off to put an end to it. He walked over to the kitchen, placed himself a few feet from the event, and shouted, "Hey guys!"

Heads turned, the kilt went up, and a picture was snapped.

Grandpa Joe started laughing immediately, because it should be impossible to remain tense when a fat, kilted man is showing you his green penis. But, somehow my father managed to maintain his composure. Dad gave Baxter a quick "thumbs up," then turned right back to Grandpa Joe and continued his sermon.

Baxter waddled off, his best efforts defeated.

After it all ended, I asked Grandpa Joe what had happened. In good spirits he shook his head and laughingly explained he had received a lecture on "inappropriate behavior." This included:

- Sitting among the family (Grandpa Joe wasn't my father, and shouldn't have been in the front row)
- Donating money to the cause (same reason)
- Giving a toast at my sister's first wedding (same reason—he's not her father; despite the fact my sister had asked Grandpa Joe to give a toast)
- Meddling in family affairs (attending the wedding?)

There were other such silly things, but I didn't take notes and no longer remember them. Grandpa Joe said he mostly let my dad vent, not wanting to make things worse by turning a lecture into an argument, but he did swing the pendulum back the other way. Grandpa Joe asked my father how he thought it made Mom and I feel when they looked up at the ceremony and saw he wasn't sitting with the rest of the family. The response was, "No one told me I was supposed to sit there." Given both ushers told me they tried to steer him to the front, combined with the comment Mom's therapist overheard, this was nothing short of an outright lie.

Fortunately, Grandpa Joe has an easygoing attitude and didn't let it ruin his day. My sister, however, is not always laid back and was tired of our father's behavior. I was not witness to what happened between them, but a little while later he told me, "Well, your sister just said she hates me, you hate me, everyone hates me, and that she never wants to speak to me again."

I laughed and shrugged. It was my wedding day, and I was having too good a time to care about invented drama. In fact, of everything I've listed so far, not a single thing bothered me. Skipping the rehearsal, offending the Matron of Honor, skipping the pictures, sitting in the wrong place, ignoring the reception line... I could have gotten angry, or not, and I simply chose "not." I've (obviously) known my dad my whole life, and knew what to anticipate regarding the day.

Or so I thought.

As the evening wound down, one of my groomsmen, Barrett, found me for some alone time while other guests were dancing. He and my dad are friendly with one another, and Barrett said they had just spent a little time catching up. My dad expressed a bit of sorrow to Barrett, information Barrett was passing on to me to do with what I pleased. Apparently the slideshow of my childhood had wounded my dad. He told Barrett that he had many photos of me, and it would have been nice to be asked to contribute some to the montage.

I nodded my head, a bit upset with myself. Given his belief my mother was in control of the wedding, asking him for childhood photos would have been the appropriate thing to do. I thanked Barrett for the information, and continued celebrating.

The evening eventually ended. We had to be out of the rental space by midnight, so at 11:45 the lights went up and a few close friends and family set about straightening up, that we might avoid a huge cleaning fee. I cannot remember if my father was there or not. No matter how hard I search my mind I cannot recall when he left, or if goodbyes were made.

Baxter, now nicely drunk, stood on a table and incoherently slurred his "Hulk Smash," lifting the kilt and disgusting any women left present.

A bar was chosen, and a precious few friends and family made their way over to finish out the night.

At closing time, Mom and I waved farewell to our friends and hopped in the car to away to our hotel. As we drove, I told her about my conversation with Barrett, and how even though my dad had acted pretty much as I figured he would, we still should have included him in the picture choosing process.

Mom grew immediately livid.

"Goddammit!" she yelled. "I emailed him several times asking for pictures, I emailed Alice, and even *talked to him* about it! When I asked, he said we could talk about it later, and then he never responded to any of my emails or messages!"

I wasn't angry like Mom was, but I was disappointed in myself. It had been years since I let my dad get to or trick me, yet he had been able to do so that night. He had been playing the victim for Barrett, trying to gain a little sympathy while ignoring the facts at hand, and I fell for it like a rube in front of a snake oil salesman. Well played, Dad. Well played.

Fortunately, a few minutes later, when we arrived at the hotel, we discovered a wonderful surprise. Mom and I had found a bargain rate for our room online, and paid $60 for a normally $150-a-night stay. At the desk, we were given our key, then took the elevator up to discover we were staying in the Presidential Suite. A tenant at our rental property worked at the hotel, and when she saw our name on the register switched us to the un-reserved room. We entered to find wine, candy, roses, and hearts. It was a damn fine finish to a goddamn decent day, and quickly removed all anger I felt over the "I wanted to be included" ruse my father pulled.

And it really was a great day. I know it's a horrible cliché to say so, but it was one of the best days of my life, easily. Naturally, your birth topped it, but having so many friends come out to visit with me was overwhelming, amazing, and a slew of other descriptors that cannot give emotional resonance proper justice. Old friends, current friends, Internet folk, and people I've met doing comedy... it was profoundly touching and great fun. I've had many tell me the party was so enjoyable they felt they should have paid admission to attend. I credit their joy to Mommy. Though a wedding is supposed to be about the bride, she turned that concept on its head and tried to make it about the guests. From having a short ceremony, to throwing the reception immediately following our vows and whatever else you can think of, she buckled down and pretty much planned it all. I could not have asked for a better, more beautiful bride, nor could I have asked for a better partner since.

It's odd how one day can be a juxtaposition of celebration and stupidity, how two diametrically opposed paths can be created from one event, toward one person, away from another. I didn't end that day with the thought in my head to stop talking to my father, and we have exchanged a couple emails since then. It's been maybe five at the most, all small talk with nothing relevant ever being written. He sent me a birthday card; Mom and I invited him and Alice to our house for Christmas and didn't hear back, so we sent gifts before the end of December. I think that's when I finally noticed the fade, when our invitation was put on the back burner and no response to our gifts was given. I realized we hadn't actually spoken, and somewhere in my mind I thought, "Well, let's see how far this goes."

And so it goes.

The reason I bring all this up is because you will be meeting your grandfather for the third time very soon.

I think.

In the beginning of December, we exchanged a couple emails involving dates around Christmas he and Alice could visit and spend time with you. These emails ended with my saying, "Pick a weekend and let me know."

Since that day, I have heard nothing. I offered two dates, and Sunday the 29th of December was one of them. So, knowing the way my father's brain operates, he may be ringing our doorbell tomorrow. Or not. We won't know until the day passes into night.

As I finish typing all this up, the most important thought of all comes to mind: nothing I've just written matters.

My relationship with my father is my relationship with my father. It has absolutely no bearing on how you will interact with him. A chunk of me feels like deleting everything written... but I almost wonder if that would be considered a lie of omission.

Your grandfather loves you, and I tell you everything I have so that you may reflect back and glean a little understanding of why my interactions with him may have been strained at times.

I absolutely refuse to do or say anything negative about him to you as you grow. Your relationship with him will be defined by how he treats you, and my baggage will not be a part of that. I think, in part, I needed to get all of what's written above out of me, if only to get to the conclusion I just have.

Maybe I took the long way around, but familial relationships are as messy as politics. You'll begin to understand that all too soon, unfortunately. For now, you are one happy, loving, and clueless toddler. I hope you retain your innocence longer than most people.

Love,
Dad

January 3, 2013

Dear Hillary,

I am in Des Moines, Iowa, and missing you dearly. I know I begin most of my letters similarly, but it's true. The city changes, the emotion does not. If it seems silly to you, I apologize. It is astounding how quickly the longing to snuggle you up begins. It's almost like pre-missing, where a malaise starts to wash over me as I pack my bags. As I ready myself for departure, the thought I will not be there for nighttime kisses or midnight nightmares is ever-present in the back (and sometimes forefront) of my mind. I am all too aware I won't see you for three or four days.

You do give "kisses," by the way, and they are adorable.

You have figured out when Mommy and Daddy want to smother you with affection, we enthuse "Kisses!" You lean toward us to receive love, and if in the mood you return the gesture by opening your mouth wide. You awkwardly push your open mouth against our pursed lips, which is your version of a kiss. It is nothing short of hilarious, and adorable. Sometimes you decide whether or not to kiss us, but you always, always, always respond to "Can Elmo have a kiss?" No matter what you are doing, or where you are, if Mommy or I say, "Can Elmo have a kiss?" you come sprinting over to kiss your favorite puppet.

And we smile every time.

This past week you and I listened to a band called The Clash. Mommy has put me in charge of your musical education, and I am going to do my best to head off something I fear is inevitable.

As I write, a "band"—and I use that term loosely—
called "One Direction" is the most popular group in the world.
They are a construct of five feminine boys taught dance moves
and songs written to appeal to immature minds. By the time
you read this, they will have not existed for many years.

Do not search for them in history books; they will be
but a footnote, an unimportant blip on the musical spectrum.
Like Menudo, New Kids on the Block, or The Backstreet Boys
before them, One Direction was designed to skyrocket in
popularity, then fade into obscurity. Their career arcs begin
with girls entering adolescence and end when those girls leave
puberty in the rearview.

My goal, and I know I will fail, is to steel you against the
onslaught of pre-packaged garbage assailing your senses as you
grow ever more aware of the world. Boy bands are churned out
every few years, timed to hit a market of squealing girls who
want nothing more than to feel connected to something or
someone. If your Mom and I can make you feel loved and in
touch with yourself at home, maybe you'll escape such silliness.
The chances are slim, but attempts have to be made.

In your short life you have been given shakers, a
keyboard, and access to musicals. You and I watched The Blues
Brothers together, skipping from song to song, and you were
transfixed. You loved what I consider the high points of the
movie—James Brown, Ray Charles, and Aretha Franklin. I have
a photo of you glued to the TV as James Brown danced and
sang gospel music.

(Mommy made you watch Sister Act 2, which is why
I'm in charge of your musical education. Under Mommy, you'd
be listening to God knows what.)

Every day you hear The Police, The Ramones, U2, Miles
Davis... "Classical Morning" is a playlist that sounds
throughout our house several times a week. You may not be
able to name "The Barber of Seville" today, but you will when it
matters.

As you grow into a young woman, I'll infuse you with
the music of powerful women like early Melissa Etheridge, Ani

DiFranco, and Liz Phair—women who will help guide you through your emotional development in a way that I, as a man, cannot.

If I can instill in you an appreciation of music, there is an outside chance that when you hear nonsense, you'll recognize it for what it is.

Yes, all art is subjective, but response to art says more about the responder than the art. A person that hears Rihanna and says, "OMG, this is like the best, *evar!*" is probably not a very enlightened person.

In my experiment/tutoring, I am also hoping to instill in you a sense of how important originality is. I shall explain.

One of my favorite bands is the Red Hot Chili Peppers. They are fronted by a man named Anthony Kiedis, who—and this is important—cannot sing.

I don't know that I ever realized that, or even gave it much thought up until possibly my ten-thousandth listening of *Under the Bridge*. At that pivotal moment, the instant his voice sounded through the speakers it hit me like a truth I'd always known but was never conscious of, that Anthony Kiedis has an "ugly" voice. Not "bad" ugly, just "not pretty." And because of that, his voice is perfect for the Chili Peppers. Their music is unique, and so is Anthony, and when it comes to art, originality is far more important than "perfection."

Think of interesting singers: Tom Waits, Leonard Cohen, Janis Joplin, Tori Amos. Remember the first time you heard the high-whine falsetto of Sting on Roxanne. Not a single person listed has a "good" voice in the classical sense. Many are limited in range, and therefore have to write music to suit their restrictions. If they cover another artist's song, they have to completely change the arrangement to make it work.

Now list singers with amazing voices, those who can hit notes all across the aural spectrum: Mariah Carey. Beyoncé Knowles. Rihanna. Whitney Houston in the 1990s. Each of them can... or could, given when you'll be reading this, sing any song they wanted to and did so with the confidence of a perfectionist. The thing is, they all did so without any emotion.

They all *emoted* very well, but that is something completely different from *emotion*. Emoting doesn't involve soul. It's as if each singer studied human feelings, but couldn't quite replicate them. They knew the notes, they understood they were supposed to convey love, sadness, etc., but internal disconnect kept it from actually happening. The separation kept aware listeners at arm's length, and ultimately when comparing the singers in the first batch to those in the second, the "ugly" voices and songs are superior every time.

There is an intangible something in true artists that comes from within and creates soul. It is well known Beyoncé was trained from childhood to be a perfect singer, dancer, and performer. This means her drive came from without, not within. Her father instilled it in her. On the other side of that spectrum, Bono once said he raged to have his thoughts and ideas heard. He would hit a single key on a piano, and immediately want to find the corresponding note he could hear inside his head. That desire created passion, which is something lacking in a performer who sees art as a series of pantomimes, not a form of expression. Yearning creates a more unique confidence than aspiration, because yearning leaves a shade of doubt hiding behind the performer's eyes. Aspiration can be programmed, while the human touch known as uncertainty will never be found in a robot.

Contrast some polar opposites in the music world. In 2003, South Africa held a concert to raise awareness for World AIDS Day. Both Peter Gabriel and Beyoncé performed. Peter, older and with a tired voice, sang *Biko*. This song, originally written in objection of South African apartheid, evolved into a song defined by protest of injustice. That day, *Biko* represented the frustration felt by those who believed first-world nations were ignoring the violence AIDS was ravaging upon their continent. As the song played, a stadium full of people shot their fists in the air, demanding acknowledgment.

Beyoncé, for her selection, played *Crazy in Love*. She and her singers writhed around the stage and created a sexual energy/tension that could almost be considered inappropriate, given the focus of the concert. Though Beyoncé's performance was a thousand times more energetic and modern than Peter's, her show was a failure on two fronts. One, because she had nothing of substance to offer the proceedings, and two, because she just didn't understand that fact. At no point did she or any of her handlers ask, "Is this relevant?" It was like watching the telecast of the 9/11 fundraiser all over again. On that night, Sting performed *Fragile,* while Bon Jovi sang *Livin' On a Prayer.* The former is about violence being an untenable solution to world problems, the latter an anthem designed to be shout-sung at karaoke bars by drunken louts.

But both Jon Bon and Beyoncé probably had the best of intentions, but each was in over their head. Maybe it could be argued that charity concerts take on too much weight, and to prevent things from collapsing under serious earnestness lighter fare is sometimes needed... I don't know. It certainly didn't feel like that was the objective in either situation.

But I've digressed.

The idea "original is better than perfect" runs the creative gamut. It can be argued in cases involving art, writing, or comedy.

- Thomas Kinkade was a hack painter that appealed to the masses, but Jackson Pollock became a respected legend. If anyone ever makes a film about Kinkade, it will not be an honoring biopic like Ed Harris did for Pollock, it will be a Lifetime movie showing his drunken escapades and Disneyland urinations.
- Nicholas Sparks may be an author successful beyond words, but no one could ever argue he is a good writer. Erik Larson, on the other hand, has probably sold far fewer books, but draws people in intellectually with his work.
- In the world of comedy, legend Richard Pryor surprised listeners with sudden left turns within stories. His jokes developed organically, and drew listeners in. On the flip side, Jay Leno crafts "perfect" jokes—set up, punchline,

set up, punchline—but he garners almost no respect in the artistic or critical community.

Obviously mediocrity can be successful—every example offered involves a multi-millionaire—but it is rarely admired, even when honored. Ordinary has been awarded Oscars, Grammys, and many other statuettes, but such an offering is hardly a guarantee of historic relevance. Which movie is more widely remembered and respected, *Crash*, which won the Oscar for Best Picture for saying "OMG, racism is bad," or *Brokeback Mountain*, which was a landmark film that examined homosexuality? The devaluation of once-important awards is most likely one of the reasons fewer and fewer viewers tune in to witness the glad-handing these days.

Maybe this is all nonsense I use to justify what I do on stage. In the end, my attempts to be creative are what fuel my thoughts about art and the human imagination.

To me, attempting to be original—talking about my life and ideas over asking, "What's up with airline peanuts?" or stating "Things be CRAZY!" as a punchline—is more important than writing standard, albeit banal, jokes. It might be easier to swim with the masses, but I didn't get into my field of work to be like everyone else.

And in the art I surround myself with? In that I would much rather have the "ugly" of an Anthony Kiedis over the beauty of a Rihanna. As far as my attempting to keep you from the wonders of Boy Bands? Well, "Rudie Can't Fail."

Love,
Dad

January 11, 2014

Dear Hillary,

I am in Forest City, Iowa, and missing you dearly.

My whole life, I've watched parents swat at their children's hands in stores.

The action is usually accompanied by the words "Don't touch," which come out in the most unusual combination of whisper and shout; hushed yet somehow still roared. Sometimes the children whimper or cry, sometimes they just look defeated. The adults are alternately embarrassed and irritated. "What if someone saw me allowing my child to grab an item? They'll think I'm a bad parent!"

On occasion, the swat is followed by a yank of the arm; "Come with me, now!" said via physical intent, not verbal interaction.

It's always made me cringe.

Oddly enough, I never played any "What if?" games in those moments. I never put myself in the position of the parent, and thought, "I'd certainly react differently" or "What would I do in that situation?"

Well, here I am.

You are officially a toddler now—sixteen-months strong and interested in walking everywhere and grabbing everything. When we go to the store, you're more interested in exploring than sitting in the cart.

So what do we do?

We explore.

And we grab.

You walk where you can, and try to pick up everything. Sometimes you fail—as with bags of flour—sometimes you succeed. When you discover an item you can lift, one of two things happens: you either carry that item around the store, or you begin taking multiple amounts of said item off the shelf and setting them on the floor. It is then my job to pick each item up and place it back where it goes, so you can repeat the process and believe we are having "fun." Because it *is* fun. To you. And that, in turn, makes it fun to me. Shopping isn't really fun for anyone, so if you can make it interesting for us, hell, more power to you.

If we make it through our shopping experience with an item still in your hand, I'll swap it out with something we're actually purchasing. "Good trade," as Wind in his Hair might say. We then return the unneeded item to its place on the shelf, because that's what happens when playtime is over, toys get put away.

You don't get to play with everything; certain items are off limits. We're not going to toss eggs or anything else fragile around. But instead of swatting and yanking, I monitor my body response carefully. I generally pick you up and start making faces at you. You understand "No," so I exaggerate it mightily, shaking my head as I smile, "Noooooooo." It's my way of letting you know you're not going to get to play with everything you want, while maintaining that just because you don't get your way doesn't mean it's all bad.

At Target the other day, the two of us ended up in the vitamin aisle. Your eye spied small items; something easily grasped by your tiny hands and limited dexterity.

Immediately you began picking up the pill bottles.

Ever the helpful father, I showed you that if you shook them, they made a neat rattling sound. This made you grin from ear to ear. You began experimenting with a multitude of containers; each one picked up, shaken, and then either handed to me or placed on the floor.

Knowing this could take a while—there were quite a few options available for all your shaking needs—I pushed the cart aside and sat down next to you. You would grab a bottle, sometimes two, and shake and wave them in the air, and look at me, beaming. To me, this was the most important moment, the interaction. Children take their life cues from us. They absorb how we relate to the world and reflect it as they age. So as you would look to me, I would smile and grab and shake my own pill bottles. It was my way of letting you know you were doing nothing wrong, everything right, and that I was enjoying myself just as much as you were.

Which, of course, I was.

Discovering which vitamins carry which maraca tone was a much more interesting way to spend ten minutes in Target than actually *shopping*.

At some point, a couple turned the corner into our aisle. From my vantage point all I could see was from knees-down, but I know they paused at the sight of a grown man and his daughter playing among the pill bottles.

Sometimes you don't need to see a face to understand intent. Sometimes you don't even need words.

"Oh..." sounded forth from what sounded like an elderly woman.

I didn't need to see her to know she was smiling; the warmth contained in her "Oh" could have melted butter.

I looked up, and she and her husband were gazing down at me in a way only grandparents can, love glowing through their eyes.

Some people won't understand a grown man sitting on the floor in Target shaking pill bottles with his daughter.

But some will.

Here's to hoping there are more of the latter on this planet than the former.

Love,
Dad

January 14, 2014

Dear Hillary,

    I do not care how many times it happens, the dog farting, and then jumping up startled and turning around to see what the noise was that came from behind him, is endlessly amusing to me.

    Love,
Dad

January 17, 2014

Dear Hillary,

I am in Negaunee, Michigan, and missing you dearly. Mommy and I attempted to Face Time with you earlier using our phones, but things did not turn out so well. The instant you heard my voice, you burst into loud, confused tears. You could see and hear me, but I wasn't there. You didn't know why I was inside a tiny little box and not by your side, and you were so very, very sad. It was heartbreakingly endearing. Knowing you missed me terribly made me the most odd mix of happy and miserable.

Mommy and I hung up quickly, and then she bounced with you on the bed and you forgot all about me. Because, hey, bouncing on the bed is FUN.

This week was Squeak's first big checkup. There are milestones in the development of a fetus, and we crossed one a few days ago. According to our doctor, the fact Squeak had a strong, strong heartbeat meant the chance of miscarriage dropped to less than 5%. Which is fantastic and relieving, but we're not out of the woods yet. Next comes the genetic screening, where we learn whether or not Squeak has any birth defects or illnesses.

As a parent, you never stop worrying. In fact, you learn to worry more. Becoming a parent means your heart gets kicked open and worry can creep in at any moment, even when supposedly peacefully asleep...

I had my first nightmare in 1979.

I was 10 years old, and had just watched the made-for-TV miniseries *Salem's Lot,* a movie about vampires. The

"Window Scene" and The Master were two things that nestled frightening images into my mind.

That night, thoughts of vampires had me wake to find that in a sleep-driven panic I had launched myself out of bed. Wide-eyed and shaking, I took in my bearings from the floor and noticed that my breathing was shallow, and fast. I was hyperventilating, even if I didn't know that word.

No matter what evil dreams I've had over the years, that moment remained the benchmark for horrific thoughts that run through my subconscious.

Until October 20th, 2012.

As a rule, dreams are stupid things. Not aspirations—"I wanna be an Airborne Ranger/I wanna live a life of danger"—but the imagery that bounces around our brain while we sleep. Everyone can attest to having had dreams that make absolutely no sense, but were real to us at the time.

On October 20th, my unconscious movie started out very, very silly. It ended in a way that scared me like I had never felt fear before.

The dream was a cartoon, playing out in my head, and the theme of the cartoon was a basketball game of "Aliens vs. Babies." Maybe it was inspired by the movie Space Jam, which I saw once, in the theater, and hated. Maybe I just have dumb dreams. I don't know.

I do know Maggie Simpson was in the dream, and from what I remember the events transpired as follows: The Aliens were winning handily, so the crafty cartoon babies started using trickery to gain the upper hand. Maggie Simpson unleashed a clever ploy that ended in Kang (or Kodos, it's difficult to keep track of which is which) throwing her through the hoop, and for some reason that counted as scoring more points than using the basketball. Soon all the Aliens were throwing all the Babies through hoops, and all was done in the typical form of cartoon hijinks. Everything was ridiculous, and no baby was in any form of danger, this despite their being tossed about like rag dolls.

All at once, the scene changed. Without warning, it was no longer a cartoon, there were no more aliens, no more Maggie Simpson. In a cruel twist of mental psychosis, suddenly my own infant daughter, *you*, Hillary, were falling to the ground.

Before I could react, you landed with a thud.

The sound of human flesh and bone landing forcefully against hardwood floor reverberated inside the hall and within my head.

I looked to Mommy, who shouted in complete terror, "I thought you were going to catch her!"

You weren't moving. Whatever damage had happened was severe enough you couldn't even cry in pain.

Your eyes were open, and they stared lifelessly at me.

I started screaming.

And screaming.

And screaming.

And then I woke up.

My heart was pounding furiously; Gene Krupa on cocaine.

I was paralyzed, my whole body tense with fear as a thousand thoughts and emotions ran through me. I didn't know if I should rush and check on you or throw up over the side of the bed.

On the nightstand, the clock told me we were somewhere in the 5am hour.

Calming as slowly as if molasses, I began gathering my wits about me, and came to a conclusion: the reason the dream happened is because when Mommy and I retired to bed the evening before, we attempted "extinction" with you.

If you are unaware of the term or practice, extinction is a way of teaching your baby to learn to sleep on its own. When your baby cries, instead of rushing in to check, you let the child work it out until she finally exhausts herself and sleeps. Mommy—ever the baby-book reader—had information in her head that stated, "At any point after an infant is two months old, you can begin sleep-training them using either extinction, or graduated extinction." Well, you were just over two months old, so...

We chose that night, because earlier that day I noticed you were very aware you had us wrapped around your baby-fingers.

I had been administering Daddy Day Care while Mommy was at work, and at some point during your afternoon nap you began to whimper. I listened for a few moments, ultimately deciding to let you work it out a little. Babies usually whine or make crying noises as they transition between sleep cycles. More often than not, it is worse to interrupt their slumber by picking them up rather than to just let them be.

Within a few minutes, however, your mewling began an ear-splitting crescendo that announced, "Hey, Dad! I'm up! This is real!"

I walked into your room, and the instant you laid eyes on me, the crying stopped. You gave me a very clear look—*Oh, hey. There you are. Yeah, I was calling for you*—and waited patiently to be picked up.

Laughing and thinking, "Well you little shit," I raised you to my shoulder and we bounced out to the living room where we sat and watched The Daily Show.

When Mommy got home, I informed her you had connected crying with Mom/Dad rushing in to save the day. It was decided that we could either break the habit now—ten weeks into your life—or continue down the path of placation and end up with an attached, needy daughter still wanting to cuddle at age twenty-six.

So extinction it was. That night, as we lay you down to sleep, should you fuss, you would weep.

When bedtime came, Mommy was already snuggled in and reading. I had been bouncing you around in my arms, gently cooing a made-up "Hello" song until you looked sleepy enough to be put down. I lowered you into the crib. Everything went smoothly, and I gave Mommy a "thumbs up" sign.

After twenty minutes, it all went south.

Mommy was asleep when it started. I was awake, staring at the ceiling, and wondering if I'd be able to nod off myself anytime soon, when you fired off an opening salvo.

This was nothing that started small and grew until eruption; this was Spinal Tap at "eleven." You were unhappy, and wanted the world to know.

And just like that, I started crying.

If there are ties between logic and emotion, I have yet to find them. In my head, two very clear separate streams of thought began pounding war drums. On the logical hand, I knew you were fine. You were safe in your bed, in a warm room, had a full tummy, and a clean diaper. On the other, emotional hand, I understood you were just a ten-week old baby that—even though unable to formulate coherent thought—knew two things: one, you used to be in a very warm womb and were now in a large, frightening world, and two (and most importantly), if things get to be too much, cry and *someone picks you up.*

Except this time, no one was coming.

That's what had tears running down my cheeks as I lay in the dark, listening to you.

I wondered what sort of confusion was running through you at that moment. Were you wondering why neither Mom nor Dad was lifting you in warm embrace, holding you to our chest, bouncing you, cooing in your ear, and kissing you on the nose? Did you feel you had been abandoned; that we were gone forever, and that no one would ever come to your aid again? Were you afraid, alone in your room in the dark? Or, and possibly worst of all, were you thinking the most simple of basic human thoughts, "I want to be held and loved"?

Before that moment, I believed certain things "killed me" as they happened, like when you received vaccinations. But those moments didn't make me cry. They didn't tear at me like the knowledge my child was in her room, wondering where I was, confused by the fact that she was thrust into this stupid world without asking to be, and was now abandoned in a ~~cage~~ crib in the dark.

And worse, I was doing it to you on purpose. You needed consoling, and I was actively neglecting my parental duties. In that moment, in my head, I was the most awful father in the world.

Your cries eventually woke Mommy, who soon realized she had an even bigger baby in her bed than in the nursery. I didn't try to hide what I was doing. I couldn't have even if I had wanted to. My breathing was erratic, and I was continually wiping my cheeks with the back of my hand. What could I have said the problem was, allergies? I may be emotional, but I'm no sissy; I'm not allergic to anything.

Mommy nuzzled up next to me, her heart, in her words, "full." She had never seen me so emotional and found it playfully delightful. I took her hand, and we settled in to ride it out.

Over the course of the next ninety minutes, an interesting swing of the pendulum took place. When she awoke, Mommy was steadfast. This was all for the best, and you would undoubtedly cry yourself out within twenty minutes. When that didn't happen, Mommy's resolve started to weaken. Where up front I had been the Nancy-pants and emotional wreck, once it was out of my system I was grounded and ready to wait as long as needed.

Mommy, on the other hand, went from being resolute, to capitulation. When your cries tick-tocked past the twenty, then thirty, then forty minute marks, Mommy turned to her phone. Using the World Wide Web, she went about researching sleep training.

"We did this too soon!" she hissed. "Everything I'm finding says you have to wait three months! My book that said two months is garbage!"

I did my best not to roll my eyes. If there is anything you can find on the web, it's absolute "truth." If you need to know what really happened in Dallas on November 22nd, 1963, or what's in Area 51, or the truth about chemtrails, just look to the Internet. It was my turn to promise her we were doing the right thing, but Mommy would have nothing of my assurances.

My guarantees didn't have the backing of anonymous posters on Internet message boards, and therefore held no weight. I had to cede to her demands; if the crying continued to the ninety-minute mark, we could quietly pop in to the nursery and make sure all was well.

Because the Gods are cruel Gods, you did not stop crying, and we had to endure the pain of knowing you were suffering needlessly because we were being stubborn. There were respites of almost thirty to forty seconds, and once almost a minute, where we were certain you were done... but no. Those were only pauses to rejuvenate the air in your tiny lungs and rest the cords in your baby throat.

When the allotted time had passed, Mommy darted out of bed and noiselessly dashed into your room. I followed less quickly, still hoping we could get this extinction thing banged out in one night.

When I got to the nursery doorway, Mommy was crouched next to your crib, where she could monitor you without being caught. She looked at me with worried eyes, and motioned that she wanted to go in for the save. I stopped her and whispered, "Not during an outburst. Wait for a moment where she's at a low-ebb."

Mommy waited, and a few seconds later a break came in your crying. Mommy reached in and cupped her hands under your armpits, gently raised you up, and pulled you in for a hug. She whispered a song of apology into your ear, begging forgiveness for the neglect, then eventually nursed and laid a relaxed you back in the crib. You then slept soundly for a nice stretch of time, until right around the 5am hour.

Unbeknownst to you, at that moment, one room over, the most evil of nightmares was shocking me awake.

Staring at the ceiling as I had when trying to fall asleep, I wondered why something so awful would be rooting around the recesses of my mind, when I heard you squeak.

I wondered if you were awake, or just transitioning, so I got up.

As I tiptoed into your room, your first actual cry erupted. This wasn't a transition; it was definitely "awake time."

I quietly positioned myself aside your crib. Your eyes were opening and closing, opening and closing. Due to the crying, you couldn't focus and see me, so I reached down and lightly grasped a foot.

Your eyes went wide instantly, and the crying stopped as if I had hit a "mute" button.

You looked at me with a casual expectance: *Oh, there you are. Picking me up now?*

I smiled and said, "Hello, beautiful baby girl."

I lifted you to me; you nuzzled into my shoulder, contented.

And my heart went to bursting.

And we never made you wait for us again.

Love,
Dad

January 24, 2014

Dear Hillary,

I am in Brimley, Michigan, and missing you dearly. I have been harboring an irrational fear lately, which is redundant because most (if not all) fear is irrational. Specifically, I have been having a thought I do not appreciate; a thought I label as "wrong," or "inappropriate," instead of recognizing it as natural. If anything it is an emotional hurdle to be overcome.

What I am discussing, in my roundabout way, is your future sibling, Squeak. Every so often, *What if I don't love Squeak as much as I love Hillary?* flutters across my unfocused brain.

I try to justify it with more questioning, like, "Is that a normal thought?"

As a first-time father, they are questions I can have but am unable to answer. The best I can do is research it out given the experience I have.

When Mommy was pregnant with you, I received some odd words of wisdom, thoughts that were anything but wise. A friend of mine was visiting, and noticed me loving on our doggy, Kitty. In a tone that carried no emotion, he said, "When you have your kid, you'll love your dog less. You can't help it. It just happens. You don't have time for him anymore."

His words made me confused, and somewhat sad. I love our doggy, Kitty. This is a given. Kitty looks at me with such deep, brown eyes. He is a dog full of tenderness.

So when I heard I would love him less because of you, I didn't like it. I brooded, not wanting it to be true. I had heard horror stories about pets and children my whole life; I know first-hand people who stopped caring for the animals that had brought them such joy only a few months prior to their child's birth.

Eventually, I informed Mommy of my worries, and she laughed and shook her head.

"I don't think it's anything like that," she explained. "I think the heart has the capacity to love more, the more there is to love. I think that when something new arrives, your heart expands."

The idea that love is finite, and that if something new arrives we must displace old love in order to accommodate new, was nonsense to her.

It might sound like a Hallmark card, but Mommy said it, and hearing the concept articulated made me happy. I liked Mommy's explanation, and found it to be true.

At least, true for us. Maybe there are people for whom love is finite, where they can only love a certain amount and then have nothing left. Thankfully, I don't think your Mommy and I are like that. I don't find myself loving Kitty any less because you are here, and I don't find myself neglecting him like I was told I would. He still looks at me with his deep, brown eyes, and I still find myself smiling at him because of it. I lean in, go nose-to-nose with Kitty as I scratch his ears and gaze into his doggy eyes. Because even though I have no way of knowing whether or not this is true, I believe it makes him happy.

So.

Believing like I do that the heart expands and love is infinite, why do I still have the random thought, "What if I don't love Squeak as much as I love Hillary?"

Maybe it's because I don't know Squeak yet. Maybe it's because the more I watch you grow into a little person, the more your personality develops, the more my heart expands and I love you.

I don't know.

But I do believe that fear is irrational.

And I have to believe that when Squeak is born, I will look into her (or his) eyes and my heart will expand even further to accommodate the love she will need when entering this big, scary world. Because if I didn't believe that, what hope would there be for the future?

Love,
Dad

January 29, 2014

Dear Hillary,

Earlier this week we watched one of the many Sesame Street episodes on our DVR. As it played, I marveled at how long the show has been around. I watched it as a child, and am now happily introducing it to you. The show is educational, informative, enlightening, and many other praise-worthy terms.

Your favorite character is Elmo, which isn't surprising. Many kids love Elmo; the marketing department really hit a home run with that puppet. He's even on your diapers, which makes you smile and laugh and wave them in the air. I'm not sure how you'd feel if you made the connection between having your idol on something you use to eliminate bodily waste, though.

When you see the TV remote or a smartphone, you point and ask, "Elmo?" You know he can be found on those devices, and you revel in the defeat Mommy and I feel when we realize we didn't hide our electronics well enough.

(It's not that you aren't allowed to watch television, but we do try to limit it.)

When you get hold of one of your magical "Elmo" devices, you smile and thrust it at us. You know where Elmo exists, you just don't know exactly how to make him appear. Not for any lack of trying, mind you. You push the buttons on the TV remote like mad, and on occasion even turn the set on. You also grasped so very quickly the concept of Siri, the Apple voice-command app. When you manage to hold down the button that gives a "beep-beep" tone of acknowledgement, you garble your delightfully incoherent toddler language into the phone immediately, holding it up to your mouth in understanding that somewhere inside the gadgetry is a woman's voice trying to help you.

Sometimes Siri exclaims, "I'm sorry, I didn't catch that," and sometimes she comes up with the oddest translation of your word salad, such as, "I found several trash compactors in your area. Would you like me to call one?"

(Side note: your current fascination is all things with buttons that go "beep beep." I'm not sure exactly when it started, but one day as I was carrying you past the house thermostat, you reached out with a pointed index finger, saying, "Beep beep! Beep beep!"

I had to pause while you pushed several buttons, causing the display to illuminate, which amused you.

Now we cannot pass a vending machine, the thermostat, an ATM machine, or the microwave without stopping.

If it has a button, you reach for it eagerly, stating quite clearly, "Beep beep!"

But I digress.)

Sesame Street picks a theme for each episode, a "life lesson" to instill in the young minds watching. The show tells children they're unique, teaches them how to deal with frustration and disappointment... truth be told, the show tells children things most people forget as they become adults.

(Which means watching over your shoulder is sometimes a guilty treat of mine, because there's nothing wrong with continuing emotional education through adulthood.)

Gold medal-winning Olympic skater Evan Lysacek was on a segment of the episode of Sesame Street we watched, discussing "confidence." What the word means, what confidence is, and why the children watching should be confident as they pass through life.

(See what I mean? Good life lesson for many adults.)

There is sometimes a fine line between confident and arrogant, and I hope teaching aids such as Sesame Street help you learn and understand the difference. Confident is usually quiet, while arrogance is loud. Confident people carry themselves with dignity, arrogant people less so. Unfortunately, all too often in life you will run into the latter masked as the former. It might sound strange, but when people lack confidence they act arrogant as a substitute.

In my lifetime, I've watched the rise of the Internet, something that didn't exist when I was young. Now the whole planet is interconnected by bandwidth. Connectivity is a double-edged sword; the best and worst thing the Internet did was to give everyone a voice. On the plus side, it allowed oppressed people the opportunity to speak up and be heard, to overthrow tyrants and dictators. The drawback is that the Internet allows arrogant and inconsiderate people to shout their oft-unwarranted thoughts to the world. Sometimes when you have nothing to say, you want to be heard all the more. It doesn't make sense, but little in life does.

Take Elmo, for example. As stated, you love Elmo. He's pretty much your favorite thing in the world. However, there are people who hate Elmo. They hate Elmo as much as you love him. Because they are insecure in their belief/opinion, they want other people to think like they do. They post on message boards, being as negative as possible, telling the world how much they hate Elmo, and how if anyone likes Elmo that person is stupid. They write online reviews, and post their thoughts on personal blogs: "I pound my chest with my opinion!"

It is this way with everything. Your favorite movie, your favorite book, your favorite TV show... If you love it, someone out there hates it. And opinion is a two way street. Anything you hate, someone out there really loves. A movie you couldn't stand is someone else's favorite movie.

This isn't a bad thing; people are entitled to different opinions. But are you confident in your opinion, or insecure? If you are confident, you like what you like and allow others to like what they like. "Live and let live," as the saying goes. If you are insecure, instead of just quietly thinking to yourself, "Well, this isn't my thing," you feel the need to tell everyone what you dislike, and get angry when other people don't feel the same way. The key to navigating life is understanding that, and deciding how to react when confronted with something you don't enjoy. As someone who attempts to swim in the world of creativity, I see all too often the dark side of people's thoughts.

I bring all this up because something interesting happened to a joke of mine. I mentioned in a previous letter that I post my comedy online. Sometimes I'm well received, sometimes I'm ignored, and sometimes, well, other things happen.

I shall explain.

Earlier this week, I posted a joke on a website that allows people to do three things. They can vote anonymously as to whether or not they like what they see, leave a comment for me to read, or both. For this particular joke, the overwhelming majority of the comments were negative. Right off the bat people began insulting me, calling me names, and showing me the worst side of their personalities. But as this was happening, anonymous viewers voted the joke positive. Many people really enjoyed my offering and let it be known, albeit silently.

Unfortunately, three or four people were so insecure regarding their dislike they felt the need to shout about it. Instead of either voting down my joke and moving on, or just looking at it online and deciding they didn't like it and leaving well enough alone, they felt the need to attack either the joke, or me personally. Even worse, anyone who said, "This made me laugh" was ridiculed and insulted. The negative few didn't want anyone disagreeing with them.

I was sitting back and letting everything unfold without intervention, and some people asked why I wasn't stepping in to defend myself. The only answer I had was because I generally don't get involved with such nonsense. Once a joke is out there, it's out there. People are going to react how they will, and there's nothing I can do about that. Plus, I found it laughingly ironic that as people were calling names because they didn't enjoy a joke I made, I was sitting on the floor with you, making you giggle. I would tickle your toes, boop your nose, and raspberry away on your tummy, and the whole time you would squeal with glee. Then I'd look at my phone to see another person over-analyze my joke in order to sound smart and shake my head in response. The dichotomy of their fiction and actual reality was insane. Internet Warriors, being self-righteous from the obscurity of their homes.

How very noble.

Anyway, I tell you all this for two reasons: one, if you ever do anything remotely creative, you will face the same scrutiny. People have opinions on everything, and they value their own opinions above all else. You will have to steel yourself against judgment, and trust in yourself and your art. How you express yourself—music, paint, poetry—is an opportunity for someone who doesn't have those skills to judge you for yours. Don't let their negativity weigh on you; their words are more a reflection on who they are, not who you are.

Two: remember, no matter how vocal negative people are, there is always more good than bad in the world. Sometimes good is more subdued than bad, and bad more boisterous, but good has greater numbers. Even when working silently.

Is it nice when people comment "This was great!" on my comedy? Absolutely. But even if people are silent in their support and the detractors are vocal, knowing the anonymous many are out there in greater numbers makes me smile. And, as the numbers showed, the masses enjoyed my comedy far more than the detractors wanted them to.

Whatever you choose to do with your life, always remember to be confident. People may attack or slander you, but they don't matter. Negativity isn't worth your time. Positivity is.

Positivity, and belief in yourself.

Love,
Dad

January 31, 2014

Dear Hillary,

I am in Quincy, Illinois, and missing you dearly. Because I am gone most weekends, I get my "Hilly Time" every Monday and Tuesday. You stay home with me, and we go on whatever adventures we can find. On Monday we generally head down to the mall, because they have a play area for young kids. Tuesday we usually go to the local rec center, because they have "Tot Time" at the library, where books get read and songs get sung. Sometimes before, sometimes after this reading/singing event, we go to The Campsite, an indoor children's play area.

The Campsite is smaller than the play area at the mall, but it's also much nicer because the rules are enforced. In the mall, parents are supposed to take their shoes off, but they don't. At The Campsite, everyone—adults and kids—removes their shoes before entering. No food or drink is allowed in either play place, but people pay no heed to the sign at the mall, and coffee, soda, and whatever else people drink gets spilled everywhere. At the rec center, if someone brings coffee in, a staffer escorts them out. Basically, without enforcement, people treat the things they don't own without respect, which is sad. That, as they say, is why we can't have nice things.

The mall does have its selling points, however. Where The Campsite is enclosed, the play area at the mall is wide open, and therefore easily escaped by wandering children. And you, dear one, love to wander.

For a while, you will play on the soft, pliable edifices designed to be crawled and hopped upon, but after a spell of time you notice there is a larger world surrounding you, and you want to examine it. You make your way to the exit, and sometimes glance over your shoulder to see where I am. Sometimes you just go for it. There is so much space to roam that you are overwhelmed by possibilities. Should you stick to the corridors? Should you enter store after store, seeing what they have to offer?

I follow at a safe distance. You are always within eyesight and a three-second sprint, but I never linger too closely. I want you to explore, to learn limits, and test boundaries.

And that probably makes me an oddity among the parenting world.

In the many months we have been coming to the play area, I've observed three styles of parenting: helicopter, indifferent, and interactive.

The helicopter parent, a term coined years ago, is someone who frets and worries about their child constantly. They hover above their child, ever vigilant to outside threats such as tripping, falling, or sneezing. They are the Kings & Queens of "No-no," and "Don't touch!" Always said with the child's best interest at heart. They see danger in everything, and fear the outside world.

The indifferent parents are almost worse, because they check out immediately upon entering the playground. They sit on the bench, eyes affixed to the cell phones in front of them, playing games, Facebooking, texting... anything and everything but paying attention to their child. Every so often I see kids looking at their parents. I have no way of knowing what goes through their minds, but I do know I never want you to see me and wonder if you are less important than the cell phone I own.

These first two parents never let their kids leave the play area. Many children are like you. They see the rest of the mall before them, and eyes go wide as they wonder, "What's out there?"

But if they make for the exit, or worse, forge their way into the mall proper, the resounding word "No!" comes shouted from their parents' mouths.

With indifferent parents, it's somewhat sad. They look up from their electronics to see their child has strayed several dozen feet from the play area, then rush out and scold the child for being a child, instead of looking inward and examining their poor parenting skills.

I personally do my best to be an interactive parent, meaning I play with you when I can, and leave you to your own devices when you are with others. Whenever you look up, I am looking at you happily. When we lock eyes—when you find me, making sure I'm still around—I smile, and then you smile. All is well in the world. What you're doing is OK, and I'm nearby making sure you're safe. Like a security blanket you don't always need to hold, but like having around just in case.

But, as good as I am, I pale in comparison to Mommy.

My parenting fun involves making silly faces, and picking you up and wiggling you around as you giggle.

Mommy, on the other hand? She gets down and dirty. In fact, I'm going to step aside and let Mommy take over for a while. She wrote an open letter to the parenting community at large, and I think she did a bang-up job discussing the concept of parenting.

"About six weeks ago, I took my daughter Hillary to the community center's indoor toddler playground on a chilly Saturday afternoon. Only one other family was there — a dad on his tablet, headphones on, accompanied by three kids ranging in age from six to one and a half. The middle child, a girl, was adorably precocious and introduced herself (and her brothers) to me immediately. "I'm Charlie, and this is Joshua. The little one is Noah," she informed me. At exactly that moment, her brother tooted and Charlie's jaw dropped. "Joshua. Say excuse me."

He sheepishly did, and I immediately liked this little trio.

Hilly isn't really into other kids yet—she's just a little too young—so I got down on the squishy floor with her and crawled around. Soon Charlie and Joshua were following me, so I decided to play along. "Joshua! Charlie! We're out of gas! What will we do?" I asked as they clambered into the squishy plastic Jeep. "The frog! He's got the gas! Go get it, Joshua!"

While he retrieved the fuel, Charlie and I crawled across the "water" on the carpet to the troll bridge, where we tried to figure out the magic word that would make the troll come out. Then we all lumbered into the canoe where I taught them how to "paddle" with invisible oars. Suddenly, a big storm blew us all out of the boat, but we swam to safety with the help of a giant fish.

The entire time, Noah toddled around after us, as did Hilly. We kept up our game for almost half an hour before taking a break. The kids' father glanced at me sideways a few times, making comments about how I had "too much energy."

Dad finally gave up his spot on the bench after seeing Noah climb into my lap, wrap his arms around my neck and deliver an open-mouthed kiss right on my face. It was adorable. I was smitten. And Dad was self-conscious.

He got down on the floor and tried to play with his kids, but he had a hard time going from "grown up" mode to "Hot lava! Quick! Get on the rocks before you're melted by hot lava!"

Admittedly, it takes a while to remember how to play make-believe. Dad tried but ultimately called it quits, and herded his kids out the door soon after.

I felt bad for them. Their daddy was lacking imagination. Or maybe his was just so out of practice he couldn't find it amidst the cobwebs.

This past Sunday afternoon, we returned to the playplace. To my delight, Charlie, Joshua, and Noah were there again. They didn't remember me at first, but they soon recognized me, and were rarin' to play again. We had a blast, throwing our balled-up socks at my husband (he was an energy-sucking troll) and their dad (he was a troll that, if touched, would put you into a coma). To his credit, he tried to participate this time around. He even started the sock-throwing, which was the best he could do. Dad still couldn't play make believe, hard as he tried. Hilly and Noah got into it a little more this time, too. (And I got another kiss from Noah at the end. Yay!)

I'm not that unique and special of a parent, I'm sure. But I've been to the playplace a lot over the past few months, and never seen another parent playing — really playing — with the kids.

So here's my request for you, parents:

I know you're tired. We all are. I'm not asking you to play every single time. But every so often, when you're at the playground, don't veg out.

*Get down on the floor. Take off your shoes. Forget about how you look, and ignore what other parents might think. **Play**. Be a kid. Play pretend, play make-believe, and make up nonsensical stories. Throw socks. (Someone else's stinky socks, even.) Pretend they're hand grenades. Fight bad guys, typhoons, and talk to turtles. You can do it. You should do it.*

When I think back on my own childhood, I have very clear memories of the rare times my parents put aside their adult responsibilities and played with me and my sisters. Having mom or dad visit our little kid world was the Best Day Ever.

Make tomorrow your kids' Best Day Ever. Because all too soon they'll stop playing make believe, and you might just wish you'd played with them when you could."

I couldn't put it any better than that, which is why I didn't try. I think between the two of us, we're going to do an OK job with your playtime.

Love,
Dad

February 6, 2014

Dear Hillary,

I am in Williston, North Dakota, and missing you dearly. Though I am forever thinking of you, it was recently driven home how important my role of father is.

I'm not completely stupid. I *know* it's my job to be a good father and that you will receive your life cues from me... but this past week it was branded into me just what it means to raise a *daughter*.

There is an old joke: when you have a boy, you only have to worry about your boy. When you have a girl, you have to worry about every boy on the planet. The idea is boys want to take advantage of girls, and girls need protection. Which, in my opinion, doesn't give girls much credit. I feel that if I raise you correctly, you will find self-worth in who you are, not who you date.

That lesson is something I learned the hard way.

It is popular knowledge that the way a woman dates is directly tied to her relationship with her father; the confidence and self-esteem instilled in any child is tied to the lovers they take in adulthood. My parents did not have the most loving, tender marriage. What I absorbed growing up was that relationships are built on pain, mistrust, and dishonesty. Though such things were never verbalized, the presence and power those emotions had under our family roof was palpable. I internalized all too well the idea relationships were about frustration, not joy.

At some point during my scribblings to you, I'm going to reminisce about the three relationships I had before meeting your mother. Each taught me something new about myself, and allowed me to grow into a man that was ready for a healthy, loving relationship by the time Mommy and I met.

I will start today, with Karen.

A fellow traveler in the comedy world recently tossed a nugget of information my way, "Did you hear Karen got married?"

Karen is the last woman I dated before I met Mommy, and no, I hadn't heard she got married. I hadn't thought of her in years, actually. We were only together a handful of months, which over the span of a lifetime doesn't add up to much.

Turns out, she not only got married, Karen married a man as old as your grandparents, someone 30 years her senior. The age gap between Karen and her new husband is larger than the gap between my mother and me.

I would almost like to say this news surprised me, but it did not. Karen marrying a man with an AARP card was as expected as gravity. Where my childhood experiences led me on a quest to fix wounded doves, Karen embarked on a lifelong scavenger hunt for a father figure.

Karen liked a certain kind of man, one who would drink a beer and start a fight if the mood struck him. Someone who voted using hot air or anger, not intelligence, as his North Star. Someone that would hunt for fun, because if you don't kill animals, you're a sissy. Someone who drove a truck, because economically sensible cars are for gays. Men drive *trucks*, not cars. Men listen to country music, not jazz. Because I did not fit the mold she needed to feel feminine, we were doomed from the start.

There is nothing wrong with trucks, cars, country music, or jazz. The problem is in believing there is only one way things should exist; stereotypes shouldn't be standards. When someone states, "That's the way life has to be, and anyone different is wrong," they are too narrow-minded for my tastes.

I look at you and imagine a man saying, "You're going to be a stay-at-home wife who has babies and lives in the kitchen." That would anger me. Now, if someday you *choose* to be a stay-at-home mom and raise children, I will respect you, for it's a difficult task. But no one should force you to do such a thing because they believe in specific gender roles; no one should box in another person because of the limitations of their own imagination, or the blinders they wear through life.

My goal is to raise you to be full of poise and self-respect. I want you to observe my interactions with Mommy, to see how I treat her, and absorb them. I want you to know you deserve respect and love from your partners, because you are worth it. Nothing would disappoint me more than knowing I failed you as a father, and that your self-worth was tethered to less-than-stellar lovers. As judgmental as this sounds, when I think about Karen, I see all the things I want to be better for you. Hearing of her marriage slammed home to me how important my role as father is.

As stated, I heard of her nuptials via a fellow comedian, Scott, and apparently he was also a part of Karen's romantic history. I met Scott in the green room of a comedy club, and he introduced himself in a vulgar fashion involving the fact we shared sexual conquest of her.

I've been blessed with a fairly decent Poker Face, so if my eyes betrayed either surprise or shock at his words, I am unaware. My face remained placid, that much I know, because maintaining a neutral expression is a skill I possess. I do admit to having arched a mental eyebrow at the statement. No one had ever given me such a greeting, so it caught me unprepared.

Apparently while I dated Karen for just under a year, Scott slept with her for a weekend. For some reason, my name came up repeatedly during his two nights with her, and for years he wondered who I was.

I was and remain curious: why had I been the focus of attention during their weekend romp? It's been several years and I still have no answer for that question. It didn't feel appropriate to contact her just to ask, "So, why were you two talking about me, all these years later?"

Upon first hearing the other comic had been with Karen, I didn't feel any single way about it. Karen was so far in my rearview she only remained as a wisp of memory. She had, however, dumped me, which at the time hurt. Rejection always hurts, and anyone saying otherwise will Pinocchio their way to an elongated nose. But I moved on, met Mommy, and became quite happy. So while my first response to hearing of Karen's nuptials was indifference, the more the weekend with Scott progressed, the more I learned I had dodged an enormous bullet.

Scott cheated on his first wife with Karen, and before our weekend together was finished he would cheat on his current fiancée with an employee of the club. He had an addiction problem—prescription pill bottles littered his hotel room, making it look like Heath Ledger's last stand—and his nights were a blur of alcoholic imbibing. For someone in their early twenties, this could *almost* be forgiven as "normal," but for a man on the dawn of forty it seemed a bit immature.

I examined him as a scientist might a specimen, wondering what kind of transition Karen had to go through to shift gears from me—someone honest and monogamous—to a walking mess of a man who was desperate to convince the world he wasn't going bald.

(Note: Hats, hair plugs, and growth-gels don't fool anyone, my follicle-challenged friends.)

It was an informative few days. I learned that after dating me Karen had become a trampoline for comedians passing through her town, and that she had a child and wasn't in a relationship with the father. I was shown pictures that had her looking at least fifteen years above her given age, meaning time was a robe she did not wear well.

(It did make her look closer to her husband's age than her own, though. Hey oh! #MeanJoke)

I'm not proud of it, but these enlightenments gave me an ego-swell, and probably a mild case of schadenfreude.

Pre-marriage motherhood, by the way, is a trait Karen shared with her younger sister. Because their parents treated religion as a set of rules to be obeyed and not a vehicle for enlightenment and compassion, both daughters went a little boy-crazy when given the opportunity. It has been proven time and time again that wagging a finger and saying "NO!" does nothing but create the desire to experiment and explore. My job will be to teach you cause and effect.

This doesn't mean you won't date casually, and/or be in relationships that don't last. The "high school sweetheart turned lifetime lover" match is a rare one. But it also doesn't mean you have to view short-term relationships as failures. While some people see disappointment in past relationships, I see "failed" relationships as building blocks; they are steps to be taken as you progress and grow as a person. The only question is, *will* you grow? All too often we squander opportunities to pause in self-reflection and use them to finger-point instead. Rather than examine what could be done better next time around, we double down on personality problems and poor decisions that got us in trouble in the first place—imagine if I had tried to date another "Karen," just to prove I could. It was only when I decided to find someone wise on her own terms that I realized unions are partnerships of equality.

The point is: every misstep I took led me to the place I am today. There are those that say, "If I could go back and change one thing in my life...", but I harbor no such fantasies. To change one thing would be to change my entire timeline, and then who knows where I'd be today? I might not have met your Mom, and we might not have had you. The idea I couldn't have you as a daughter is a far greater tragedy than any heartbreak I suffered after an unsuccessful relationship.

I hope to instill in you the confidence to like what you like. That way, you will choose lovers based on how well they treat you, not because you feel you have to live up to their approval or expectations. Or, even worse, because you feel someone subpar is all you deserve. I want you to have confidence, so you don't seek out anyone who uses a false swagger and arrogant disposition to cover up their intellectual shortcomings.

Over the course of your life, I will do my best to take lessons learned throughout my life to give you better footing than I had when dating.

And I will support you as you make decisions, because that's what I'm here to do, support you as you grow.

Love,
Dad

February 15, 2014

Dear Hillary,

I am in Duluth, Minnesota, and missing you dearly. When I am home, there are things I know I shouldn't do, yet I do them anyway. Case in point, one day many months ago, when you were learning to crawl, I picked you up out of your crib at the exact moment I realized I had to pee.

You were post-nap groggy, so I figured—even though you've been mobile for a while now—putting you dead center of our king-size bed would be safe.

One toy to distract you, always within sight by me. Yup, safe.

I plopped you down, walked seven feet into the bathroom, and let fly my yellow stream of freedom.

Which is exactly when you decided to laugh and beeline it straight toward me.

Ever ready, I was aiming with my left hand just in case my dominant right hand needed the freedom of use. I pinched off and dove toward you, arriving just as you tumbled over the edge, rug-burning the hell out of my left knee in the slide.

You were giggling, so I did the same; no reason to get you all panicked.

I set you on the floor—which is what I should have done in the first place—stood, walked back to the ceramic god, and finished up, proud of myself. Seriously, it was almost as good as Antonio Freeman keeping the ball off the ground to win against the Vikings in OT.

(You'll have seen it on YouTube by the time you read this, trust me.)

Anyway, your daddy is not a bright person. I make no secret of this. As proof, I offer up my latest achievement of stupidity, something I could get an award for if such a thing existed.

On my Facebook friends list, there are two women with nearly identical names. By that I mean they share the same first name, and have oh-so-similar last names. Naturally, it would be easy to assume I would confuse the two.

The other month, a woman popped up in my "Hey, it's your friend's birthday!" feed. After a glance, I quickly surmised it was the fitness instructor whose classes I like to attend. As one might expect out of a fitness instructor, she's muscular from top to bottom, with rips and cuts aplenty to flaunt. It was Wednesday, her day to teach, so I scribbled a little ditty on her wall: "Happy Birthday! In honor of your special day, I'm skipping the gym tonight and going out to eat pizza and get fat, just for you!"

Get it? It's a joke! She's a fitness instructor, and I was going to skip her class to eat unhealthy food! Ha ha! So funny!

A few weeks later, I received another notice for my fitness instructor friend from that lovely birthday monitoring service on Facebook. Confused, I went to her wall and wrote, "Didn't I just wish you a happy birthday? Geez, how many do you need a year?"

And that was that.

For about an hour.

Before long, my mind started putting together pieces of a puzzle I didn't even realize existed, and I decided to log back on to Facebook and scroll down some other profile walls.

My "Pizza and get fat" comment was nowhere to be found on the fitness instructor's profile, so...

...where was it?

Turns out, I had left the comment on the *other* woman's wall, the one whose name is *two letters* different from the fitness instructor. A woman who was, as chance would have it, a little larger than your average woman, but probably right in line with your average resident of Mississippi.

That's right, I went to the profile of a woman who was overweight and told her I was going to get fat in her honor.

I felt like the biggest idiot, ever. I wasn't sure whether to apologize, explain, or ignore, and in the end settled on the last option. The larger woman never brought it up, which in my mind means I hopefully dodged a bullet, but probably means she harbors a silent resentment against me.

Oh well, I suppose that's what people get when they use avatars instead of personal pictures to represent themselves.

Situational awareness is something I try to be better at, but usually fail. One of my best friends, Mr. Brian Jones, came to visit me when I lived in Los Angeles. Well, to be fair, he traveled to LA for business, then stayed a couple extra days to hang out with me.

Due to the fact we were (and continue to be) obsessed with music, I took him to Amoeba Music. It's a world famous, independent record store with a location on Sunset Boulevard. It carries everything. New, used, hard to find, impossible to find, and I-didn't-know-that-existed bootlegs.

While standing in one of the wider aisles, I noticed a copy of *Californication*—the CD, not the TV show—on the end cap display. Brian introduced me to the Red Hot Chili Peppers in 1987—he played the song "Backwoods" for me, from *The Uplift Mofo Party Plan*—and I was hooked. As a bass player, the song ripped into me something fierce.

I immediately bought *Freaky Styley*, and when they came out, *Mother's Milk* and *Blood Sugar Sex Magik*. Brian and I finally saw the Chili Peppers live on the Blood Sugar Sex Magik tour. At first, we were excited, because it was the second date on the tour. They were playing Madison, Wisconsin, and then we were seeing them in Milwaukee.

"How cool is that?" we thought. "We get to see them before anyone else!"

Little did we understand the band was getting the unimportant dates out of the way, so the kinks would be taken care of before the important markets: Chicago, LA, New York, etc.

Not that it means anything, but it was a triple bill that night. RHCP, Smashing Pumpkins, and opening for both with a short, thirty-minute set, an unknown band called Pearl Jam. Eddie Vedder was still stage diving back then, and he rode the audience around the entirety of the Eagle's Ballroom while crowd surfing. Pearl Jam really should have had a longer set; Billy Corgan's nasal whine really couldn't follow their energy.

Anyway, after Blood Sugar, things fell apart for the RHCP. Anthony's drug use was a problem, John Frusciante quit the band, and they seemed destined to fade away, releasing 'greatest hits' albums ad nauseam for the rest of their career.

Surprisingly, in 1998, Frusciante returned, and with him the hope the band would reclaim their iconic sound. Which, if you look at the *sales* of *Californication*, they did. But to me, the gap between Blood Sugar and Cali had been too long. Maybe I changed, but to me, while I could still listen to *Mother's Milk* beginning to end, I could only listen to a song or two on Cali. To me, they sounded like a fantastic Red Hot Chili Peppers cover band, not the Peppers themselves.

I know I shouldn't complain—it is near impossible to maintain vitality for three albums, much less thirty years—but maybe that's why I like The Police so much. Five albums, each entirely different in sound, style, and texture from the one before it, and then bam, break up and walk away on top. Or, to put it in a famous way, "Better to burn out, than fade away."

One of my main fears regarding the RHCP is that I am one of those curmudgeons who speak only of what Bruce Springsteen labeled "Glory Days," meaning I'm stuck in the past, and the problem is mine. Or maybe I'm right, and after a while their ability to really nail a song—something I think they absolutely did with Rain Dance Maggie—happened less and less often.

Either way, standing in Amoeba Music, I picked up and held *Californication* for a moment, saying to Brian in a resignedly depressed tone, "God, I used to love them, but this just... it's just not good."

I placed the CD back on the shelf, and turned to see their bass player, the iconic man named Flea, standing about 10 feet away.

His back was turned, and he hadn't heard me and wasn't paying attention to us in any way, shape, or form, but damn if I didn't feel stupid.

He was my favorite bass player, and the man who inspired me above almost all others regarding the instrument, and I had just insulted him. Plus, had I not just said that and felt like a complete moron, I would have taken the moment to rush over and shake his hand and thank him for the music.

To do so after slandering him would have been hypocritical, even if he were unaware of the insult.

Flea eventually wandered off into the Big Band section and ended up walking out with a handful of discs.

I don't remember what Brian or I bought, if anything.

Yup.

Your Daddy the dummy. At least you haven't figured it out yet.

Love,
Dad

February 22, 2014

Dear Hillary,

I had a local gig this weekend, which is my favorite kind. It means I get to perform and get paid, while also sleeping in my own bed and being there for you when you wake up. And you, dear one, are waking up differently these days, which is why I'm writing with a gentle smile right now.

As always, on Tuesday we went to the library for 'Tot Time'—a three-book reading event for children your age—and followed that with a visit to 'The Campsite,' the playground for toddlers I've already mentioned. It is filled with spongy structures to climb upon, meaning if anyone tumbles or falls, they bounce back no worse for wear.

This week, as always, you made straight for your favorite toy, the mock Jeep. You love sitting behind the steering wheel and cranking it left and right. When you arrived another girl was already there, but as there is room for two, her presence did not deter you. Up you climbed, and as you started throwing a leg over to fully scramble inside, she looked at you in a mix of horror and agitation and shouted, "Hey! You're not my friend!"

She then jumped out and darted off.

You didn't mind, because you don't yet comprehend every spoken word, just a precious few you hear from Mommy and Daddy.

(Plus, it meant you now had unfettered access to the steering wheel you love so much.)

I laughed, because... well, it was such a pure moment. So like a child to be completely without candor. Would that adults acted similarly.

Years ago I knew someone I labeled a friend. We met online in a large political debate group, and eventually established a friendship outside it as well as outside of virtual reality. I was introduced to his wife, we dined together several times, and I even spent a night under his roof while between gigs.

One day, he stopped talking to me, and the next I was no longer a part of his online social circle. The last message I sent him was "All well in your world?" and I never got a reply, just radio silence.

Which was fine. We had been drifting apart, and to quote John McClane, "I got enough friends!"

He had gone through a rough patch in his marriage, a time when he was actively having an online affair with another woman, and I did my best to be supportive... but I probably failed a bit. Having been cheated on myself, I didn't appreciate the lack of respect he was showing his wife. It wasn't my place to say anything to her, but every so often I did toss a question or two his way. I'm sure there was a hint of judgment in my voice, even though I consciously did my best to just be there for him. Unfortunately, after listening to his laments, I would ask, "Any plans to actually work on your marriage, or are you just focused on the new woman?"

When he disappeared I figured it was because I knew too much, or because he patched things up with the Mrs. and needed a scapegoat for his extramarital dalliances. Pointing a finger and saying, "It was all him!" is an easy way to cover your tracks in such a situation. He also may have been ashamed of his actions. Distancing yourself from your worst behavior often involves distancing yourself from the people around you at that time. Hell, he also may have sensed I didn't approve of his actions and wanted more supportive friends around him. I don't know, and while it doesn't gnaw at me, I always thought it would have been nice to get one email explaining why he stopped talking to me. No matter what it said, even if it involved anger and accusations, at least then I'd have something to nod my head at thoughtfully. It may have been harsh, it may have been sympathetic, but it would have been tangible.

Mommy used to have a lifelong friend, one she actually considered her best friend for many years. I mentioned her in an earlier letter, "Jamie."

As you know, for two years Mommy and I were unsuccessful in our journey to make you. When the natural way didn't work, we enlisted the help of medical professionals. First came fertility medications. When those didn't work, insemination was attempted, and at the end of it all was the process of in vitro fertilization.

Mommy handled the adversity like a champ, but as can be expected she was occasionally frustrated and emotional. Having been pumped full of hormones nightly for weeks at a time did not improve the moments of frustration or sadness.

One of her go-to friends during this time was Jamie, someone she had known twenty-five years. They had been friends since elementary school. Jamie had been Mommy's matron of honor, and I met her for the first time at our rehearsal dinner.

From what I was told beforehand, Jamie didn't like me. Not me specifically, but the idea of me. Many times people from small towns have small minds and see life using a very narrow worldview. They like things to fit into easily understood boxes: men are breadwinners, women make babies. Families own a house with a white picket fence, you buy a dog and have 2.5 kids, and everyone goes to church. Needless to say, I fit none of these little stereotypes and was therefore immediately suspect.

Because I wanted to clear up any misunderstandings, I went out of my way to make nice at the rehearsal. I wanted her to have an opportunity to poke and prod at me with the sort of questions protective friends like to ask. My memory of her was pleasant enough, and aside from that evening—combined with the following day, our wedding—I never saw her again.

Around our one-year anniversary, Mommy was speaking with Jamie about the fertility issues we were encountering. We had discovered that making a baby wasn't going to happen naturally, and it was frustrating. It was a time of great pain for Mommy, and she needed all the support she could get. While on the phone with Jamie, however, she got something different. A statement was made that was so stunning, Mommy felt as if she had been physically struck.

"I don't like Nathan, and think you can do better. I think you should leave him."

Mommy said the words poured out of Jamie as if said in great relief, like Jamie had been holding in for a long time and was happy to get them off her chest.

Mommy was speechless, the thought "Why would my best friend say such a horrible thing about someone she doesn't know, and who I love?" running through her head.

But Jamie didn't need to know me; she knew what she wanted to judge. Did I drink, do drugs, cheat on, or hit Mommy? Of course not. I just didn't fit into the idea of what a man should be to Jamie, and that was enough.

While Mommy didn't like her friend's attitude or statement, she was willing to look past it. Mommy tried to rationalize the judgment any way she could, and even tried understanding Jamie's point of view. They were different people, and different people like different things.

In fact, Mommy actually didn't like Jamie's husband too much. This was a man who went drinking (under the guise of fishing) on weekends, leaving Jamie home with the kids. Jamie would call Mommy crying in frustration over being abandoned so often, and Mommy would listen and support. She knew Jamie's husband didn't cheat on or hit her; it was that small town mentality rearing it's ugly head, where men work and drink, and women raise the kids. Never once did it cross Mommy's mind to say, "You deserve better." Sometimes you just have to listen to friends and be a sounding board for them to bounce their frustrations off. Not everyone wants a solution to their problems, they just need to get them out of their system.

While Mommy was willing to look past Jamie's lack of tact, in Jamie's mind the problems in their relationship just kept building.

Mommy is agnostic. She doesn't believe in any conventional religion and isn't shy in her convictions. Her friend is Christian in belief, if not function. Mommy shares her problems and life difficulties openly; she keeps a very popular blog describing her life, even the "bad" parts. Jamie believed "good folk" do not discuss such things openly, and told Mommy so on several occasions. People aren't supposed to tell their thoughts to the world like that. In fact, polite people do not have problems, they have game faces.

Unknown to Mommy, the differences festered until they reached a breaking point.

On the eve of her first round of in vitro, a time when she was supposed to be stress-free and as relaxed as possible, Mommy sent Jamie an excited email offering the measurements on all her eggs. The emotion behind the email was hope. After all the failed treatments, Mommy's fingers were crossed so hard they were white in anticipation and pressure. Would this procedure give us our child?

The response was as unexpected as Pearl Harbor: "We are different people and I don't think our friendship is working. Good luck to you. I will continue to pray for you."

And like Kaiser Söze, twenty-five years of friendship were gone.

Mommy suspects the last line, "I will continue to pray for you," was more than a throwaway. Apparently frustration over Mommy's refusal to step in line with the "blinders-on" way of life always rubbed Jamie the wrong way. The big, outside world is a scary one, and if you don't approach it the "correct" way, you were doomed. That Mommy feared neither judgment nor punishment for her beliefs became an increasing bone of contention her friend refused to let go of. Mommy believes it pushed a friendship teetering on the brink over the edge.

Mommy was hurt, but the more time that passed, she felt better and better about what happened. Jamie was right, they were two different people. Sometimes you can make a friendship work, but if it is constant effort and involves friction, what's the point?

Like the child who yelled "You're not my friend!" Jamie was straightforward with Mommy. Straightforward in a way my once-friend with the wandering eye had not been with me. Because of this, Mommy went from hurt, to appreciative.

In the end, it's always, always for the best. You won't be friends with every person you meet, and that's OK. At the end of the day, you want supportive, caring people around you.

Here's the best part of the whole story. About ten minutes after the one child yelled, "You're not my friend!" another little girl smiled at you. She reached out and touched your arm, almost checking to see if you were real or not. She then turned to me and said, "She's so pretty..."

She wanted to be your friend.

Those, dear one, those are the kind of people who should be in your life.

Love,
Dad

February 26, 2014

Dear Hillary,

You have an exciting new way to eat breakfast, something that takes place in five separate but important stages.

1. When Daddy asks "Toast or cereal?", request cereal.
2. After Daddy places the bowl of cereal in front of you, dump it and all the milk over your high chair tray.
3. Pick through cereal with right hand, eating individual pieces, while holding spoon uselessly in left hand.
4. Splash both hands in remaining milk.
5. Giggle at Daddy as he sighs.

The excitement, it never ends.

Love,
Dad

March 1, 2014

Dear Hillary,

I am in Rochester, Minnesota, and missing you dearly. You are in Des Moines with Mommy, visiting your cousins. From what I've been told (and shown through a couple pictures), you absolutely adore your cousin Sam. He makes you laugh, and laugh, and laugh. Which isn't surprising; Sam has always had younger cousins around—your Aunt Kayla's children—and his interactions with them were always geared toward selflessly keeping them amused. Sam is a good kid. I'm glad you enjoy his company.

I had a very tough decision to make this past week, because I got a fantastic work offer. Whether or not I could take it? Well, that was another thing.

A cruise ship was looking for a comedian, someone to entertain their passengers. Did I want the gig?

Yes and no. Yes, because it was solid work, with great pay. Really great pay. It could have covered an entire quarter for me. Three months of no income worries, gone with a snap of the fingers. No, because unfortunately they sprang it on me quickly: could I leave next week and be gone an entire month?

That was the tough question.

I have a few gigs lined up here and there; it will neither be a fantastic nor an awful month money-wise. So to take the gig I would have had to cancel all my shows...

...and burn people I had made commitments to in the process. That didn't seem honorable, cancelling on contracts because I had the opportunity for *more* money. But I also wonder if that isn't that what success is built on, ruthlessness. Is my willingness to honor low-paying gigs hurting me? You'd think that being an honorable person would pay off karmically, but I unfortunately know way too many selfish bastards that are very successful, and part of the reason could be their near-sociopathic nature.

One gig I have involves an eight-hour drive. The person who contacted me for it is new to the comedy game, and he emailed me out of the blue: "I saw you a few years ago, am producing a comedy show in my town, and I want you to be a part of it." He has a passion for stand up. How could I email him a middle finger a week out from my date, simply because someone with more money wanted to buy my services? I wanted to... I mean, I really wanted to, but couldn't bring myself to do it.

On top of the last-minute issue, being away from you for an entire month would have been difficult beyond words. It would have been hard on Mommy, yes, because she wouldn't have had me around to help with you and household needs, but emotionally it would have been near impossible for me. Simply put, I cannot imagine an entire month away from you. My three and four day departures are difficult enough.

While I do miss Mommy, it is easier because she is an adult and understands things. She gets the concept called time; "Nathan will be gone for three days, and then return home."

You don't get "time," you greet me like our doggy does. Whether I've been to the gym for an hour or away for three days, when I walk in the door you bum-rush me like I'm front row at The Who circa 1979, Ohio. But what would you think as the days turned to weeks? Would you wonder if I was ever coming back? Would I just fade from your memory entirely? I don't know, and without enough time to digest these questions I'm not able to arrive at any conclusions.

Hopefully, this is a "problem" I will get to address again in the future. Best-case scenario, I get the offer again and can take it. Because the way the cruise ships pay, I could be gone one month and then stay home two. And wouldn't that be nice? Morning Snuggles every day! I suppose that's the trade off, and the reason they offer so much money. Sacrifice, reward. You have to have the former for the latter.

I'm worried, though. Sometimes opportunities come along with extreme rarity, and if you lose your place in line you go all the way to the back. I'd hate to think I shot myself in the foot by doing the honorable thing, but do understand that business doesn't always reward honor.

As odd as it sounds, this whole scenario has me thinking of timing, and how so much of life is built off accidental moments. Your mother and I met by either accident, or fate, depending on how you look at it. I happened to be passing through Iowa on the right weekend, and she happened to have a series of events happen in her life that brought her to the very comedy show where I was performing. I may or may not be alive, walking, or in a coma because of timing, accident, or fate.

As you age, you look back on moments when one of two things could have happened, and either the better or worse outcome affected you. There is an importance to recognizing certain moments in life; moments that might seem like nothing at the time, but when looked back upon held significance you should have recognized.

From the early-to-mid 2000s, I lived in Los Angeles. I worked in the film industry as a "Site Rep," which is short for "Site Representation." Basically, I acted as a liaison for film productions and office buildings that allowed filming on their property.

Film crews work long hours, and one day I worked a shift that went from 10am Tuesday to 2:30am Wednesday. I had to be back on duty at 6am Wednesday morning and considered just sleeping on the floor in the office building—I'd done it before and it was actually sometimes more tolerable than driving home, napping for an hour and driving back—but ultimately decided that even if only for a short snapshot of time, my own bed would feel a million times better than concrete covered with a half-inch of industrial carpet.

I shut down the area being rented, made my way to my car, exited the parking garage, turned east on 7th street, pulled up to a red arrow at Figueroa, and waited.

And waited.

And waited.

And waited.

After what seemed like hours (but was most likely only several minutes), the arrow remained red even though the light allowing traffic to move forward on 7th switched to green.

I looked around and decided I had had enough. Downtown Los Angeles became a ghost town after 10pm— sometimes even earlier than that—and I wanted to get home. With no one around to witness my move, I made an illegal turn north onto Figueroa, then pulled up to a red light at Wilshire and waited again.

Next to me was a lovely Maserati, a car that probably cost more than I had made in my entire lifetime to that point.

This time the green came quickly, so instead of illegally running a second light I was able to be a happy motorist and drive within the lines of the law. As one would expect, the Maserati jumped out in front of me without even trying to. I was in a manual VW Golf, which handled like a tank and most likely weighed as much as one. As I accelerated, the next light up, 5th street, turned green.

"Good times," I thought. Karma was working in my favor, and I wouldn't have to slow down again.

The Maserati drove into the intersection of 5th and Wilshire, and for the one second it was there the intersection became crosshairs. A Mercedes Benz doing about 60 miles per hour flew through the eastbound red and smashed square into the Maserati.

The impact was as loud as a thunderclap.

The two cars spun together a moment in a pirouette of violence, then the Maserati broke free and slid sideways into a light post.

When the Mercedes unlocked from the Maserati, it shot backwards 75 yards over the sidewalk and up several steps in front of the corner of a building, losing both front tires in the process and knocking an extraordinary chunk of marble and concrete off the stairs of the building.

My foot had left the gas instinctively, and I popped my car into neutral and coasted to a stop as I pulled to the side of the road. I was calm, and created a sort of mini-checklist in my mind: "Get out of your car. Get to the Maserati. Make sure everyone inside is OK. Ignore the people in the Mercedes, who ran the red light and whose fault this is."

As I was exiting my car, I noticed two other cars pulling over.

Gawkers, or witnesses? I wondered.

Two teens jumped from one of the new arrivals. They ran over to the Mercedes, stopped at passenger side, and reached in the window.

I immediately wondered if the car was about to blow up, and looked for flames underneath the hood or by the gas tank.

The teens then began violently yanking a person out of the Mercedes, changing my thought from "explosion" to *they're going to beat the hell out of that guy. They're angry because he caused the accident.*

Half-jogging to the Maserati, I noticed the teens at the Mercedes were Latino, and ragged-looking. Looking closer, it appeared like the driver of the Mercedes was kin to them. And then I put it all together. The moment they got the driver out of the car, they began rushing him back to their waiting vehicle, literally dragging his injured body.

My thoughts crystallized in an instant. *They stole the Mercedes. They're getting their accomplice away from the scene of the crime.*

Which is exactly what happened.

As embarrassing as it is to admit, I became a cliché, a person at the scene of a crime who is unable to process information quickly enough to be of use to any police investigation. Instead of immediately leaping into action, I froze for half a second and that instant was all it took for them to get away. Not that I would have tackled anyone or attempted to fight three Latino teenagers, but as I ran at the exiting auto I realized they were going to be up the highway ramp and on the 110 Highway before I could memorize a license number. I felt like an idiot as their taillights sped off into the night.

Frustrated with my incompetence, I turned to find two Japanese nationals staggering out of the Maserati, teens themselves and thankfully not hurt. Well, not seriously hurt, such as crippled or comatose. They were shaken, and one was holding his arm, bent like a broken wing. He looked at me and repeated, "Please help me." His eyes were filled with confusion and pain, his voice cracked with pain, and he used pigeon-English that would probably get him mocked or beaten in rural America.

"Hey, hey, hey," I said as soothingly as I could. "You should sit down."

"They run?" he asked, pointing to the Mercedes.

"Yeah, they're gone," I said, noting with absolute disgust that the only other witness—the other car that had pulled over—was pulling away himself, deciding not to get involved.

The devastation to the Maserati was amazing; the whole car was reduced to a twisted marriage of plastic, metal, and rubber. The Mercedes was barely recognizable as having once been a drivable machine.

Building security came outside and started taking pictures of their damaged step, showing more concern for it than the two stunned and possibly injured men wandering their property.

I got on my phone and tried calling the police, but "911" wasn't an option for cell phones in the mid-2000s. I ended up calling security at the property I was working at several blocks away, and they phoned everything in for me.

The paramedics and fire department arrived shortly thereafter. I gave my statement, and everyone agreed the Latinos were most likely stealing the Mercedes.

I drove home and gave minor thought to the things that could have shaved ten seconds off my trip and therefore put me directly in the path of the Mercedes. Had I run the second red light, had I punched it a little harder off the green, left work moments earlier... By sheer happenchance I was witness to violence and not a part of it. Was something on my side that night? Luck? Karma? Neither?

At the time, the event didn't really affect me. Some people take "almost" and turn it into a rallying cry for change, vigilance, or added responsibility to life's fragility. Not me, not back then. I went home, went to bed, got up, and went back to work. Routine continued as the watchword to my existence.

But becoming a father has changed me. Now I notice things little and large. I reflect back upon witnessing the accident, and wonder what kept me out of the path of the Mercedes a little more than I did back then. I also think about all the little puzzle pieces that had to fit just right in order to allow Mommy and I to meet when we did. I'm not sure I believe in fate, luck, or karma...

...but I look for it more often these days.

While I hope I haven't burned an important cash cow of a bridge by turning down the cruise line work, I have to believe the timing of it just wasn't right. I have to believe there are still opportunities out there for a comedian living in Iowa, and that the harder I work, more of those opportunities will present themselves.

Only time will tell.

Love,
Dad

March 8, 2014

Dear Hillary,

Another local gig, another chance to sleep in my own bed and wake up for Morning Snuggles with you...

...something you took advantage of big time this week. On Monday, you were feeling a little under the weather. You were fussy, and wanted to be picked up and held quite often.

When you're like this, I generally pick you up and then lay down on the couch. You roll your eyes at me, saying with your face, *this isn't what I wanted, Daddy. I wanted picked up, not couch time.* And then you scurry off until you notice I've started up a task—laundry, dishes, Facebooking—which is your cue to rush to my knees and howl. *I need picked up again!*

On Monday, however, when I laid down on the couch, you snuggled right in to me and fell asleep.

And I was trapped.

Five, ten, fifteen, and twenty minutes went by. You snored lightly, happy in your perch.

As the minutes turned to an hour, I began to wonder if I was going to have to Aron Ralston my arm off.

Some people say I spoil you; that I should have rolled you off me. I wanted to make very sure you didn't wake up. I attempted to sneak out from under you once before, and you didn't like it.

Now when you fall asleep on me, I wait it out. Because that's my job as Dad: make Hilly happy.

When all was said and done, you lay atop me for two hours. You woke very happily, looking at me lovingly with an appetizer of smile, and main course giggle.

Which is the other reason I don't mind being trapped underneath you, you wake up so much happier with Mommy or me around. In your crib, you wake to sniffles and little cries, sadness that ends when one of us enters and picks you up. But for the whole tenure of your time as our daughter, when you wake up and we're right there next to you, you're undeniably happy.

It makes the time memorizing the ceiling worth it.

Love,
Dad

March 14, 2014

Dear Hillary,

I had a Tuesday night gig this week, which puts me at home with you and Mommy for the weekend. Grandma Janet and Grandpa Joe—my mom and fake dad—are here, as Mommy and I are taking a date night to celebrate her birthday a little early.

The gig was in Marquette, Michigan, and it was one of the reasons I didn't take the cruise line offer I mentioned a couple weeks back. Could I have cancelled a one-off show on a Tuesday night in order to make more money? Yes. But they would have had to print new posters, change all the promotion they had already done... Yes, they could have found a new comic easily, but it would have been inappropriate to ditch out on my responsibilities for the sake of greed.

Plus, I got this job from someone who saw me four years ago. When he started producing his own comedy shows, he specifically reached out to me. Which I really liked; I was booked on merit, not because I hung out after a show and got stoned with the owner of the club (which happens all too often in my line of work, where hanging out and being "cool" is more important than being original or funny sometimes).

Anyway, you, dear one, were interesting this past week. And I mean that in the best of ways, even though you were in the worst of tempers. You've begun having meltdowns, generally over very small things. For example, you wanted to bring a dripping washcloth out of the tub with you, and wouldn't accept a trade for a dry one. When Mommy and I wouldn't let you take it out of the tub, you threw a ten-minute crying fit. The next day a hair tie broke, and when Mommy threw it away, same thing: complete meltdown. The morning following that, you didn't want to get dressed, which led to back arching and leg kicking while you screamed and cried.

The meltdowns are loud, and you lose control of your emotions quickly, as if a switch is being flipped. One second you're fine, but the moment you're denied exactly what you want, exactly when you want it, boom, World War III.

At first it was funny, in a way. I mean, we didn't realize it was about to become a pattern. When you were in the tub, crying, Mommy and I were talking you through it as best we could. "Hilly, we understand you're frustrated, but getting water everywhere just isn't on the menu tonight." As you began throwing your tantrums at the drop of a hat, however, we grew resigned to the fact this is something we're going to have to ride out. I've no idea how long this new phase will last, but I hope it's a short one.

However disruptive you become, there is one thing that will never happen. I will never strike you. I say this because on Wednesday I opened the newspaper (Google it. By the time you read this, newspapers won't have existed for many years) and read about a couple who beat their six-week-old child with a wooden spoon when it "was not listening, would not be quiet, or was getting mad."

I don't understand it.

I cannot wrap my mind around it at all.

The idea that any child, much less an infant only six weeks alive, is something to be reasoned with, controlled, or hit... I am at a loss for all peaceful words. The only emotions I have are revulsion due to the act, and anger combined with a desire to commit physical violence against the parents. An infant of six weeks knows only one thing, "I was in a nice, safe womb, and now I'm in a big, scary world." If an infant cries, it's because something is wrong, not because it needs to be disciplined.

If you, Hilly, are having a tantrum, as a one-and-a-half year old, it's because you are having problems being understood. You're trying to figure out how to express yourself, and it can grow frustrating when Mommy and Daddy don't understand you. As you grow, you'll learn what "No" means, and there will be consequences—time outs—for not listening. As a toddler, however, we just have to be patient and let you tantrum as we wait it out.

Sometimes you just want basic things; the washcloth, the hair tie, etc. But I'm certain that's just a small part of a larger whole, the fact you haven't gotten your words yet, and you don't know how to impart upon us what you need us to know.

It must be incredibly exasperating.

Sometimes, you might be testing us, because we haven't heard of behavior like this happening at daycare. Chances are, like most toddlers, you're on your best behavior around others, but Mommy and Daddy? Well, those are buttons you can push, and boundaries you can test.

It did lead to one small ego boost for yours truly, I must admit. On Monday, I prepared to leave for my gig. You were in the midst of one of your new meltdowns, and unfortunately it was for reasons neither Mommy nor I could discern. You had spent all day with me, and were perfectly fine. But as the day grew long, even after a great nap, you broke down around 6pm. Witching hour? We don't know. But Mommy spent about an hour settling you down, talking to you, letting you cry, talking you through it... and she had you calm-ish, where the remnants of the storm were all that was showing...

...and then I took my suitcase to the car.

You lost it.

I heard screaming and crying from inside the house, and when I returned you were red-faced and looking toward me.

"This is because you left," Mommy sigh-smiled.

You lunged for me when I came back into view, as if to say "Don't go, Daddy!"

When I reached back and took you, you put me in your death grip. You didn't want me going anywhere.

They are truly horribly wonderful moments, when you feel so happy to be loved, yet so sad because your daughter is sad.

You've done it twice before. Once, over the phone. Mommy called me for Face Time, a video chat on our phones, and the instant I popped up, you took one look at me, realized I wasn't at home with you, and lost it. Your fingers were grabbing at the phone frantically, your crumpled face saying louder than words, "Daddy! Where are you?! Why are you in that small box?"

The other time, well, that was the first time.

I left mid-morning on a Saturday. I was driving two hours to watch my best friend lay his father to rest. I suited up and left without incident.

Made the drive, shared some good moments with my friend even though we were surrounded by the very tragic loss of his father, and then drove home.

As I was nearing home, Mommy sent me a text: "We're at the rec center indoor play place, if you want to join us."

And why wouldn't I?

The Campsite is a long corridor of a playroom, with windows spread across one of the two long ends and one of the short ends. Plenty of sunlight; plenty of opportunity to see the outside world.

I parked and made my way to the building, and while hopping up the stairs and into the structure I spied you, and you spied me. You smiled, "OMG! It's Daddy! Yay!"

But then I had to leave your sight to enter the building proper, and make my way around a wall to the play area entrance.

And the instant I was out of your sight?

You lost it.

The tears started immediately, and Mommy started laughing gently.

You wanted Daddy so bad.

I rushed around the corner and back into your sight; you were near-pounding the glass for me.

I took my shoes off and hurried into the room and you melted into me. *Don't do that, Daddy. Don't leave my sight.*

I hugged you for a good five minutes, and then you looked at me and laughed and smiled. All better.

Well.

Two quick updates. You had your 18-month check up, and the doctor gave smiles and thumbs up across the board. You're a healthy, growing girl, and all is well.

And, good news, so is Squeak. The blood screen for serious diseases came back negative, which is very positive for us.

Love,
Dad

March 21, 2014

Dear Hillary,

You know I love you more than words. You are my
everything, and I orbit around you as does the earth the sun. I
love spending almost every moment I can with you.
Note that word, "almost."
As much as I love you, you do not need to hunt me
down every time I sneak off to relieve my bowels. Pooping is a
nicely private time to me, and I try not to male it up too much,
with a newspaper and twenty minutes of solitude. No, I'm a fast,
one-minute get-it-outta-me-fast pooper.
(I have a healthy colon.)
I also, for the record, find it a bit disconcerting you feel
the need to go peering into the toilet after I stand up. I know
you're just an inquisitive child, but the arch of your eyebrow
that signifies interest on your little face... Yeah, it's poop.
Nothing interesting there.
I would close the door, but you crying and pounding on
it is good for neither of our mental states.
Maybe you think, "But Dad, you see me poop all the
time! I make quite a show of it!"
And you do.
You furrow your brow and gain a look of intense
concentration.
Your face becomes red with pressure, as you try and
work out exactly what's going on with your little body.
And like a summer storm, everything passes quickly
and you go on about your day happily.

Or, you try to, but I scoop you up and it's time for a diaper change, where you fuss and squirm and flail all four appendages as I try to wrestle you into a clean Pampers.

Anyway, I can only hope the day will soon arrive that when you notice I have stolen away for a moment, you grant me a quick respite from your presence.

Love,
Dad

March 29, 2014

Dear Hillary,

I am in Brimley, Minnesota, and missing you dearly.
I sit here wondering about decisions I have made. The past few weeks have seen me knocking off little one-night-stand shows on my calendar, shows that meant I couldn't take the cruise line gig. One reason I didn't take the cruise is because I was supposed to be part of a "comedy festival" being thrown in Iowa. The festival was pitched as a way of meeting "industry insiders from Los Angeles!" and "making connections with power people!" but in reality has turned out to be a sloppy money grab by the organizers.

A friend, Gerald, got hooked up with the festival because he runs a successful comedy night in Des Moines. His show was given a slot at the festival, and Gerald believed this was because the festival producers were interested in Iowa comedy. Unfortunately, the producers just wanted to *appear* interested in Iowa comedy. In reality, they just wanted the branding; "Look! We have an Iowa staple in our lineup!" After Gerald lined up professional Iowa comedians—including me— to perform, the festival producers dismissed his list and offered slots to amateur comedians from out of state, people who paid entry fees to become a part of the gathering.

I'm inventing numbers here, but the way the scam works is like this: say 100 amateur comedians pay a $25 submission fee, then $2,500 goes into the pockets of festival producers. If 200 amateur comedians submit, it's $5,000, and so on. Considering many of the performers are not receiving compensation for their efforts, and the producers are also making money off ticket sales, it becomes a nice way of pocketing a little cash for the select few people running everything.

I was initially supposed to be on the bill despite not paying an entry fee, but only because I did some promotional work for the festival before discovering their ugly underbelly. I wrote a nice article for the producers, and then was tossed aside like trash. It's not a nice feeling, being used, and all I can hope at this point is that elusive energy called "karma" bites those in charge in their collective butts.

Bringing this back to where it started, the festival was something I thought of as a good reason not to take the cruise line money. "Why take quick cash now if I can meet someone important at the festival?" Well, since I'm not at the festival, that stings. On the plus side, there are apparently no industry insiders there, either; the festival website is devoid of anything or anyone interesting. Turns out they scheduled their shindig right atop a well-established comedy festival in Atlanta. From what I've been able to gather, anyone of any importance is there, and not in Iowa. Thankfully, I was able to pick up the paying gig I'm at now, which saved the weekend from being a total loss.

Well, enough complaining.

Your future sibling has been hitting all marks and growing well. Every checkup gets a thumbs up from our doctor, a wonderfully happy woman who smiles easily and is open and honest in a fun, upbeat manner. She isn't "professionally clinical," but in fact playful and (at times) delightfully sarcastic. I don't know if she is this way with all her patients, but she picked up on the fact that Mommy and I are not "normal" people very quickly. Since I am a comedian, I am generally considered "off" by some, and since Mommy tolerates me, she is generally branded as "fun," too. Our doctor, Dr. Ward, says she enjoys giving me flack. And I enjoy receiving it. There is something nice about having a slightly-less-than-professional relationship with your doctor that makes visits fun.

This past week, on Wednesday, they did an ultrasound and found that Squeak has all hands, toes, feet, and everything else important. They measured bone length, skull circumference, and counted the beats in Squeak's very strong heartbeat. They did a gender check, too, but Mommy and I weren't interested in that information. That's a surprise we get to discover at the end of this journey.

As of a few weeks ago Mommy started feeling movement and kicking, too. Every so often she'll say, "Squeak is giving me a pounding!" and smile.

Given the stage of development we are at, we have begun "brainwashing" Squeak, just as we "brainwashed" you.

What do I mean by that?

Well, it's time to let you in on a little secret, something Mommy and I did by accident.

When reading all the baby books while you were in her womb, Mommy discovered the importance of talking to you. The ears develop early, and even inside a mommy's belly a baby can hear the big world outside waiting for them.

Mommy made fun of me for whispering A Christmas Song to her belly in the month of July, and she rolled her eyes when I read *The Love Song of J. Alfred Prufrock*, but she was pleased with a musical selection I made.

Originally, the idea was to play a multitude of different styles, but as happens often, life, time, and exhaustion got in the way of best intentions.

Instead of many songs played over time, one song became a part of our nightly ritual. Mommy would lay down for bed, and I would hold my phone to her belly. Every night, before bed, you would hear the relaxing tones of "Obiero," a song by the Kenyan musician Ayub Ogada.

It is a simple melody, and a relaxing song. We played it because we had the mild hope that it would lull you into allowing Mommy a nice night's sleep. If you were relaxed, you wouldn't be interested in all the gymnastics you performed so often in Mommy's belly. Somersaults, twists and turns, kicks and pirouettes... you were quite the acrobat.

We played the song to you repeatedly, and without meaning to set in place a pattern of recognition.

After you were born, we noticed that if you were having a bad moment and shaking your fist and crying at the world you were now a part of—*I miss Mommy's belly!*—if we put that song on, it would calm you. No matter how worked up you might be, we would play Oberio and you would freeze. Something in you recognized what you were hearing, and you would forget to cry and just listen.

Once we discovered that, we weren't sure what to do, save it for emergencies, or continue down the path? We decided to keep using it as a relaxation tool, and now play it as you near bedtime. You've been alive for around two years; a year and a half on your own, and nine months in Mommy's belly, but we still play you the same song nightly, something you can associate with peace, warmth, and relaxation.

Now it's time to start playing something to Squeak.

It wouldn't have been fair to use Obiero again—that's your song, special to you—so we chose Open, by Peter Gabriel.

It too is a slow, relaxing tune. I used it to propose to Mommy, which you probably know by now.

I think it will be good for Squeak.

We shall see...

Love,
Dad

April 1, 2014

Dear Hillary,

In honor of what is known as "April Fool's Day," I present you with a series of nonsensical things I have done in the past few weeks. I don't do it to be a snot, it's just that...
...well, sometimes my mouth gets in front of my brain, and it's all downhill from there.

* * *

You had an ear infection, and I was sent to Walgreen's to pick up a prescription of antibiotics.

Pharmacist: "Okay, you're going to give her three ounces, twice a day. There will be extra."

Me: "Can I drink it?"

The pharmacist became visibly confused and stammered for a second.

Pharmacist: "Is this... I thought this was for... Are you the one with the ear infection? It says this is for Hillary."

Me: "That's my daughter, yes. But you said there would be extra."

The pharmacist was very confused by this point, and repeated herself.

Pharmacist: "Right, so you're going to give your daughter three ounces, twice a day, and there will be some left over..."

Me: "And I can drink that?"

The pharmacist stared at me several seconds, still confused, then said flatly: "I wouldn't."

Me: "OK."

Some people get flummoxed so easily.

* * *

You and I go to Target quite often, especially over the winter. When it was colder than should be humanly allowed outside, the mall was a safe haven of warmth and space for you to roam. Unfortunately, after a while I would have to find a way to amuse myself while shopping.

Me, after buying eggs, milk, butter, and orange juice at Target: "May I please have a gift receipt?"

Target Clerk: "Um... sure."

Me: "You know what? That's OK. I don't need one. If they don't like the butter they can deal with it."

I walked away, leaving the clerk bewildered.

* * *

Bewildered is better than angry, for the record. I don't act like an idiot to be frustrating or bother anyone; I just amuse myself by being dumb. Unfortunately, not everyone has a great sense of humor.

For the longest time, I refused to sign my name on the electronic pad at Target. I would write "NO!" on the signature line, because the statement above the line reads "I agree to pay these charges..."

I began drawing smiley faces, male genitalia, and other stupid assorted things. Somewhere along the way, you, dear one, took up an interest in drawing, so I started letting you sign the keypad for me. Ninety-nine percent of the time the clerk didn't care, or actively laughed, but once I had a dour woman frown and state, "I need YOUR signature."

I pointed to you, and said in all seriousness, "She's authorized to sign for me."

The woman walked off, frustrated.

* * *

I don't always pick on clerks; random people are sometimes innocent victims to my moronic behavior.

Because I'm always traveling, I am often eating alone. I wandered into a restaurant once, and as I was waiting for the hostess two women stepped in line behind me. When the hostess arrived, she looked us over and asked, "How many today?"

I turned to the two women and politely questioned, "Three?" as if we were a trio dining together.

After two confused (and somewhat nervous) looks from them, I returned my gaze to the hostess and proclaimed, "Just me."

I'm a people person.

* * *

Mommy doesn't escape such treatment, for the record. No, if anything she gets it worst of all. Her mom (your Grandma Diane) was visiting, and I came home to find the two of them talking in the kitchen.

At some point, I heard my name being called...

Mommy: "Nathan? Nathan?"

Me, looking up: "Huh?"

Mommy: "What do you think of that?"

Me: "What do I think of... what?"

Mommy: "We were talking to you, weren't you listening?"

Me: "Oh, no. I tuned out. I thought you two were just clucking away at one another."

I ran for the bedroom quickly, before Mommy could hit me.

(Remember, Mommy is a hitter!)

Love,
Dad

April 5, 2014

Dear Hillary,

I am in Milwaukee, Wisconsin, and missing you dearly. I lived here as a child, returned for college, and spent much of the 1990s here. It's a nice city, one I can finally appreciate again. For a good half-decade Milwaukee held too many memories, and one ghost, for me to enjoy it when I visited.

But that is a tale for another letter.

Today I'm thinking about how happy I am with where we live, where Mommy and I are raising you. A small town with a big college is a good place to be, because you have the best of both worlds. "Small town" generally means safer, and "university" means traditional thoughts are challenged, progressive attitudes are held, and the insights into life are numerous.

My formative years were spent in a small town, only one that lacked an institute of higher learning. This means I was exposed to the negative aspects of isolation.

Due to the wonders of social media, I'm still in touch with people from that era of my life, and it is disheartening when I discover many of them still think small thoughts, and hold a narrow worldview. It's as if the past twenty-five years never existed. No technological breakthroughs, no advancements in medicine, no examination of history to show what is beneficial to mankind and what is detrimental.

Some of them assume being born a certain color grants them certain rights, and that anger and willful ignorance is the best approach to any problem. They don't understand why everyone on the planet cannot either (a) believe the same things they believe, or, lacking that, (b) just leave them alone. "I've got mine, you get your own!" is almost their religion.

When interacting with them, I try to avoid subjects that have depth and gravity, because when they get in over their head—when challenged with facts, figures, science, and history—they clam up and resort to either name-calling or silence. When they realize they've nothing to defend, instead of opening themselves to the world around them they shut down even further, entrenched in ancient thoughts or long-ago-proved-false ideas. It is depressing to know they are attempting to raise their children to remain small-minded in such a big world.

Several days ago during an online discussion, someone I went to high school with showed up to add his two cents. In the past, he has offered up gems such as "The American military is full of baby killers," "Policemen and firefighters should be paid minimum wage," and everyone's favorite, "Rape victims had it coming." As if it needs said, he is simply not a good human being.

When I called him out on those outrageous statements, he—in his mind—justified them. He went on a lengthy diatribe about how he believed the American military works, and explained why he thought firefighters are overpaid. Neither explanation is worth going into, but it was his comment about rape victims that was beyond upsetting. In full arrogance, he claimed that if a woman went out in public dressed like "a hooker" and got raped, "then she should not put herself in that situation." He then went on to say he believes his line of thinking "empowers women."

As a father, this made me want to vomit. Were I the father of a son or not a father at all, I would find his statements abhorrent, but they wouldn't affect me personally. As a father to a daughter, however, the idea some men out there think like him troubles me to no end.

I hate the fact that as a woman, you will have to keep your radar up 24/7 just because men like him exist. I am sickened by the idea some men believe that the onus of arousal and control is entirely on the woman, and that men have no control over their urges.

In the most recent moment, he was so bereft of rational thought all he could muster up was "I graduated top of our class in high school and took advanced classes. Didn't see you in any of them."

In his mind, he was insulting me. But all I saw was a man hung up on the fact he peaked over twenty-five years ago, someone trying to revive old glories to cover the fact he hadn't done anything with his life since then. It was mix of pathetic and sad. I almost felt sorry for him.

It is my intention to raise you to become the polar opposite of ignorance, to expose you to different cultures and manners of thought, and with a fish-eye lens to the world. I hope you will neither fear nor judge people of a different color, background, or sexual orientation. Every interaction you have during these formative years will be based in experiencing something new, not fearing something different.

Even though I might not like it at times, I will expect you to challenge me, and not accept everything I say as law. And I think that will be good, because I do not intend to raise you with an iron fist, desperately clinging to the idea I know everything and you were put here to obey me. I plan on raising you using guidance, trial and error, and allowing you the freedom to experiment and fail on your own.

I will do my best to keep you attached to the present, not remain mired in the past. Every day will be an opportunity to accomplish something, not relive faded glories.

Not that there is anything wrong with revisiting the past—you just shouldn't live there.

Two of my oldest friends came to visit with me after Friday night's performance, men I have known for almost thirty years now. There is nothing more enjoyable than a conversation that takes place almost telepathically. When a sentence can begin, "That one time, with the shoe..." and before the words have exited one person's mouth, the next is saying, "...and the dishwasher broke!" To outside ears, the juxtaposition of "shoe" and "dishwasher" are random, but that's because they aren't on the inside track.

Mark, Ed, and I were in a heavy metal cover band back in the day, and spent as much time with one another as should be heterosexually allowed. As we visited after my show, most of the stories we regaled one another with involved the imbibing of alcohol, as well as the stupidity that comes with it.

Here, daughter of mine, are my two favorite stories from that evening...

* * *

I have been to two AC/DC concerts. I have seen AC/DC once. If you read those statements and cock your head like a confused puppy, I will let you know that a substance known as Absolut Vodka played a big role in my missing one of the two shows. But that will be my second tale.

Both concerts took place at one of the best music venues of all time, Alpine Valley. An outdoor theater, it sits nestled at the base of rolling hills in southeastern Wisconsin forged by glaciers. In the 1980s, the location was legendary. Dave Matthews has called it his favorite place to play, Mötley Crüe filmed their video 'Same Old Situation' there, and the Monsters of Rock tour began under its tri-arched roof. It also took the life of Stevie Ray Vaughn; his helicopter crashed into the side of a mountain there after a show with Eric Clapton.

The parking lot at Alpine Valley is an enormous, gravel wasteland. The amphitheater seats 40,000, so the space needed for all the cars bringing those patrons needed to be vast. Tailgating was a must before shows; you could bring a grill and make a day of it. I think the gates would open as early as 3pm for 8pm concerts.

My friends and I would take in several shows a year, because back then a concert ticket was less than $20. The trek from our hometown of Oconomowoc to Alpine Valley involved taking the two-lane highway WI83, and that took us through several small towns along the way.

For one of the AC/DC shows, it was my turn to drive. I'm not sure what made us smart teenagers, but we always knew to designate one non-drinking driver. I don't particularly recall being wise beyond my years, but apparently we were (at least regarding that single aspect of life). I'm guessing we didn't want to deal with the hassle of a ticket more than we had any fear for our safety, but however it happened, we were actually a conscientious little crew.

As we drove along WI83, we came to a bridge that was down to one lane, as half the bridge was torn to shreds and being re-constructed. To cross, you would pull up to a stop sign and wait. Across the bridge, another car would do the same. Depending on who arrived first, one car would cross the bridge, and then the other. While crossing you could look out both windows and see the river below. On one side was the guardrail, on the other broken concrete and rebar.

There were four of us that day, Mark, Ed, me, and a friend, "Josh." Josh wasn't officially a full-time partner in our posse, but he loved AC/DC and was an agreeable enough fellow to bring to a show.

Josh was an enigma. He was both an incredible athlete, and an enormous drug enthusiast. In high school, he broke numerous state records at swim meets—some of which he still holds today, thirty years later. He was being groomed for Olympic tryouts. Imagine knowing Michael Phelps in high school, and I don't use that comparison lightly. Josh was so fast in the water that during one race, as he swam he actually waved at a couple friends in the stands, mid-stroke. He never broke form, but everyone saw it. As his in-water arm rose to begin its downward thrust and his head turned sideways to take a breath, he gave a one-handed "Yo" of acknowledgement. He also still won that race easily. It was an incredible display of both athletic ability and callous attitude toward it.

When we arrived at Alpine Valley for the show, everyone pulled out the stash of liquor they brought and started preparing for the concert. Once sufficiently drunk, however, Josh decided he needed more to dull his senses and wandered off. No one knew where he went, but we knew what he was up to, and sure enough when he came back Josh's eyes were wide and his pupils dilated.

"Dude, I found acid. They gave me two hits and I'm tripping balls," he informed us.

Acid was a little too intense for the rest of us, but in Josh's world it was just another day of mind-altering intake.

The concert came and went—good times were had by all—and everyone piled into my car to begin the drive home.

We eventually arrived at the one-lane bridge, and noticing that Josh had succumbed to his vices and was snoring in the back seat, I devised an evil plan.

"Hey," I whispered to my co-pilot, Mark. "Have my back on this."

Mark didn't know what I meant, but he have me a shrug of "OK, whatever."

When it was our turn to cross the bridge, another car was patiently waiting their turn at the other side. As it was now midnight, its headlights shone directly upon us, and that's when I started yelling.

"HOLY SHIT!! WE'RE GONNA DIE!"

To my right, Mark immediately started both laughing and yelling, "JESUS CHRIST NATHAN!! JESUS CHRIST! DO SOMETHING!!"

It took about a half a second for Josh to snap-to. His eyes popped open, his head jerked up, and he took in his surroundings. Straight ahead, headlights "coming right at us." To the right, a two-story fall to our death in the river. To the left, a two-story fall to our death in the river. We were on a single-lane destination to a head-on collision. Drunk, possibly stoned, and still tripping on acid, Josh went into meltdown. He started howling like a banshee, screaming at the top of his lungs as the rest of us howled along in unison.

And then, when we reached the end of the bridge, I simply pulled back into the open lane, and the car that had been waiting good-naturedly at his stop sign rolled forward past us.

Josh was panting and in a cold sweat; a state of "What just happened!?" And then he was out; dropped like a sack of potatoes into the drug-induced coma he had been in moments before.

In his right hand was a piece of yellow foam. Josh had been so panicked that in a moment of super-strength he had dug his fingers into the seat cushion and torn a chunk of it out. I repeat: he dug his fingers into a car seat cushion and had the strength to pierce the fabric and pull out foam. That takes some doing.

I didn't care. The joke had been worth it.

* * *

The next time we went to AC/DC—again at Alpine Valley—it was my turn to drink. Someone else was driving. Back then, a couple friends and I would each take a bottle of Absolut Vodka and race. We would drink as much as possible as quickly as possible and see who could finish their bottle first. I don't mean a flask or mini-bottle; I mean we would each take a full-fledged bottle of vodka and go nuts. Nothing says stupidity like teenagers with ideas.

That night I made it three-quarters of the way through mine. It was more than enough to do me in, and in fact it probably should have killed me.

The group I was with stumbled to our general admission lawn seats and sat down. I looked up and saw two enormous banners, one on each side of the stage, depicting a white lion. Apparently some genius thought the band White Lion and their hair-"metal" song *Wait* would make a good opening act for AC/DC and their straightforward blues-rock.

After a mere three (or so) minutes, I had had enough. Whether it was the vodka or a primped-up blonde singer crooning, "When the children cry" I don't remember, but I do know my stomach became queasy. I needed to empty my bladder, so I announced my departure to the group. Like The Terminator, I informed everyone I would "be back."

I was somehow lucid enough to know that I was too drunk to go wandering around in search of a bathroom, so I devised a plan. I knew the Porta-Potties were always kept along the back fence, so I decided to walk in a straight line until I hit the edge of seating and go from there.

I ended up in the furthest back corner of the amphitheater, tucked away at the opposite end from any building or fixed structure. Luckily, there were Porta-Potties along the fence in this corner.

I made my way into a lovely-smelling blue toilet and started to relieve myself. During my yellow-stream of relief, I suddenly decided I was going to be sick. I half-tucked my peen back into my pants and dropped to my knees to heave. As I was in a Porta-Potty, this was not the most sanitary place to stick my head.

Nothing came out, but after a few minutes of remaining in a "safe-to-puke" position, I suddenly believed I was about to crap my pants. So, I stood up, found my balance, dropped trou, and sat back down.

Now, since 1981 AC/DC has ended every concert the same way, by playing *For Those About To Rock, We Salute You* as the final song of the night. If you're unfamiliar with that particular song, it ends with lead singer Brian Johnson bellowing out, "For those about to rock... FIRE!" followed by cannon explosions, and then the subsequent, "We salute you!" Played live, mock cannons usually line the back of the stage and are fired at the appropriate moment during the song.

So it is with that information I tell you that back in the Porta-Potty, without knowing why, I was jolted awake. My pants were around my ankles, my wiener flopped between my legs, and my face was imprinted with the plastic I was leaning against.

I sat there a half-second, wondering where the hell I was and how long I had been in blackout mode. And then I heard a somewhat distant, somewhat muffled voice, "For those about to rock... FIRE!"

There was a pregnant pause for dramatic effect, followed by one of the loudest explosions I'd ever heard.

BOOM!

"We salute you!"

And it hit me. I had just slept through the entire concert, in the plastic bathroom, naked from the waist down. I quickly crossed myself and thanked whatever power was out there that even though the music had been quiet enough to sleep through, the cannons weren't. Waking up in a latrine the following morning would not have been the most exciting moment in my life.

I took in my surroundings and didn't like what I found. I grabbed some toilet paper to clean myself, and discovered that I hadn't even pooped like I thought I needed to.

I exited the toilet, and to this day I can't remember whether or not I had bothered to lock it. If that had happened today there would most likely be pictures of me all over the Internet.

I paused to find my bearings. As everyone was enjoying the finale, I was alone. I decided as that I had already missed the entire concert, there was no point in my trying to see the last twenty seconds. I knew I was by the back fence, so I walked along it until I found the exit and made my way into the parking lot.

We had parked on the end of a row, this much I remembered, so I figured there was nothing more to do than walk up and down each aisle until I found my friends. Fortunately, this only took a few minutes; somehow I ended up in the correct row on my first try.

I lay down on the hood and half-fell asleep. As the concert ended, people flowed by me, laughing.

Eventually my friends showed up, both amused and stunned, asking, "Dude, where the hell were you?"

I did my best to explain, then crawled into the back seat and promptly fell asleep until I was nudged awake in my driveway.

I got out of the car and realized I didn't have my keys on me, so I set about breaking into my bedroom window. This took climbing through four-foot high bushes, which was not overly enjoyable.

The next morning, my mother found me, a mess on my bed, still dressed, my window still decapitated by my entrance.

"You dummy," she scolded me. "I saw you forgot your keys, figured you were coming home drunk, so I left the front door unlocked."

Oh well. At least my keys weren't at the bottom of a Porta-Potty.

* * *

I didn't drink a lot when in high school, but when I did, I went all out. Mark, Ed, and I all survived our teenage idiocy just fine, as did many of the classmates I visited with while in Milwaukee.

Josh, sadly, let substance abuse get too strong a grip on his life. Once destined for greatness, Mark said that if I wanted to see a life gone awry I should look Josh up on the Wisconsin court database. Multiple arrests and paternity lawsuits were now his life. Athletic achievement was not.

Depressing, but that's the roulette you play when experimenting with drugs. Sometimes you can remain casual; sometimes there's a round in the chamber.

You may be wondering why I told you these stories; most fathers don't entertain their children (much less their daughters) with tales of drunken debauchery, especially those ending half-nude in a plastic bathroom.

But I am being as honest with you about my teenage years because I know you, too, will go through a phase of what is called "experimentation."

Maybe it will happen in high school, maybe college. I don't know.

Mommy and I have to walk a fine line between freedom and... well, not "oppression," exactly, but something along that line. Maybe caution.

If we give you too much leeway, you may wander down a path like Josh, and end up with an unfortunate adult life. If we keep you too much under our thumb, the instant you are away from us you will explode with bad decisions. Mommy has a good friend that was raised under such strict conditions that as soon as she got to college, she got pregnant. The girl had heard so much about sex while being told "NO" by a wagging parental finger that she was bursting to find out what all the fuss was about.

It's frightening, thinking of what lies ahead in the future for me as your dad.

As I write, it is well known that my generation is trying to protect and shield their children from everything we lived through. We played on concrete playgrounds; today's kids play on spongy ones. We drank water from a hose; today's kids have to have filtered water. And so on.

I don't want to shield you. I want you to experience life.

But safely, armed with knowledge of the good and bad that can happen with each decision you make.

Goddamn if that doesn't scare me awake some nights.

Love,
Dad

April 12, 2014

Dear Hillary,

One of your favorite things is splashing in the tub during bath time. You splash and laugh, giggle and splash. It makes you joyous.

As the water hits me and makes a mess, I wonder as I laugh, *what kind of person would get upset by this?*

I know they're out there; you read horrible stories in the news of parents who lost their patience and hit... I trail off there, because the mere thought of violence against a child offends me, and I don't feel like finishing the sentence. But I have to wonder what goes through their head. Do they not understand what they are dealing with? Do they think babies are born miniature adults, able to reason, understand, and think?

You are a small person, but all you want to do is laugh and enjoy yourself. You want to experiment with your surroundings, to learn and grow.

And if that involves splashing?

Well, until you are old enough to know otherwise, I think I can handle cleaning up a mess nightly.

Your independence has been amusing me lately. It's independence bordering on belligerence.

Which I love.

You have begun taking the feeding spoon away from Mommy and me, and attempting your best to scoop and place food in your mouth all on your own.

Naturally, as dexterity isn't your forte quite yet, more food ends up strewn about than in your mouth. Sometimes you attempt to use the spoon upside down, and if Mommy or I try to correct you, you throw a fit: *NO! I'M LEARNING,*

DAMMIT! So we let you be. Or, I let you be. I'm not sure if Mommy is as patient with food splatter as I am.

As you flick the spoon and food goes flying, I smile and shrug my shoulders. It's all I can do.

Should I force you to eat without holding the spoon yourself? You're growing and developing; you're curious. You want to do things you see Mommy and Daddy doing.

It is somewhat odd, however, that as you grow more independent, you are also going through a bit of an attachment phase; dropping you off at daycare has been challenging lately. More and more you are sad at the idea of being left there.

When Mommy or I pick you up, we sneak in and spy on you for a moment, and you are always, always, always playing happily. Whatever you happen to be doing, you are engrossed in it fully, a smile on your face. So you do enjoy daycare, you just don't enjoy being dropped off there.

You love Mommy and Daddy, and want to be with us, always.

I took you the other day, and kneeled on the floor to take off your coat and put it in your cubby. You immediately went to the cubby, grabbed your coat and hat, and carried it back to me. *No, Daddy. I don't want to be here. I want to put my coat on and leave with you.*

You nuzzled your head into my chest, refusing to acknowledge anything around you. Your little arms tried to wrap themselves around me. I hugged you back, and placed my chin upon your head.

After a minute, I tried to turn your body around, so you could see all your playmates and snap out of your sadness, but you were having nothing to do with it. As long as you were tucked into my chest, you were safe.

So I allowed you to remain there.

It actually took all of my resolve to leave. I wanted to scoop you back up and carry you out with me, but couldn't. Daycare is good for your social development, and I know the women there are kind and loving to you—as said, when I arrive in the afternoon you're full of joy. It just takes you a couple moments to remember you're OK with being there.

When I pick you up in the afternoon, I literally pick you up.

I sneak in, and you rush over when you see me, dropping whatever it is you are doing. A smile hits your face as you dart, and a giggle exits your tiny body as I scoop you up. You immediately turn to all the daycare ladies and smile and wave, smile and wave.

So I cannot believe anything bad is happening when you're there alone; I have no reason to believe your sadness is anything but separation anxiety.

I just hope it is another stage of development, and you'll move through it sooner rather than later. Seeing you weep when I drop you off ruins my whole day. Convincing myself it's all for the best is a difficult, difficult task.

Love,
Dad

April 19, 2014

Dear Hillary,

"They say goldfish have no memory, I guess their lives are much like mine. And the little plastic castle, is a surprise every time"

~Little Plastic Castles

    I remember clear as a bell one of my favorite moments dealing with a scam artist. I was leaving my gym in Los Angeles—where I lived when I met Mommy—and walking toward my car. A man in his thirties approached and started talking.

    "Can I ask you a question?" he asked.

    "You just did," I responded with a smile while not breaking stride.

    He was momentarily stunned and paused to figure out what had just happened. I gained several feet on him, and he had to jog to catch up.

    "I need to ask you something," he stated, using a new angle.

    "Go ahead," I said kindly, still walking.

    "OK, see, I live like twenty miles from here, and my car is all busted up, and I'm not sure if it needs gas or if I should be taking a bus or what..."

    He paused to see if I would fill in the blanks with an offer of cash. Instead, I moved in a different verbal direction.

    "That's not a question," I informed him.

    Frustrated, he finally just blurted forth his intent, "Hey man, can I have a dollar?"

"Nope," I responded, still smiling. "I'm leaving the gym. I don't have any money on me, just my driver's license."

And that was that; each of us went our separate ways.

(Some-day, love will find you...)

As a rule, I generally don't give money to panhandlers. Mommy and I donate food to our local pantry, but I don't give directly to people. I live by the age-old adage about giving a man a fish, versus buying him cable so he can watch the fishing channel.

Or something like that.

I was in San Antonio, Texas, a while back and did a one-eighty on this stance while in line at a little Mexican restaurant.

I didn't know the city or the restaurant. I had been driving, saw the place, suddenly realized I hadn't eaten in seven hours, and pulled over.

Wandering in and examining the overhead menu, I figured it was worth staying, so I got in line. Fairly soon after I arrived, a homeless man arrived and stood behind me. I didn't think anything of it, until he got out his money.

He had one dollar.

One dollar, and some change.

I saw him look at the menu, and then down at the change in his hand. As he counted through it—the change in one palm and the index finger on his other hand shuffling through it for accuracy—I was asked to order. I picked a $5 enchilada platter, got out my wallet and paid, and looked at the homeless man.

"Hey," I said. "You got enough there to get what you need?"

He was either startled or embarrassed, because he answered so quietly it was barely audible.

"I think so. Thank you."

I nodded and went and found a table to wait for my number to be called. The man collected a soda cup, filled it with iced tea and took a table on the other side of the restaurant.

My number was shouted out; I went up to collect my food. While returning to my table, I heard a gentle voice say, "Excuse me."

I turned to see the homeless man looking at me with sad eyes.

"Does your offer still stand?" he asked politely.

"Absolutely," I said, reaching for my wallet.

"I was only thirsty when I ordered," he explained, "but I should probably eat."

I gave him a couple bucks, he thanked me, and I returned to my table and stared at my food.

Though I had entered somewhat ravenous, I became completely uninterested in my food. I picked at it a little, then decided I had to leave; I no longer felt like eating. I didn't want to be there, I wasn't hungry, and something was wrong inside me.

I got up and walked my tray over to his table, and where I had ordered the enchilada platter, he had a simple, small bowl of Spanish rice in front of him. It was without doubt the cheapest item on the menu.

I set my tray down, "I didn't really touch this," I said. "I filled up pretty quickly."

He looked up at me heartbreakingly, thanked me with a shy, soft voice, and I left.

I got into my car, pulled out my expensive and seemingly self-indulgent phone, and emailed Mommy. I told her what happened, and said that for reasons I didn't understand, I felt awful. She did her best to cheer me up; her warm words filling a cold screen, trying to assuage my first-world guilt.

Safe in the cocoon of my car, reading, "Why do you feel bad? You did a good thing!" I teared up and began to cry. It wasn't sobbing, the tears just trickled out of me, an uncontrolled sadness doing its best to escape my guilt-ridden body.

I don't really know why I felt so horrible, but the thoughts going through my head were: "Should I have just

192

offered to pay for his lunch while I was paying for mine?" "Did I give him enough money?" "Where would he get dinner?" "Why didn't I do more?"

The last question is the one that haunted me.

I didn't know anything about this man, or his history. He may have beaten his wife and kids at one time. He may have had a great job but abused alcohol or drugs and wasted away his fortunes and talents. I have no clue. In the moment I saw him, in that one moment he was counting the change in his hand to see if he could afford to feed himself, all I saw was a fragile human in need. A man searching for the most basic of all needs, sustenance. And that moment hit me in places I don't like to admit exist.

My tears only lasted about twenty seconds, and a mere ten minutes later I was swearing at my GPS for taking me to a residential neighborhood and telling me I was at the location of a car wash.

You have moments in life that reach the core of who you are supposed to be and how you are supposed to think, and then they fade. Just like that I was back in the safe world of blinders and apathy.

I'd like to pretend that a moment like that changes a person, but I think it's just a bump in the road, a momentary shift of consciousness. A bump where it is knocked into us how lucky we are. And the very next day, we are somehow left wanting. Our current phone isn't powerful enough, our television isn't big enough... somehow our magnificent life pales next to those with more.

How soon we forget.

To better remember our blessings, Mommy and I watched a documentary, *American Winter,* on HBO. It was about poverty in the United States, filmed in Portland, Oregon, using eight diverse families to make up its storyline. The eight families were all dealing with various problems. A single mother—her husband passed away—living with her son in a windowless, one-car garage. A woman whose daughter needed medical treatments struggled to pay the $49,000 bill. A 50-year-old man who once pulled in a $50,000 annual salary was laid off, leaving him to care for his Down syndrome son with no income. The myriad stories all carried tragedy within their covers.

These were not people who lived large and were caught unaware by the economic downturn of 2008; they didn't buy mansions in the housing boom when rates were low and get underwater when the variable rate shot up. They lived in trailer parks, impossibly small-looking homes, and apartments. And yet they struggled to put food on the table and keep the electricity on.

As I watched, I was taken to a time in my life I don't revisit often, my very early childhood. When I was young, my family was on food stamps. My parents were dirt poor, and we were what would be considered "White Trash" today. I ran around barefoot on a farm, and all my clothes were secondhand.

Because of this, I am incredibly thrifty when it comes to money. For example, I have been eyeing a $28 Batman shirt on Amazon for several months. It is something I can easily afford, and yet I don't buy it. Many thoughts go through my head as I window-shop it repeatedly, first and foremost being *you have several Batman shirts already, dummy.*

Above and beyond that is the idea that spending $28 on a T-Shirt is just silly.

I almost bought it once, but after clicking "Add to Cart" became irritated by the fact there was a shipping charge. Mommy and I are members of Amazon Prime, which generally means two-day shipping is included free. Unfortunately, in the case of my Batman shirt, the seller was a second-party vendor, meaning our perks didn't apply.

"Not happening," I thought as I deleted my order.

I was angry enough I was spending $28 dollars for something I didn't need, so I wasn't adding $5 on top of that.

Again, I can afford the $5 shipping fee, but it was a convenient out for me, a way of being mock angry instead of dealing with the real issue swimming in my subconscious, fear.

In almost every situation I have an opportunity to spend, the niggling little thought in the back of my mind screams, "What if I need this money for something more important later?"

This idea has swelled my bank account, as I find saving greenbacks easier than tossing them around casually.

My point of view is also, unfortunately, one that makes me see poverty from a sometimes-cruel angle. When the documentary showed a family struggling to pay their electric bill—the husband/father unable to find work—my first thought was, "Well, why didn't he hoard the cash he spent getting those tattoos? That could have been money to pull from a bank account right there."

I am not proud of such moments, but do admit they freight train through my mind uncontrolled.

If marriage is a system of opposites and balance, it makes sense Mommy is the yin to my yang, as she can spend money as easily as she sneezes. Our 2013 tax return was higher than either of us expected it to be, and before you could say "blueberry pancakes" Lydia had her sights set on American consumerism.

The Sunday after receiving our tax refund, we went shopping for a new dining room table. There was nothing wrong with our current dining room table, but Mommy didn't like it.

That alone was enough of a flaw for her to want it replaced.

"It's too big for our dining area," she claims. "I'm tired of always bumping into the damn thing."

At the furniture store, my input was desired, but what I was willing to give was all-too-honest. "What do you think of this one?" was responded to with "I think the table we have at home is fine." I wasn't saying it in a rude tone, more a mix of "confused-we're-spending-money" and "matter-of-factly."

Mommy eventually settled on two tables she liked, a high top and standard height. I liked the high top, she liked the standard height. Because she is a generous woman who likes to placate her pouty husband, we ended up ordering the one I preferred, and that was that.

Until we started watching the documentary, and I saw eight families watch their lives disintegrate in mere months. Every story contained the arc from loss of job, through debt, to desperation. The mantra repeated throughout was, "This could happen to anyone."

As trained by my childhood, I said to Mommy, "This is why we shouldn't buy tables we don't need."

Mommy was frustrated with me, and rightfully so. She thought on it a minute, then said, "You know what I was thinking while that documentary was on? I was thinking how good it made me feel that every year I donate so much time to the food pantry I support." That, of course, is why I married her.

Everything in life is perspective, and if Mommy tolerates me long enough, her positivity and kindness might just shine through the doom-and-gloom scenarios I always default to. And maybe, just maybe, I can nudge her a little toward my ant-like behavior, and help her dial back her grasshopper's song.

Hopefully you will turn out to be a generous mix of the two of us. You'll save as much as possible—but won't feel guilty when deciding to spend some of it—and you'll never forget how lucky you are. Best case scenario, Mommy and I raise you to be more mindful of your blessings than I usually am.

I may not have known the story of either man, the one outside my gym in Los Angeles, or the man in San Antonio, but I only responded to one of them kindly. That failure is on me.

I hope I raise you to be better than I ever have been.

Love,
Dad

PS: I never bought the Batman shirt, in case you were wondering.

April 26, 2014

Dear Hillary,

This was not your best week. On Monday, we went to the doctor because you weren't feeling well. Your doctor wasn't available, so we saw a random practitioner. You were diagnosed with a pretty strong ear infection in one ear, and a slight one in the other. An antibiotic was prescribed, and home we went.

Nothing changed from Monday to Wednesday, so back to the doctor we went, this time seeing the one who has observed you from birth. Things were worse. Now you had severe infections in both ears, a croupy cough, and a fever of 102°. The prescription was altered, and Mommy and I crossed our fingers things would be better after this visit.

On Thursday, you bottomed out. Nothing was right in your world, and you only wanted to be held. None of your favorite activities mattered to you; if you weren't in my arms, nothing was right in the world. We snuggled on the guest bed, we snuggled on the couch, and I carried you everywhere with me. I took you to Target, thinking the outside world would distract you from what ailed you, but that didn't work. I had to push the cart while carrying you around the store. If ever I tried to set you down, you would enact your death grip. Your tiny fingers would claw into me, and your little legs would clamp around me tightly.

Friday was a mix of better and worse.

The day started off fine. You were happy, and Mommy took you to day care. Mommy said drop off was fine, and that you went to Miss Sydney for hugs, but at noon they called and I had to go and retrieve you. Unfortunately, not long after

Mommy left, you wouldn't leave Miss Sydney's embrace. When I arrived, she was sitting on the floor with you, and you were asleep in her arms. Using a sad tone, she explained what I already knew: if she tried to tend to other children, you howled loudly, tears streaming down your face.

I brought you home and the depression continued. Unlike Thursday, not even snuggles placated you. For thirty minutes you cried into my chest and belly, as I did my best to rub your back and calm you. All I could think is how confusing and frightening—maybe—it must be for you. All you knew is you hurt inside. You didn't know why, you couldn't articulate what was happening, you just wanted it to stop.

You've been sick in the past, but it's never been for an extended spell before. One, two days tops, sure. But a full week? No, this was new.

There is no worse feeling than that of powerlessness, and that is what I was, powerless. I could not assuage your pain, I couldn't end it, I couldn't explain it to you. All I could do was speak as soothingly as possible, so that even if you couldn't fully comprehend my words, my tone suggested hope. Hope that your pain would soon end.

Today you finally took a few steps toward normalcy. I got up at 3:30am—because sleep is not always my friend—and you were coughing. There was still some croup left in your system, and it took you over an hour to work it out. Your sleep during this period could be described as restless at best.

You announced you were ready to get out of the crib at 6:15, so I went in and retrieved you. I nuked your milk, and we had a very lovely extended version of Morning Snuggles. Usually when you finish drinking, you hand me your cup, then slide off me and explore the house. What toys haven't you played with in a while? What's the doggy up to? Does the animal's water fountain need splashed in? Better find out.

But today, you finished drinking, handed me your cup, and snuggled deeply into the crook of my arm. You popped a thumb in your mouth and stared wide-eyed at the ceiling above us. Occasionally you would arch your neck to look back at me, just to see what I was up to, and I would look at you, smile, and whisper "Hello." This seemed acceptable to you, so you would go back to taking in the room around you from the safe vantage point of my arms.

After twenty minutes had passed, Kitty came sniffing around. You smiled and pointed, shouting your favorite word, "Doggie!"

You scrambled off me to pet at him, and seeing an opening, Kitty jumped up and sprawled out atop me, conveniently taking the warm spot you created and vacated.

Well, this wasn't part of your plan; no way Kitty was having Morning Snuggles alone. You climbed back on me and stretched out next to Kitty.

Now I was trapped under two little heat-makers.

Eventually you began to nod off. As said, it had been a rough morning full of coughing and poor sleep. We remained like this for almost an hour; you snuggled up next to Kitty, the three of us early-morning napping together.

The sun was ultimately too much to bear, however, and the room became too bright to sleep in. You woke up, rolled over on to your (and my) belly, looked me square in the eyes, and laughed. A new day! How exciting!

You pushed off me and went to find Mommy. You were fussy at first, but we went to the mall and did a little shopping, and you enjoyed exploring.

By afternoon nap you had stopped coughing, and it seems a corner in your sickness has been turned.

Mommy and I could not be more relieved. Watching you sick has been less-than-fun, to put it mildly.

As your infection was taking hold, by the way, you somewhere finally attached the word "No" to its meaning. Now instead of shaking your head furiously when met with something you don't want to do, you dismiss Mommy or me with the most adorably definite "no."

"Hilly, are you ready for bed?"

"No."

You respond without even making eye contact. We're not worth your time. You're doing something very important, such as drawing on the table or taking all the silverware out of the drawer and placing it on the floor.

"Hilly, would you like some toast?"

"No."

Sometimes you say it so casually, as if Mommy and I are the most dumb, dense people on the earth for even thinking you might want whatever it is we are offering.

Sometimes you still shake your head, but now that you have found the word that harmonizes with it so well, it is more delicate than angry.

Though you don't do it, it is almost like you are rolling your eyes using a shake of the head. "No" is only one word, but it sounds forth from you like a full sentence: *No, Daddy, don't be dumb, geez...*

Ninety percent of the time Mommy and I laugh, but I have the feeling it's going to wear on us like Chinese Water Torture: repetition to death.

Sooner before later, we're going to have to deal with tantrums as we explain that your "No" doesn't always cut it. Given the way you howl, it's not going to be fun, but better to do so now than in a few years.

Sigh

Parenting.

No one said this would be easy, but you're worth it.

Love,
Dad

April 29, 2014

Dear Hillary,

Today while you napped, I got into an argument with Simon, our gender-confused cat.

It went a little something like this:

Simon: "MEOW!! I WANT TO GO OUTSIDE!!"

Me: "It's raining, you don't want to go outside."

Simon: "MEOW!! I WANT TO GO OUTSIDE!!"

Me: "It. Is. Raining. You don't want to go outside."

Simon: "MEOW!! I WANT TO GO OUTSIDE!!"

Me: "Fine, go outside!"

I opened the door, Simon stepped outside, realized it was raining and turned around just in time to see me close the door and give him the finger.

I warned him.

Love,
Dad

May 3, 2014

Dear Hillary,

I have written this before, but it is absolutely worth repeating: I cannot wait until you have reached the age where you are no longer fascinated with my bathroom activities.

This week, you had extra-special fun with me "going number one," because it happened in a public restroom. We attended Music Time with Nancy, a multi-week class we signed up for in order to get a little socialization into you. It was the first class for me—last week Mommy and Grandma Diane (Mommy's mom) took you—so I wasn't too sure of the protocol.

We walked in as everything was about to start, and Miss Nancy asked me to put a nametag on you. Since you were wearing—as you usually are when I am in charge—a Batman shirt, I wrote "I'm Batman" on the tag. Not only would it represent accuracy, it was also a nice bit of nostalgia for those who would get the dual meaning.

When I affixed it to you, I had no idea the instructor was going to sing her way around the arc of children facing her. "Hello Sarah! So happy you're with us today! Hello Kennedy! So happy you're with us today!" When she got to you, there was a moment's pause, but then, given no other option, she went right along with it, "Hello... Batman! So happy you're with us today!"

All the other parents giggled, meaning my stupidity was a success.

I cannot explain why, but I've always lied on my nametags. Early on in our relationship, it caused a minor moment of friction between Mommy and me. We were attending some sort of nonsensical social get-together, a "Young Professionals" event. Someone created the gathering under the guise of "building connections with people in the community!" and with nothing better to do, Mommy suggested we go network.

Upon arrival, we were given nametags to fill out, and without even thinking, I grabbed three. I began writing, and before I knew it had scribbled "Xenu is my God. Ask me about Scientology. I <3 Tom Cruise" across them.

I plastered the trio to my chest, and went about entering the room when Mommy grabbed my arm.

"You can't wear that, it's embarrassing!" she hissed.

"To who?" I asked, bewildered.

"To me!"

"It's fine, trust me."

Mommy was anxious, but I wandered off with my head held high. Time to meet new people!

I don't know if this needs said, but my nametags were a hit. They garnered more attention that night than just about anything else. Were they funny? Maybe, maybe not. Were they different? Yes. And different is all that mattered. In a sea of social normalcy, I had done something just a smidge off, and that was Robert Frost's road less traveled. Where my idiotic mind thinks it's normal to write stupid things on nametags, it doesn't even cross the thoughts of most folks, so my idiocy was (in the very least) an icebreaker.

So.

Back to Music Time.

We completed our session with ease, and you, dear one, had bunches of fun. You danced (a bit), shook musical shakers, hit timing sticks together (albeit to a different beat than the music), and both laughed and smiled. Because you were happy, I was happy. Watching you revel in the silly events made my heart grow three sizes that day.

(Or some other stolen reference involving love.)

After class ended, you wanted to explore the rest of the recreation center where Music Time was being held, so we wandered hither and dither, to and fro. You spun the handles on the foosball table, reached your wee hands into the pool table looking for the cue ball, and eventually wandered into a corner of the room and paused.

I knew what was coming next.

You turned and looked at me, your little face and delicate features growing quite stern. A hue of crimson appeared around your eyes as you concentrated. Something serious was taking place.

You, my dear, were pooping.

Your poop face is hilariously endearing. It is a wonderful beacon with which to let Mommy and me know what you are up to, so we can change you quickly and not let any of the nasty stick to your skin and create a rash.

When you finished impersonating a bear in the woods, I scooped you up and away to the bathroom we went. I placed you on the changing table, took your stinky diaper off while you squirmed (and managed to plop a socked foot into the poop; kudos to you on that maneuver), and tossed everything into the handy-dandy wastebasket by the sink.

I then reached into the diaper bag... and discovered no spare diaper. Nada. Zip. Zilch. Oh, the joy I felt in that moment.

I looked at you and sighed.

Technically, I should have checked the bag for all necessary supplies before leaving the house, but since Mommy was the last person to change you in public, I felt it easier to blame her for the lack of necessary provisions.

What to do?

I pondered the idea of plucking the dirty diaper out of the garbage, scraping it clean and re-using it, but you had piddled as well as pooped, meaning it was trashed. Because you had seemingly vacated all your waste, I decided that going diaper-free until we got home would be safe. And if not? Well, that's what a washing machine is for.

I put your pants and shoes on, helped you to the floor, gathered up the diaper bag, and we made moves to Elvis the building. While doing so, however, I decided it wouldn't be a bad idea if I paused to relieve the pressure mounting on my bladder.

Which is where things got tricky.

I had hoped you would wander around safely and ignore me, but your interest in my bodily fluids knows no bounds. The instant I started a healthy stream, you tried to scooch as close as possible in order to get a glimpse of what was happening.

Now, I'm no prude, and I know you're just curious, but it's not an image thing. I don't mind you seeing me naked (and lord knows you do constantly), but in a public bathroom things are sketchier than at home. I didn't want you getting too close to the urinal, because the multitude of less-than-hygienic people using it daily creates a surface unsafe for a toddler's hands. Or anyone's hands, for that matter.

I began to pivot while I peed, as if playing basketball. My foot was constantly in motion, turning my body, blocking you, frustrating you... I thought all was won when you disappeared behind me, but no, victory was not mine to have.

A moment later you re-appeared and rushed right up to the next urinal, the one aside me. You grabbed hold of the lip and happily arched your chin up to look inside and see what it was.

My shoulders slumped.

So. Very. Gross.

After my bladder emptied a few seconds later, I scooped you up (to minor protest: *Daddy! I wanted to see in there!*) and rushed you to the sink. I fired up the warm water, rinsed your hands, soaped and scrubbed them, rinsed them again, paused, lathered them up a second time, performed a surgeon's sanitizing ritual, and then rinsed them a third time.

Had I been so conscious, I would have then grabbed an anti-bacterial wipe from the diaper bag and battled all the germs on your hands with that, too.

Frustrated with my inability to be a decent father, I carried you to the car, buckled you in your seat, and watched with sad eyes as you shoved a thumb in your mouth.

So. Very. Gross.

Telling Mommy the story later, she smiled and said, "She's going to get hepatitis on your watch, just you wait."

My hope is instances like this won't happen when you realize that waste exiting my body isn't in the least exciting. But until that day, I will no longer use a public bathroom if you're with me. Better to soda-bottle it while driving than allow you another opportunity to do that ever again.

One final note for this letter.

Last night I drove to Dubuque and back, because I got myself involved with something I don't particularly like, a comedy contest.

There are many reasons I'm not a fan of comedy contests. Unlike sporting events, an artistic competition is based upon opinion, not athletic achievement. In a high jump, there is one clear winner, because one person simply jumps the highest; in a football game, one team outscores the other. In a comedy competition, the factors for judgment are completely personal, because comedy is subjective, not definitive. I've also been in several contests that were fixed; the judges knew going in who they were picking regardless of whomever did the best. Years ago, an outside source told me three weeks in advance who was going to emerge victorious in a multi-round contest.

For this specific competition, preliminary rounds ran Wednesday through Friday, two shows a night, seventy-two comics total. Each comedian performed for six minutes, and two comics from each round advanced to the semi-finals.

I was on the second show Friday.

I put together a five-minute set, because in a competition it is better to go short, than long. If you go over your time, you lose points. I felt my set was a nice mix of quick quips, personal stories, and character definition. And I was mostly right.

A countdown clock was set stage right as you performed, one you could monitor it to make sure you didn't run long. I figured that—as my set was five minutes—I wouldn't need to watch the clock.

This was almost a very costly error.

When my slot arrived, my name was announced and I walked center stage and began speaking. There was laughter, applause, and more laughter and applause. When I waved my hand in the air and said, "Thank you, goodnight!" I turned to discover eight seconds left on the clock. The cacophony of merriment I had been hearing—laughter and applause—added 52 seconds to my time. The audience enjoyed what I had done so much that I almost ran long.

Amazing.

There was a small café near the showroom, so after my set I went there with an old friend. We caught up with one another while the other performers let fly their best jokes.

After forty-five minutes, I returned to the showroom and saw something incredible. Two large screens were broadcasting a live, running tally of the audience vote; people were texting in their favorite comedian's name. Out of everyone, I was in the lead. Seventy-some comedians, over several days, and people were voting for me like mad. It was exciting and humbling.

The show was just finishing, and I went backstage to await final judgment. It arrived, and I had not made the cut; two other comics were advancing. According to the host, "It was the narrowest vote in the competition's history." I had missed out by one point.

I began to exit the showroom when two very interesting things happened. I was walking by some tables, when an arm shot out and took tight hold of me. I turned to find one of the most well-connected and powerful booking agents in the country speaking to another man, but holding on to my arm.

I paused, and he let go while motioning for me to wait a moment.

As I waited, I reflected on something I had been told a half-dozen times over the course of the evening, that this particular judge had been a ghost all week. Every comic wanted to get near him, but no one could. He was avoiding everyone, and yet he had stopped me.

When his other conversation finished, he turned his attention to me and we had a nice chat. Nothing serious, but he asked how you were, brought up Squeak—asked when the arrival date was—and made general inquiry about my life and family.

When all was said and done, he told me to stay in touch.

There was no promise of work, but I couldn't neglect the fact that while every comic said they wanted to talk to him and couldn't...

...he went out of his way to talk to me.

Another judge cornered me; walked right up to me and stopped me in my tracks.

"You should have advanced," he said. "I'm very angry with the other judges right now."

I smiled and thanked him for his kind words, but he had more to say. He gave me his credentials, and they were impressive. He had been in the comedy business for thirty years, managed a prominent club in Vegas, and had many powerful connections.

And he really, really liked me.

I do not know what will happen from this point forth, but he gave me his contact information and demanded I get in touch with him.

"I need a four-minute set from you, so I can pass it off to the people booking late night television shows," the man explained.

Television.

Wouldn't that be something?

If I could lose the sprint, but win the marathon?

I don't want to get my hopes up, but...

...yeah.

We shall see.

Love,
Dad

PS: I really do <3 Tom Cruise. If you haven't watched *Oblivion*, *Jack Reacher*, and *Jerry Maguire* by the time you're reading this, I've really failed you as a father. More so than if I've allowed you to get hepatitis from a urinal.

May 10, 2014

Dear Hillary,

I am in Merrillville, Indiana, and missing you dearly. Two nights ago I was in Traverse City, Michigan, performing at a casino. The venue is only important because for reasons that defy all logic, smoking is still allowed indoors in Midwest casinos in 2014. I say Midwest specifically, because for the most part the United States has gone smoke-free. By the time you are reading this, my hope is the last few vestiges of smoking zones will have disappeared. When I was a child, people could light up anywhere and everywhere. In restaurants, on airplanes... it didn't matter if it was an enclosed space or had no proper ventilation. If you wanted a cigarette, you grabbed one and went to town. Now that I think of it, even students could smoke at high school. All you had to do was go to an entryway and have at it.

When I began my comedy career, smoking indoors was still widespread. I'd go out for a night of comedy and return home bathed in cancerous nonsense. I'd immediately jump in the hottest of showers to bleed free my pores and wash the smell off me as best I could. My clothes would be isolated from my day-to-day laundry, so they could be washed twice in an attempt to get the stench out. Now that smoking in public is slowly being eradicated, the rare occasions I have to deal with it boggle my mind.

A customer approached me after the casino show. He was missing a couple teeth, had unkempt hair, was quite jovial in his greeting, and smelled of a person allergic to soap.

(Bath? What's a bath?)

Smiling wide, he paid me an odd compliment, "I enjoyed ninety-nine percent of your show!"

"Fair enough," I responded. "What one percent didn't you like?"

"Eh, some of your fag jokes," he explained unashamedly. "It just seemed like you actually like them."

By "them" he obviously meant gay people, because my jokes involving homosexuality are, to put a label on them, "pro gay." I don't tell jokes to demean or slander homosexuals, I just tell a few jokes that happen to have homosexuality as a theme.

I would like to say that his bigotry surprised or shocked me, or that I was taken aback, but all too often I run into less-than-desirable people in my business. They approach me with the most sexist and racist jokes possible, always delivering the closing line, "You can use that in your act."

Gee, thanks.

Over time, I've found the best way to handle these situations is using Judo, turning their misguided positivity back on them. In the case of this particular man, I returned his smile, chucked his shoulder, and said, "You're into a book of fairy tales, aren't you?"

He laughed back, because I'm not sure he caught the fact I was mocking him. Which is the point of being upbeat instead of confrontational. Had I confronted his narrow-mindedness outright, he would have gotten defensive.

I'd like to pretend that by the time you read this, racism, sexism, and homophobia will be as far in the rearview as smoking, but there are certain areas where humanity doesn't seem to make advances.

Earlier this year I was watching a TV program called The Daily Show. It is a mock news program that usually contains more facts and relevance than many traditional news outlets. On the episode that night, a correspondent named Jason Jones was in Russia covering the issue of gay rights.

As I write, Russia is currently decades behind many developed countries when it comes to both human rights and equality for all people. It's like a first-world country with third-world sensibilities, which is sad. "We have technology, but not enlightenment!" could be their rallying cry. The situation is so medieval that Russia technically made being gay "illegal." It's a little more complicated than that, but the overall situation is that gay is viewed as wrong.

Jason was interviewing an average Russian citizen, a man who said, "I can only imagine taking my kid to school and seeing two dads bringing a kid, and me trying to explain to my kid what's going on here... how to find the words?"

Jason responded, "Yeah, it's tough to explain, 'That kid has two daddies'."

This dumbfounded the man, who was so wrapped up in his prejudice that he couldn't understand that the simplest way to explain something, is to just say it. Because he saw the world through skewed eyes, he couldn't wrap his head around the fact children are malleable. Everything is new to a child, and they can be raised to either accept differences in people, or to fear and hate others.

I had run into this not-so-unique brand of ignorance a few years earlier, and had almost the same thought Jason Jones articulated so well in Russia. An acquaintance of mine had just moved his family into a gated community, because he viewed the outside world with mistrust and confusion. He didn't want to live in the city proper, because, "What if my son sees some dude in a dress? How would I explain that to him?"

He spoke these words with a mix of puzzlement and irritation, as if the issue confusing him was an expert level Sudoku or a Rubik's Cube.

I stared at him, dumbfounded. All I could think was, "Well, you'd say, 'Some men like to dress like women'."

His son would have shrugged and gone on with his day.

The reality of the situation is my friend had the problem with men in dresses. He couldn't wrap his head around cross-dressing, and instead of dealing with that he decided to push it off on his child. Because that's what emotionally immature people do.

Children take their cues from their parents, and raising you to embrace differences in other people is one of the most important values I hope to instill in you. If I am unafraid of ethnicity and sexuality—black, Asian, Hispanic, gay—then you will be unafraid of differences in people. If I am mired in intolerance, then you will be raised the same.

It's strange as an adult to look back over the course of my life and realize I've had the same thought repeatedly throughout the years. I remember thinking in high school, "It's the 1980s, not the 1950s, why are we still hung up on gay rights and race relations?" I had the same thought in the 1990s, the 2000s, and with marriage equality slowly creeping across the states, the 2010s.

("How is this still a big deal to people?!")

As I write, there is much in the news about a young man named Michael Sam. Michael is a college football player who came out of the closet just before entering the NFL draft. This shouldn't be a big deal, a gay man playing a sport, but it has upset quite a few people. A Republican lobbying firm in Washington D.C. started drafting legislation that would ban homosexual players from the NFL, and the state of Arizona recently drafted a bill that would allow private businesses to legally discriminate against homosexuals. Those ideas didn't become law, but the fact people out there are spending their time dreaming up ways to legalize prejudice is frightening. More than frightening, it is, in a word, insane. Insane to think that people are hung up on such a non-issue. Insane to think that while we look down on Russia for actually enacting legislation against homosexuals, we come pretty close to doing the same in our supposedly tolerant, advanced country.

As said earlier, I would like to pretend that by the time you are reading this the world will be one big Benetton advertisement, with people of all races and sexualities drinking a Coke in perfect harmony, but I know that won't be the case.

(I apologize for mixing decades-old advertising themes, but it makes sense in my head and makes me giggle.)

Sadly, I know too many people currently raising their children to be willfully ignorant, vote against their best economic interests, and who still believe in ancient ways and wish America was more like "the good old days."

The problem is, "the good old days" were rarely good. Nostalgia is an easy escape for people who fear change. To people who long for the days of old, it's simply a way of stating they wish black people, women, minorities, and gays knew their place once again: back in the closet, the back of the bus, in the kitchen...

These harmful ideas are still out there, being regenerated by people who refuse to celebrate differences.

The only thing we can do is hope that, over time, they become the minority, and acceptance and tolerance becomes the majority opinion. And I have to admit the tides are turning, which is nice. It might be difficult to wrap your head around what I am about to say, but I remember television first tackling both the issues of interracial dating and homosexual unions. Believe it or not, when they were integrated into television shows, the issues were considered progressive and edgy. Today each is more "normal," or accepted, but there are still pockets of hatred aimed at anything deemed "different."

"Whites should be with whites, Asians with Asians, blacks with blacks, and boys with girls!" the ignorant will yell.

I cannot really explain why people think this way, other than to say it is usually inherited. America used to be a deeply racist, homophobic, and sexist country. In fact, America shone brightly the worst examples of all three of those traits for longer in its history than it has been on the right side of equal rights for all. Believing a certain race or sexuality was inferior or wrong was widely accepted, and passed down from generation to generation. While the effects of those attitudes are fading, they do still persist, which is unfortunate.

Well.

I don't want to make this letter too serious, so I'll return to where I started, my smoke-stained clothes. You have become quite the little helper-pants when it comes to laundry time.

Sometime over the past month you discovered buttons, or as you call them, "Beep-beep." One day I was carrying you past the thermostat, and you reached out, saying, "Beep-beep."

I paused, and you extended an index finger and pushed a button, enjoying the fact the screen lit up in response. Now you enjoy beep-beeping all buttons. ATM machines, credit card swipers, and most of all, our washer and dryer.

When it's laundry time, you are generally right on top of me, sitting on my lap as I toss everything into our front-load washer. You know that when the time is ripe, I will allow you to beep-beep the machine and fire it up. After I close the door, I point to the power button and you smile, lean forward, and push it. I then point to the water temperature setting, and you push it several times until we are on "cold wash, cold rinse." Finally, and your favorite moment of all, you push "Start," and sit back on my lap as the clothes begin spinning.

It's all so very exciting.

Before I left for my trip, you were sitting on my lap as I pulled clothes from the hamper and threw them in the washer. I two-armed a particularly large batch of items, and as I tossed them into the machine you started howling. You were off my lap and head first into the washing machine before I could react. Over the shoulder you threw item after item, digging deep into the pile of stinkables waiting to be cleaned.

I sat back and waited to see where this was all going, when finally you emerged from the basin triumphant. In each hand was a pair of Mommy's underwear. Victory! You began to coo happily, and wandered off waving each in the air like a pom-pom: Go Team Go! I had to wonder if you were a reincarnated Japanese businessman.

As I returned to the task at hand, re-loading everything, you wandered back, smiling. I looked up and you had thrown one pair of Mommy's underpants over your shoulder and around your neck; you were wearing it like a sash, Miss America, dirty-underwear contestant.

It was too much for me to bear, so I took a picture and quickly posted it online for all the world to see. Because who wouldn't want to share an image like that with everyone?

(Mommy, for the record, was less than pleased with my decision.)

After that, we went to the living room, and for reasons unknown to me you decided to pluck the pacifier out of your mouth and pop it into mine. I smiled and scrunched up my face in a silly manner as you did so, which made you giggle. Which means you repeated the process. Over and over, you plucked the pacifier (now from my mouth) and then shoved it back in there. And each time I scrunched my face up, you giggled.

At some point, maybe after three minutes of this nonsense, the thought very clearly crossed my mind, "I never thought I'd be sitting on a floor, having a toddler shoving a pacifier into my mouth, and loving it."

But I do.

You keep me forever smiling in your direction.

Love,
Dad

May 17, 2014

Dear Hillary,

I am in Buffalo, New York, and missing you dearly. This week, I've been thinking about all the things that can go wrong in life, and how I so desperately hope to prepare you mentally for anything and everything I can.

Note, I used the word prepare. All too often in life, I believe parents think in terms of "protect," which means to keep safe from harm. I do, of course, want to protect you, but I know I cannot at all times, nor will I be able to your whole life. So I need to prepare you for all that life will throw in your path, so you can overcome it with flying colors.

Where did all these thoughts come from? In short, a conversation with a friend of mine, Jay.

Jay and I were on chatting online, and he was very drunk. Jay is usually a happy drunk, but as the conversation wore on, something just... slipped out of him.

"I'm gonna shoot myself, you know," Jay slurred.

He didn't say it threateningly, angrily, or even with a hint of depression. If anything, it was very matter-of-fact. Which is why I took it seriously. People threaten suicide all the time as a cry for attention, but Jay made his declaration as almost an afterthought, something said in passing. "Hey, when you're at the store, can you pick up milk and butter? Oh, and I'm gonna shoot myself, you know."

The more casual someone is in statement, the more serious they usually are. Those who peacock their thoughts have no intention of doing anything untoward.

Jay is an interesting person. He makes me think of one my favorite quotes, from the movie *Bull Durham*: "The world is made for people who aren't cursed with self-awareness."

That's not Jay.

Jay is too aware. He doesn't live for shopping, distraction, the latest cool phone, or the newest and most awesome Hollywood blockbuster. Jay lives life searching out hypocrisy and seeking truth, because he's seen the worst the world has to offer, and it bothers him.

Jay was a soldier in the Army, and he spent time in both Iraq and Afghanistan, places America waged war before you were born. I don't know everything that happened to him, but he tells stories sometimes. More often than not he makes a joke out of what happened—Jay is a comedian like me—but sometimes... sometimes the darkness is too much for him.

When we spoke, he was too vague to get a handle on, but he kept repeating, "It was a lucky shot is all..."

I asked, "By who?" and all he would say was, "The Taliban."

I could get nothing more out of him.

There is a curse called "Survivor's Guilt," where you are in a tragic situation, and you make it out while someone else does not. If you get inside your head and think upon it too much, it can eat you alive. "Why me and not him?"

Survivor's Guilt is especially prevalent among members of the military, where an incredibly strong bond is formed. On the front lines, a fighting unit isn't comprised of soldiers, it is a family bonded by blood, soul, and shared experiences. When you lose a member, it haunts you.

Jay was hurting, and we spoke for over an hour. I did my best to remind him that life wasn't fair, nothing that happened was his fault, and that he was strong enough to take whatever was haunting him head on and stare it down. I don't know how well I handled my role as therapist, but I wanted to be the best mix of compassionate, understanding, and thoughtful as possible.

Considering I have never been a member of the military, I couldn't pretend for a moment to relate to what he went through; it would have dishonored his experience for me, a civilian, to say "I understand." Because I didn't. I could not. I could listen, and I could understand logically what Jay felt, but in no way could I pretend to feel it at a gut, emotional level. I've been depressed, yes, but I've never been in his shoes. I've never witnessed a friend die. I've never been in mortal danger.

Sometimes people like to pretend that my having been in a war zone performing comedy makes me honorable, but I deny that adamantly. My comedy tours were like mini-vacations. I'd fly into Iraq, or Afghanistan, tell some jokes, and leave. In no way could I pretend that my experience allows me extra insight into the mind of a soldier who served for real. That would be rude, and wrong.

As Jay was talking, I thought about his parents. I don't know specifically what kind of relationship he has with them. I know they have a somewhat strained relationship—they speak, but are not overly close—but I could only imagine how a parent would feel if their son checked out early one day. If the demons inside his head finally won the battle and he felt the only way out was death.

Being depressed is a horrific thing, and there is no worse feeling than hopeless. When you wake up every day in a Groundhog Day of same, wanting to escape becomes an obsession.

The worst part of all of this is that when Jay sobered up the next day, he acted as if nothing was wrong. He laughingly apologized for his behavior, and when I questioned his emotional well being he laughed me off, too.

"Oh, I'm fine," he said. "Just a little drunk nonsense is all."

The problem is, I don't believe him.

Alcohol is a truth serum; a substance that loosens the tongue and allows words and thoughts that are normally locked tightly away to spill forth unfettered by ego or worry of judgment. When drunk, the pain Jay feels was able to muscle past the walls of defense he had up. He was able to let his guard down and let it be known he needs help, that he's hurting inside. To see those walls go back up was disheartening.

Jay isn't an anomaly; the majority of people on this planet feel guilty for having certain thoughts. It doesn't matter what those thoughts are—everyone feels differently about everything. Some people find shame in joy, others revel in depression, but most feel they should put on a game face when feeling sad and not let anyone know what's really going on inside their head and heart.

Being human means having emotions, and emotions are worth sharing. I have been everywhere the emotional spectrum can take you, from the depths of sorrow to the Mount Everest of happy. And, for reasons I don't really understand, I always share what I am thinking or feeling. I vomit up my emotions all too often for the world to see, and if they so choose, judge.

Which, I believe, is a fear many people have, judgment. Unless the judgment is positive, or involves praise, people want to avoid being noticed. People feel uncomfortable sharing sorrow, so they hide it away instead of being open about their discomfort.

In a neat bit of puzzle-fitting, Mommy is also all-too-open with her thoughts and emotions. She might not wear them on her sleeves constantly, but neither does she lie about them. Which is important, because being emotionally honest is yet another characteristic I hope becomes instilled in you. I will tell you as often as possible that no matter what happens in your life, you can talk to Mommy or me about it. That when you're happy, sad, hurting, or angry, we are a sounding board for your words and emotions. Nothing that enters your head should ever be squirreled away unspoken. Only by coming to light will confusion be worked through.

I don't know what's going to happen with Jay in the coming days, weeks, months, or years. I do know that current and former members of the American military have an unnaturally high rate of suicide because of their experiences, which is beyond depressing. Our legislators pride themselves on all the chest-thumping they do for America and those who wear the uniform of service, but when it comes time to help them... well, it turns out chest-thumping and lip service is all our politicians have.

I wish there was a more upbeat way to end this letter, but at the moment I cannot think of anything to say other than to repeat that I will always be here for you.

Never be embarrassed by your emotions. They are what make you, *you*.

Love,
Dad

May 24, 2014

Dear Hillary,

This week, I played the "What if?" game, and it kept me awake and staring at the ceiling well past the point I should have been sleeping.

The "What if?" game is generally unhealthy, even when hopeful. It's a series of thoughts that race through your head, always involving fantasy, and usually involving fear and negativity.

The thoughts in my head were 100% negative, entirely fear-based, and frighteningly horrific.

My dad (your grandpa) and his girlfriend Alice came to visit, and while almost everything was fantastic, one event unsettled me well after the fact.

* * *

On Monday, you had a doctor appointment at 9am. It was a follow up to your double whammy of an ear infection several weeks back. They were checking to make sure everything cleared up fine, and that you were in tip-top shape.

Grandpa and Alice said they'd meet us at the mall after the appointment, because you and I had a little shopping to do, and the mall has a play area for children that you find somewhat tolerable.

I say "somewhat tolerable," because—as I believe I've said in a previous letter—you tend to play on the spongy structures for a little bit, and then you proceed to wander the mall, me in tow.

That's what happened today.

I was wandering the corridors with you, when I noticed a friend and fellow comedian, Colin, wandering by. I waved his way, and he came over and we began chatting. Grandpa and Alice arrived, and they took over the "Watch Hilly Wander" duties while Colin and I continued our conversation.

After some time had passed, Alice came over and informed me that the bookstore was having a children's reading time, and you and Grandpa were in there. Colin and I decided to shift ourselves from standing around aimlessly to the coffee shop inside the bookstore. That way, when reading time ended I'd be right there and ready for you.

Eventually I saw Grandpa walk by, but you weren't with him.

"Huh," I thought, casually. "Hilly must be with Alice."

A minute later, Grandpa walked by again, and stopped by Colin and me.

"I don't know where Hillary is," he said worriedly. "She was right behind me, I turned around to pick up some crayons, and she was gone..."

He walked off quickly, continuing his search.

I stood up immediately, and walked the opposite direction as my father. He walked toward the exit to the parking lot; I walked toward the mall proper.

Glancing down each aisle of the bookstore, I moved with a hurried pace, but I was oddly calm. Nothing at all inside me felt panic. I just had an odd confidence I was going to see you within seconds.

And that's exactly what happened.

I made it to the line of demarcation separating the mall from the bookstore, and before taking three steps was able to see you happily wandering by some tables and chairs around the play area.

You in sight, I slowed my pace and made my way to where you could see me. When you did, you lit up like a Christmas tree.

"Daddy!" you shouted, and hustled my way full of gleeful intent.

I scooped you up in my arms, said, "Hello-good-morning... I love you!" and gave you a kiss.

You giggled and squirmed; kisses from Daddy are so yucky!

I laughed and we made our way back into the bookstore. Colin was looking around, caution across his face. Grandpa and Alice were still searching the catacombs of book passageways that made a maze of the store. When they saw I had you, sighs of relief exited their lungs.

It was a blip in our day; everything continued as if nothing had happened. And, to be fair, nothing had happened. You went on a little journey, and within two minutes were back with us.

But Monday night? Unkind thoughts kept me awake, and that's when the "What if?" game started.

What if someone had taken Hilly?

What if we couldn't find her?

What if I never saw her again?

What if, what if, what if?

The overwhelming odds are that if someone had seen you were alone, they would have helped you. The majority of people on this planet are good, kind people. But in my bed, in the darkness, all I could focus on was the idea that all it takes is one evil person to destroy everything you have.

It made me tense, frightened, and unstable.

There is no point in obsessing about the future; you prepare for it the best you can, and that's all you can do. But thinking of the times I won't be there for you—auto accidents, drunken frat parties, muggers—all the evil in the world can enter your head late at night and scare you.

I won't always be there.

It is impossible for me to be a guardian angel, hovering over you twenty-four hours a day, seven days a week.

And I hate that.

I hate that so very much because no one likes fragility in their life; the idea we are not in control of our own destiny is mind-numbingly frightening. Even though flying is inherently the safest form of travel, people on the whole feel more comfortable driving their own car. Sitting on a plane leaves you powerless, at the mercy of a pilot you don't know and inside a piece of technology you probably don't understand. When you're behind the wheel, you believe you have a say in what happens in an accident, regardless of the fact the word "accident" automatically implies otherwise.

Keeping this in mind, that, on the whole, people like a sense of control in their own circumstances, being a husband and parent can ratchet feelings of dread to absurd levels. I'm not happy with the ugly thoughts that randomly enter my head, but they are the unfortunate byproduct of love, marriage, and fatherhood.

* * *

I was having lunch with a friend. We're roughly the same age, and have a somewhat similar dating background— meaning "many failed relationships." A few years back, when he believed he had found the ever-elusive "One," he up and readied to follow her to a new city, where they would live together happily ever after. They put their ducks in a row, counted all assets, looked over the bank accounts, and in a mix of nerves and excitement, said, "Here we go."

They hopped into a car, drove to their local U-Haul dealer, and parked. She was supposed to go in and sign all the forms, but instead of exiting the vehicle sat quietly a moment, then stated, "I can't do this."

My friend, happily oblivious to what was about to happen, said, "That's OK, I can go sign out the truck."

She made herself clearer the second time around, "No, I can't do... *this*."

Her meaning was: any of it. The move, remain with him, or love him.

My friend was devastated, but manages to laugh at it today as he really has found *The One*. Now he talks of marriage, and the odd but unique and subtle difference between knowing and *knowing.* You can believe you've met your soul mate many times before you actually meet them. Given my tumultuous romantic past, which he was well aware of, combined with the fact we both settled down happily, we had a decent foundation for a conversation involving life, where we'd been, and where we planned on going.

It was with this foundation I brought up something I rarely discuss publicly.

"Sometimes I have horrible thoughts," I admitted. "Like, what if something happened to Lydia, or Hillary? When I'm away from home, they creep in and I can't control it."

The thoughts are horrible, like you and Mommy having been in an accident. Sometimes my phone rings and I will have a momentary flash, "What if it's a hospital?"

"Oh," my friend laughed, "my imagination is worse than that. I worry that I won't be home, and someone, some *man*, will break into the apartment..."

He trailed off, but didn't finish the thought. He didn't need to, because I have had the same gut-wrenching reflection myself. There is nothing so hopeless in life as feeling helpless.

We then spoke of our placing of weapons in the house—mini-baseball bat, taser—and the fact we have both occasionally considered buying guns and attending shooting classes with our significant others.

(Neither one of us is so arrogant to simply think, "I'll buy me a gun!" without training in the use of it.)

Somewhere along the conversational way, I wondered if having these thoughts was normal, as until I met Mommy, they had been foreign to me. My friend shrugged, and I laughed. My laughter was mostly genuine, but was tinged with a little extra oomph; cover used to blanket a seriousness I was too uncomfortable to admit.

When I brought up the conversation to Mommy, she discussed having occasionally evil thoughts quite openly. She admitted her imagination was as similarly unhelpful to her well being as mine is to me, and spoke of negative impulses that wake her up in a cold sweat when I am traveling. She has pictured me smashed through my windshield in the middle of nowhere, broken and bloodied, with no one around to help. Sometimes I am stuck in a snowdrift freezing to death at 3am, or run off the road by an arrogant and inattentive eighteen-wheel rig driver. Even worse than those scenarios, her mind would run an unhealthy riot when I was lucky enough to perform overseas for the military in combat zones. Much worse things can happen in war-torn areas than a car accident.

As much as I hate to admit it, and though I don't want to point fingers or lay blame, the media does not help things. It is common knowledge that "If it bleeds, it leads." The news is a product to be sold and the industry knows the most frightening tale is also the most captivating. If you play to someone's base fears, you're going to pull them in and hold their attention. "THIS BLACK MAN IS GOING TO ROB YOU. THIS WHITE MAN LOOKED NORMAL BUT WAS A SERIAL KILLER BURYING WOMEN IN HIS BACK YARD. EVERYONE IS GETTING LAID OFF AND GOING BROKE AND LOSING THEIR HOMES. CAN INNOCENT CHEMICALS IN YOUR OWN HOME KILL YOU?"

(Find out at eleven.)

So when I was in Iraq, and reports of several car bombs going off in one day would hit the airwaves, Mommy would grow scared. Because whether it is healthy or not, and whether we like it or not, fear holds great sway over our thoughts and emotions.

The flip side to all this negativity is that once you learn to love someone, you let loose a little of your natural-born self-centeredness. When I was single, or even in previous relationships, I would board a plane and casually wonder, "Huh, wonder if this thing is going down today?" It would be a passing thought, definitely not an obsession or cause to worry. Now my mind strays to you: "If we crash, how hard will it be on Hilly?"

Loving another also expands your capacity to empathize with strangers. Watching tragedy occur on the news often makes me feel for the loved ones of those involved, and at the same time whisper a prayer to a God I don't believe in for the safety of everyone close to my heart.

I remember the time in my life before I was a dad, and I know for a fact I had no clue what parenting did to human emotions. I went to see a movie called *Ransom* with a friend of mine. My friend had a young son; I was a single, carefree fella. In the movie, Mel Gibson plays a millionaire whose son is kidnapped. In a unique twist on a standard theme, Mel offers his fortune not to pay off the kidnappers, but as a huge bounty on the criminals.

I, for the record, didn't really like the movie. Though an original concept, I felt it was poorly executed, boring, and filled with clichés. Yet my friend admitted to being white-knuckled the whole film. He felt like throwing up the entire time the celluloid was running, because he was imagining his own son being kidnapped, how he would react, and how the ordeal would make him feel. The thoughts were so overpowering he could neither enjoy nor dislike the film; he was too inside his head the entire time.

I didn't understand what he was talking about back then, but Goddamn do I now.

I make fun of helicopter parents, and cringe whenever I see one protecting their child to the point of obsession, but somewhere inside me, I get it.

And if I'm lucky enough to become a grandfather some day, you will, too.

Love,
Dad

May 31, 2014

Dear Hillary,

"I know a girl... hole in her heart. She says infinity's a great place to start..."

~U2, No Line on the Horizon

I am in Cuyahoga Falls, Ohio, and missing you dearly. It's a long week for me; I got here Tuesday, and won't get home until mid-morning Sunday. These long weeks are hard, because the missing of you grows with each day, but this trip became especially trying on Thursday.

On Wednesday, my mom and her husband Joe arrived in Iowa to visit you. On Thursday, Mommy called me with news that put a sinking feeling into my stomach and kept it there for many hours. Mommy was on her way home from work early, because you needed to go to the doctor. Grandma had taken you to the park, and you wanted to go down the slide. Grandma put you on her lap, and as the two of you sped to the bottom, you put your leg out. Grandma grabbed it as quickly as she could, but it had already caught on the slide and bent a little.

Apparently you didn't really cry out, and you fell asleep in your stroller on the walk home just fine... but when you woke up from your nap, you refused to put any weight on the leg. You weren't crying exactly, but you did whimper, and couldn't walk.

Mommy rushed home, and you went to the doctor for an examination. He couldn't find anything wrong, but recommended an X-ray, your first ever.

Fortunately, it came back negative, meaning none of your little bones were broken. But you still wouldn't walk due to the pain.

For several hours I texted Mommy repeatedly, "Any change?" "Update?" "Is she better yet?" Being away from you when you were hurt was killing me; I wanted to be there so I could carry you around, feed you frozen yogurt, and watch Elmo with you.

On Friday morning you started crawling again, and by Friday afternoon I heard you were walking, so the sprain was already healing nicely, but I tell you this: it is horrible hearing your child has been injured when you are so far away. I knew rushing home was pointless, because you were fine, but part of me wanted to up and leave immediately.

I'm glad I didn't have to rush home, because I like this beleaguered little town. Maybe it's because I have been coming here so many years, maybe because the owners of the comedy club are such kind people. It's probably a mix of both.

The Cuyahoga River contains many little waterfalls, and the town has a walking path next to them. It makes for a nice little afternoon stroll when the weather is nice.

The one thing I dislike about this gig is the limited outlets for exercise. I'm staying in what's known as a "Comedy Condo," an apartment owned by the comedy club. When I'm in a hotel, there's usually a small fitness room with several weights and a treadmill, but no such amenities exist for me when I visit Cuyahoga Falls.

I've always liked exercising, but truth be told, Mommy got me addicted. Well, she introduced me to the drug. If it hadn't been so good, I wouldn't have gone back a second time. Like many men, I looked upon group fitness classes as something women did while men worked out in the main gym. But a woman whispered into Mommy's ear, "You *have* to attend this class. The instructor Jade is phenomenal," and after attending a class, she convinced me to check it out, too. Which I did. And I was amazed. Jade *was* phenomenal. She was an unbridled ball of positive energy in human form.

The neat thing about fitness classes is that the motivating is done for you. When you go to the gym solo, it's on you to step up. When you have an instructor chock full of enthusiasm in front of you, watching you, it's difficult to slack off.

After enjoying my first experience with group fitness, I discovered very quickly that—as with everything in life—not all instructors are created equal. Some limped their way through a class; others seemed to have a peak ability level that didn't register very high on the competence scale. I subjected myself to a series of less-than-stellar instructors, then began attending Jade's classes exclusively.

Unfortunately, it took one weekend to discover that banality was not only the norm at my gym, it was something instilled from the top down. Jade took a weekend off to attend a seminar on new teaching methods, a seminar created by a fitness company she admired. She also hoped to make a few connections, ones that might help work her way up the corporate ladder.

When Jade returned from her expedition, her next class was off kilter. She taught like the people I made it a point to avoid. There was no real energy, all her motivational quips were overly forced, and she wore a serious expression upon her face where a beaming smile used to reside. Instead of being fun, the class was stagnant and left me wondering what had happened. Where was the energy? Where was the positive, upbeat, inspiring person we all knew?

I wanted to know, so I asked her outright, "You seem off. Everything OK?"

Turns out, the weekend had challenged her sense of self-worth.

At the retreat, everyone around her had been acting in a certain, serious manner, and she became self-conscious. If no one was teaching like she was, then what she was doing must be "wrong," right?

I understood where she was coming from; self-doubt is a feeling I know all too well. The sensation washes over me when I watch comedy on television. I see cookie-cutter comedians performing tired, banal material, and it makes me wonder if the approach I'm taking is wrong. After all, they're on TV, and I'm not.

When I watch comedy on TV, I don't see groundbreaking, original material. More often than not, I see the opposite. One evening, a friend called me, and was laughingly frustrated. He was watching stand-up comedy, and saw two different comedians perform the exact same joke, on the same night, on two different programs on the same channel.

"Why is everyone so upset about steroids in baseball?" each bellowed with mock outrage. "It's a boring sport! I want MORE steroids in baseball, more home runs! 200 mile-per-hour pitching!"

The network didn't care the joke was so hackneyed that hundreds of comedians were doing a variation of it across the country, they just needed to fill a couple slots with material that would neither challenge nor offend viewers.

The message I got was that if you're a comic, you should actively pursue mediocrity, not develop an original voice. Triumph seems to come more quickly to those who blend in, not those who stand out. It's a reversal of what you would expect when dealing with artistic endeavors.

This attitude isn't limited to television; I can witness it in the trenches of the comedy clubs. I recently had dinner with a comic friend, and was struck by the positivity in his voice. The man had an empty calendar, yet in my mind was a one-of-a-kind character. On stage he spoke from the heart, and was truly funny and original. Yet he was delivering pizza to pay rent, because getting gigs was becoming more and more difficult. He didn't lament his misfortune, however, and in fact talked openly about how he loved what he did, and was hoping for the best from his ever-uncertain future.

On the other end of the spectrum, I worked with a man whose calendar was full year after year. Every club loved him, and he worked without sweating any dry spells. Yet all he did was complain. "I hate that club, the owners are jerks. That booking agent can go to hell, he's clueless. That audience was so stupid I just wanted to get off stage so I could get stoned."

His pursuit of drugs and alcohol seemed twice as important to him as his work as a comedian. From my point of view, his act was very bland; something any average comic could do. I would sit in the back of the room show after show, watching him pick on the people in the front row—"Hey, look at you, red shirt. What's up with wearing a red shirt like that?"—as the back of the room grew bored.

Even worse, I tried watching some of his clips on YouTube, and the shtick didn't work. In the moment, working an audience can be fun, because there's a live energy to the proceedings. But taped and rebroadcasted, it was just uninteresting. Without the vigor of being in the room as it happened, the lack of jokes his set contained was exposed.

So why was my one friend delivering pizza, while the other comic had a full calendar? It's nothing I can really explain, but I can tell you what happened at the end of my weekend with the second comic. When handing out our paychecks, the club owner sang his praises and re-booked him on the spot. When I looked for the same treatment, I was told, "I'll be in touch." This despite many of the handshakes I received after the shows came accompanied with a whispered, "You were the best one tonight."

(Not that it matters, but the club went out of business six months later. A Pyrrhic victory, I suppose. I wish it made me feel glee or even schadenfreude, but it doesn't.)

Oddly enough, I wasn't supposed to be a comedian; I originally planned on a career in music. I took piano lessons as a child, switched to percussion in school band, and ended up on bass in high school. I went to the Berklee College of Music, and after that, was in a rock band that seemed somewhat poised for success. We ended up on a compilation CD with several bands, and I promoted us tirelessly. In fact, I actually got our tracks played on a half-dozen college radio stations nationwide. We were charted as high as number one in a couple markets, and at numbers four and six in others. Which wasn't bad for a bunch of nobodies from Wisconsin.

But, as bands are like multi-person marriages, and a regular marriage is difficult enough to sustain, we fought, and I left. When I did so, I had to come to terms with that nagging little sensibility called self-realization. Maybe we are all too often defined by our own imposed limitations, but after quitting the band and standing alone, looking in the mirror, I decided I was never destined to write a song as brilliant or listenable as *Solsbury Hill*.

Here is where my thoughts cloud over. Would I never write such a song because I believe it to be true, or did I simply not have the musical skill inside me? This all ties in to my wonderment regarding the security of being average. I'm fairly sure I could have written crappy, catchy songs, but would I have wanted to bump into Peter Gabriel or a member of U2 and say, "Hey, I'm a musician, too"? Doubtful. I have no idea how Bon Jovi does it. I've read interviews with him, and he is more than OK with who he is and what he does. As he put it, he's comfortable in his own skin. Meanwhile, Sting is widely recognized as incredibly humble. Consider that a moment; the man who wrote *Every Little Thing She Does is Magic* and *Roxanne* is humble, while he who penned *Living on a Prayer* is cocksure.

It boggles the mind.

So, what is it about being average that instills such assurance? Maybe it boils down to the cliché "safety in numbers." When you don't stand out, you aren't self-aware; no undue attention is drawn your way. As most popular music isn't very good, should anyone point fingers and shout "Imposter!" All you'd have to do is aim your thumbs at those on your left and right and say, "Yup, and them too."

After entering the world of stand up comedy, I was able to meet a comedian named Dave Attell. I gave him a ride to a gig, and he flat out asked me, "Why in God's name would you ever want to do this?" Every night after every show he'd apologize for being off his game, or for not having had a good set. Which was odd, considering I had been in the back of the room staring wide-eyed in amazement and wondering what it would take to become as original, interesting, and captivating as he was.

So while I was stunned, and the audience laughed, Attell was on stage berating himself. Sadly, while Attell achieved a very good degree of fame and fortune for performing his craft, many other comics rose to greater heights than Attell on a tenth of the talent and not even a fraction of the originality.

Maybe the questioning, the insecurity, is the driving force behind those who are truly unique. At the same time, maybe it is also the anchor that holds true talent back. I have no clue.

Perhaps it's the stone-cold fact that rejection takes a lot out of you. Putting your soul on the line for something is damned difficult. To offer up your beliefs, personal thoughts, and feelings to someone—anyone—takes courage. And the wherewithal to continue doing so after realizing the game is rigged—with those of average ability easily outnumbering those with skill—takes either great bravery or massive stupidity.

Going back to where all this started, after Jade explained to me what had happened over her corporate retreat weekend and how it beat her up, I told her that people enjoyed her classes because of who she is. Her personality and how she teaches is what drew me in, and many people I talked to said the same thing. They, like me, said they skipped classes taught by other instructors.

Jade smiled, and said she knew that. She just needed to be reminded that she's best being herself, not acting like someone else.

This was several years ago, and since then the best thing has happened: Jade inspired many people who stood along side me in class to become instructors themselves.

She was just that good.

I don't know what the future will hold for you; whether you will follow Mommy's lead and become a professional, or emulate my life of art and creation. Part of me hopes you don't take after me, because Mommy's path pays much better, and is easier on the ego. There is rejection in the business world, but you aren't as attached to your job when it isn't a part of your identity.

But I know this: though originality always speaks to the soul, it is always easier to be average than exceptional.

That can be frightening to deal with at times.

Love,
Dad

June 3, 2014

Dear Hillary,

    As much as you would wish otherwise, the flyswatter is not a lollipop. That's why I took it away from you.

    Love,
    Dad

June 7, 2014

Dear Hillary,

I am in Harrisburg, Pennsylvania, and missing you dearly. I realize I haven't updated you regarding Squeak, and I think that's because of the age-old adage "No news is good news." I missed the last doctor appointment (Mommy had me home arranging furniture for carpet cleaners), but the updates are all good. Squeak is growing well, and always has a healthy heartbeat.

Squeak also, for the record, likes beating up on Mommy. You used to do that in the womb, too. You'd get all cramped and start flexing; *Hey, when can I get out of here?* You'd push and poke at Mommy's belly, and she'd excitedly grab for my hand and place it where I could feel you kicking away. A little Kung-Fu Master, we called you.

With Squeak, things are slightly different. Squeak's placenta is on the back wall of Mommy's uterus. I'm not sure where it was with you, but with it being on the back wall, it means there is precious little between Squeak and the exterior of Mommy's belly. This means that whenever Squeak gets feisty, Mommy feels it. She really feels it. Mommy has yet to see a hand or footprint, but she says it's only a matter of time.

And Mommy had a new experience with this pregnancy. You, dear one, dodged a mini-bullet, in that you never got the hiccups inside Mommy. Squeak, on the other hand, has them often, and it is tragically silly. Mommy had me put my hand on her belly, and I could feel the repetitious, tiny pulses. We both laughed, but also felt bad for little Squeak. Hiccups are notoriously annoying, the mosquito of the human body. They're not life threatening, but are still incredibly bothersome.

You had them numerous times during your first year of life, and they were the most adorable thing ever. You'd sit in your bouncy chair, looking around at the wide world in front of you, hiccupping away cluelessly.

The closer we get to Squeak's arrival, the more I remember how you entered our life. August 7th, 2012, was a day like any other day. Mommy donned her work clothes and drove off to the office; I puttered around the house, cleaning up the morning dishes, possibly throwing in a load of laundry, and performed assorted other nonsensical piddle-fart projects. I was killing time, waiting for 10am to roll around, because 10am is when Mommy had her 37-week appointment scheduled. I was looking forward to it as much as anyone looks forward to sitting in a doctor's office.

The joy of a doctor visit begins in the waiting room, where ¡Telemundo! is usually blaring at rave-level volume, and you can read about President Reagan's re-election from the most current magazine available. The waiting room is what's known as pre-punishment. You suffer the indignity of soul-crushing boredom, possibly to lower your defense mechanisms so that you are less prone to complain when finally seeing your doctor.

("You want to put your finger, where? Eh, fine. I don't even care at this point...")

On the morning in question, I dressed in my sloppiest of gym clothes and set off for the obstetrician. Having been through this a half-dozen times, I knew the routine well. Since you weren't due for several weeks, I'd hold Mommy's hand through the basic examination, then go sweat some of my many extra pounds away.

Or so I thought.

In retrospect, I should have seen it coming. The previous week, Mommy was dilated four centimeters, and Dr. Ward (no relation to Burt, unfortunately) said, "I'd be surprised if you carried this until our next checkup."

She further warned us, "If your water breaks, don't use the 5-1-1 method, just head for the hospital. The baby will come quickly. You won't have time to pack, or dilly-dally."

(The 5-1-1 method is how you time contractions. If they are five minutes apart, and last for one minute, for one hour, you're in labor. If Mommy started her contractions we weren't supposed to count them; it was go time and not the ever-popular "false labor.")

The reason I was so blasé about week 37—knowing full well Dr. Ward said week 36 showed signs baby was on the way—was because Mommy had absolutely no discomfort. I mean, other than back pain and other minor annoyances. Mommy wasn't having contractions, and was up, active, and living life as usual.

Mommy felt the same way about the scheduled visit that I did; she even left her computer running back at her office. Mommy also believed the hospital visit would be another in-and-out, and figured she'd be back at her desk within thirty minutes of leaving it.

You, however, had different plans for us.

At the appointment, Mommy's dilation measured six centimeters and her bag of waters was protruding. It was, in fact, pushing out of the cervix.

This made the doctor furrow her brow and call for tests on the fluid leaking out of Mommy. They wanted to see if amniotic fluid was part of the cocktail, but unfortunately the tests came back as "inconclusive." It was a wonderful thing to hear in 2012, "We have millions of dollars of medical equipment, and our best guess is to flip a coin."

Mommy was sent to Labor & Delivery for observation, because the doctor did not want to send her back to the office. She said "something" was "probably" happening, and it's for certainty like that you spend the big bucks on doctors.

Mommy was frustrated; I was resigned. She wanted to go back to work, not spend all day sitting in the hospital being poked at, only to be told, "Go home, come back next week" at nightfall.

I wanted to go to the gym.

"I'm fat," I probably whined.

In Labor & Delivery, Mommy was hooked to a fetal monitor so your heartbeat could be listened to, and a contraction monitor was wrapped around Mommy's belly. The contraction monitor was new to us, something previously unfamiliar in our journey through Mommy's pregnancy. It was designed to react to the tightness of skin and give an accurate measurement of contractions. Kind of like a seismograph, but for the belly, not the earth. Considering Mommy hadn't realized she was having contractions—movies and TV always showed them to be quite painful and prominent, and movies and TV are where we Americans glean most of our information—the call for this monitor was a surprise.

Mommy lay flat on her back, a position that would allow the discharge to pool at the base of her vagina and hopefully give the doctors more to work with. After one hour and a new sample, tests were no longer "inconclusive." The strip registered blue, meaning you were getting ready to pop out. Mommy's water hadn't fully broken, but it was leaking, meaning a breach was imminent. It also meant we were now within an 18-hour window to deliver you; beyond that, chances of infection increased exponentially. Which made me relieved the doctors had held us for observation. Sometimes it pays to listen to people smarter than you.

(Which in my case is almost everyone.)

Now I had to run home.

Mommy, ever the planner, had her hospital suitcase packed and ready. Considering we were over three weeks from the due date, however, it was sitting in the bedroom. She hadn't even transferred it to a waiting spot by the front door.

I had no bag-of-readiness, but as a boy I didn't really need one. I could throw a toothbrush and pair of underwear into a backpack and live for several weeks. Either way, I did have to retreat to home in order to grab Mommy's necessities, so quick-packing for myself would be no problem.

When you leave your pregnant wife at the hospital, one punishing thought enters your brain: *Now that I'm gone, she's going to go into active labor! I'm going to miss the birth of my child!*

You can't help it. The idea creeps in and takes hold.

I rushed home, explained to Kitty that I wouldn't be home tonight—our neighbor was going to take him for a slumber party; Kitty would spend the next few days wrestling and terrorizing the neighbor's cats with his best friend Jack, the neighbor dog—and sloppily packed an overnight bag for myself.

I grabbed some DVDs, some snacks (because hospital food = bleh) and hurried back to the bedside.

Fortunately, 2012 was an Olympic year, meaning the Summer Games were in full swing. Whereas on any normal day Mommy would have been subjected to the best daytime TV has to offer (a mix of "You can own this vacuum cleaner attachment for only $29.95!" and "I am not Emily Kimberly, the daughter of Dwayne and Alma Kimberly. No, I'm not... I'm Edward Kimberly, Anthea's reckless brother!"), she was at least allowed to watch the best of the best in athletic achievement.

When the Olympics became too advertising-laden to tolerate, I put in one of her favorite movies of all time, *Point Break*. I tell you this: you become acutely aware of just how often the F-bomb is used in a movie if you watch it in public while nurses probe your wife's privates.

"I'm going to adjust your pillow so I can take your blood pressure," a kindly woman would say.

"We f--king have to get these f--king f--kers!" the TV would bellow, and Mommy would turn a slight shade of pink in embarrassment.

Well then.

Mommy's good friend Kristine popped in, which allowed me to confuse the nurses by saying, "There's Lydia's actual partner. I'm just a surrogate."

Kristine is notoriously modest, and when a doctor exclaimed, "Time to look under the hood!" as notice she was going to measure Mommy's cervix, Kristine turned pale and darted out of the room. The idea she might see Mommy's nether regions was a little too much for her delicate nature to handle.

As they tend to do, the seconds turned to minutes, the minutes to hours... and those hours? They dragged on endlessly. 10am became 8pm, with no discernible change in Mommy's physiology. I mean, aside from her slightly-widening cervix. Down below Mommy expanded from six centimeters to eight centimeters, but we only knew that because the doctors said so.

In labor, discomfort is supposed to begin immediately. From one to four centimeters, women know something is happening. Pain arrives anywhere from centimeter one to centimeter four, and from there grows at a non-linear rate. Where the measurement from four to five is one centimeter, the pain can more than double, and it can increase tenfold as the dilation increases incrementally.

For reasons that defy all logic, Mommy was in labor, dilated eight centimeters, bag of waters protruding and leaking, yet she was feeling no pain. When you hear of labor, you picture women sweating, in pain, and yelling "YOU DID THIS TO ME!" at their husbands. Mommy, on the other hand, was full-ready to go back to work and carry you the several weeks needed to hit the target "due" date. In fact, Mommy progressed to eight centimeters feeling fine-'n'-dandy, something that led the entire staff to call her "Wonder Woman." At eight centimeters, women are usually ready for restraints, lest they thrash around like a possessed Linda Blair. They aren't, according to most medical journals, up and walking around carefree.

Having plateaued at eight centimeters, we would go for short walks up and down the hallways—something done to move her labor along, hopefully allowing her bag of waters to burst—and nothing would happen. No gush of fluid, no sudden exclamation of pain.

At 8:20pm, with no end to the monotony in sight, the professionals decided to burst Mommy's bag of water for her. It wasn't breaking on its own, so to get things going again, they pulled out a poking device, popped the sac, and fluid went Niagara Falls over the side of the bed. It was a torrent of warmth for Mommy, and interesting smell for me.

Within a few minutes, it was discovered Mommy's bag of waters had been pushing on exactly the right place to remove all the pain of her contractions. After the bag was popped, she finally started feeling the pressure each contraction offered. Still, Mommy noted, on the scale of "normal labor," the annoying, cramp-like contractions were nothing like what she should have been dealing with.

We returned to the process of furthering labor naturally. Again, Mommy and I went for walks up and down the hallway—me holding her hand as she shuffled—and over the next hour Mommy finally went from eight to nine centimeters. The staff shook their heads in amazement. Mommy was the only patient they could remember who made it to nine centimeters and was still up and able. Nine centimeters was the point most women were looking for morphine, heroin, or something equally powerful.

The staff asked if she wanted the ever-popular epidural, and we were given a moment alone to discuss everything. I'm not proud of this, but I am a somewhat fearful person; I don't like playing the odds. I wanted Mommy to be comfortable and pain free, but the idea of a needle being anywhere near her spine gave me pause. The slim, ever-so-slight chance something could go wrong and leave Mommy paralyzed (or worse) troubled me. Yes, it was a standard procedure, with an enormous success rate, but that .001% of the time something goes wrong...

Mommy wasn't sold on the idea of an epidural either. Mommy is no hippie, no crunchy-granola "Mother Nature" non-shaving vegan. She loves her some Western Medicine, and is a fan of going to the doctor for a prescription when the smallest sniffle arises in her system. But something about the idea of Natural Birth, something that hadn't crossed her mind to this point, suddenly took hold in her. When giving birth was on the horizon, months and months ago, an epidural was a given; Mommy believed it was just part of the process. But now that the finish line was in sight? She made it to nine centimeters without any drugs, and decided to go the extra mile without the epidural. It was explained a less effective medication could be administered later, if need be, so Mommy decided to face the pain head on and play right through it.

Take that, Jay Cutler.*

At 9:40pm, Mommy's contractions were finally shifting from "discomfort" to "holy shit," and the doctors thought a bath might provide some relief during the final push from nine to ten centimeters.

Mommy asked, "Is there any chance this will last until midnight? Tomorrow is our wedding anniversary, and it'd be pretty neat to have our first child on such a special day."

Every doctor and nurse laughed. No, this baby would be out within an hour. Two, tops.

The standard dilation in labor progresses one centimeter per hour, and Mommy did her best to match that average.

We walked and walked (at nine centimeters! Nine! Mommy really is Wonder Woman!), and when she could no longer stand it, she moved to the bed. Mommy tried some of the techniques we learned in our pregnancy readiness class, and took to all fours so I could rub her back during contractions.

She then lay on her side, and I rubbed her back and butt.

(The latter being a rare treat for me, as on any given day when I try to rub her butt, I am hit. That's right, Mommy is a hitter. Call protective services.)

When 10pm rolled around—an exciting hour filled with more Olympic coverage and Groundhog Day waiting— Mommy was finally at ten centimeters.

Now she could begin pushing. Right?

Not exactly.

When the promised measurement was reached, the big guns were called in. Whereas all day we had met with nurses, nurse assistants, residents, and students—the University of

Iowa Hospital being a teaching hospital after all—now full-fledged Doctors (capital "D") were arriving.

The head honcho, who I called Dr. White Coat (because everyone else wore algae-colored scrubs), said that while Mommy was almost ready to push, a small "anterior lip" remained. Dr. White Coat wanted to let this final piece of the cervix "melt away" before pushing started.

So, a return to the waiting game began. Which, as noted in other places, sucks.

("Let's play Hungry Hungry Hippos.")

At 10:40pm, Mommy had had enough, and called for something to dilute the pain. I confirmed her allergies (repeatedly) so nothing harmful would be put into her, and around 11pm something that would be lovely if taken recreationally arrived.

Because Mommy has smaller arms, locating a vein was difficult for the nurse. She missed the first vein, calling it "rolly," and decided to give Mommy's other arm a shot. I wondered if there wasn't a heroin addict available, since they can find a vein anywhere.

As the nurse walked around the bed, Mommy implored, "Please hurry! Run!" I understood she was now in intense pain, but still thought it amusing to ask someone to sprint around a bed. I mean, the nurse may not have been Usain Bolt, but she was by no means lollygagging.

The left arm was successful, and medication— fentanyl—entered Mommy's system at 11:12pm. The resident doctor checked Mommy's cervix one final time, and thankfully the anterior lip was gone. It was now time to push, and by 11:17pm, the room had filled with people: Dr. White Coat, Doctor Ponytail, a handful of students, and then an actual nurse to monitor the students.

Doctor Ponytail—who sat at the base of Mommy to catch you—said it was finally time to start pushing. Mommy was advised to push through the contractions, because that way they wouldn't bother her as much.

Under those orders, Mommy gave her first push...

...and passed gas.

Farted, to be less polite about it.

I laughed, because that's what boys do when in the presence of farting, but the doctors were kindly professional and assured Mommy what she had done was normal.

Normal, and about to get worse.

A short while later, an embarrassed, sad sentence came from Mommy, "I'm pooping, sorry."

I assured Mommy she was not pooping, and I wasn't lying. Or, I wasn't for the next nine minutes. At minute ten, however, I had to inform Mommy that yes, now she was indeed pooping.

To keep the odor from reaching her, I fanned Mommy's face, which unfortunately meant I aimed the poo smell directly into Dr. Ponytail and a med student, both of whom were waiting patiently between Mommy's knees for you to arrive.

My bad.

At first, everyone was upbeat and excited. Mommy asked again, "Am I having an anniversary baby?" and once again was told "no." At 11:40pm everyone was certain you would be out within minutes.

But you had different plans.

The excitement waned, and soon the room entered an odd pattern of extreme activity followed by complete silence. Monitoring contractions, when it was time to push, the entire gathering would erupt with a chorus of cheers.

"Push!"

"You're doing it!"

"Great job!"

When the contraction would end, everyone would shut down. I mean, completely. No small talk, no, "Hey, how about that sports team?" "What did you have for dinner?" or anything of the like. Because I'm an idiot, I took the opportunity to bust out one of my favorite "awkward silence" phrases. I've used it on crowded elevators where no one is talking, in "getting to know you" situations, and I dropped it like a boss during your delivery.

After a round of enthusiasm—"Go Lydia! Push!"—when everyone lapsed into silence, I counted a beat of three and then intoned casually, "So, while we're all here, I'd like to take a moment to talk to you about my Lord and Savior, Jesus Christ..." It's my favorite way of making what's already an uncomfortable silence even more awkward.

Several students looked at one another in fear—"Is he serious?"—and then another contraction arose. The time for nonsense had passed, but I was still proud of my contribution to the proceedings.

Though all assurances were that you would be out within minutes, this was not the case. The longer it took, and the more silent it got between contractions, the more worried I became. If the doctor says, "It's happening now," and then it doesn't actually happen, it must mean something is wrong, right?

Wrong.

All I did was focus on Dr. White Coat. She wore the most calming smile upon her face during the entire delivery. If ever I felt unsure, unsafe, or worried, all I had to do was look at her. As long as she was fine with the proceedings, I was grounded. My biggest fear became the idea a look of concern would cloud her face. That would have unnerved me.

At 12:01am, I informed Mommy that we had crossed into August 8th; you were going to be our Anniversary Baby.

Suck it, experts.

By 12:15am, August 8th, 2012, Mommy was spent. She was exhausted, and begging for mercy. Mommy wanted to quit, and that's when Dr. White Coat finally stepped out of the background.

In a reassuring, peaceful tone, Dr. White Coat told Mommy, "The head is almost out. Lydia, reach down and feel your baby's head."

Mommy took a weak and questioning hand and reached between her legs; there you were, waiting to come out into the world. So close, so very close...

Touching your slippery head gave Mommy a burst of energy, enough strength for one final push... and out you popped. Mommy pushed so hard, and you slid out so quickly, that you surprised both Dr. Ponytail and the med student who were poised to catch you. Instead of easing out, Mommy shot you cannonball-like into their hands.

You were seven pounds and one-point-five ounces, and a nudge over twenty-one inches long. And even though you were covered in vernix, blood, and other assorted bodily fluids, you were beautiful.

Mommy spent the next forty-five minutes being stitched up, because her last push did major damage down below. Turns out, Dr. Ponytail was the number one seamstress in the whole hospital. She took her time and did things right. There would be no accidental sewing of holes closed on her watch.

(You read that correctly. Every so often, be it because people are tired or just not paying attention, a woman will have her entire vagina sewn shut after giving birth. I'm sure there's an awful joke to be made here, but the concept of being that inept at your job boggles my mind too much to wrap my head around any humor that might be found in it.)

The three of us spent the next two days in the hospital. We were visited by family, friends, and various well-wishers. You were so popular that everyone wanted to get a glimpse of you, like a rare panda.

I had my first experience with a diaper (and put it on you backwards), and we gave the hospital kitchen one whole chance before giving up on them entirely. When your English muffin arrives not only cold, but without having even been toasted in the first place? Yeah, that's a sign someone doesn't know what they're doing.

(Side note: I brought macaroni and cheese in for one meal, and after setting everything up to eat, an obstetrician arrived to give us an overview of what to expect out of the next few days. Just as I was forking the first morsel of food into my mouth, the woman told Mommy, "You can expect to have a red, then yellowish-brown vaginal discharge for the next few weeks..." I looked at my yellow mac & cheese with brown tofu, and suddenly lost my appetite. Great timing, that.)

On Friday, August 10ᵗʰ, the hospital bid us adieu, and I drove the three of us home. Painstakingly slowly, according to Mommy. Hey, I had a new little baby daughter pants in the car! I was cautious!

Kitty greeted us excitedly, and sniffed you questioningly—"This smells like Mom and Dad, but it's so tiny..."

Our house was exactly as we had left it three days earlier, but it felt so different. Mommy and I had no clue what we were doing, but we were parents, and you were dependent on us for everything.

Everything.

Good lord, what had we gotten ourselves into?

Love,
Dad

*Jay Cutler was a quarterback who would leave the game whenever he bruised his vagina. Which was quite often.

June 11, 2014

Dear Hillary,

You and I went to the doctor earlier, because Mommy and I (though we try our best) are still novices when it comes to the whole parenting gig. On Sunday you started running a fever and drooling. Mommy donned her Sherlock Holmes cap, put a finger in your mouth, and rummaged around until she found a new, two-year molar coming in.

"She's teething!" Mommy said proudly.

Problem arose; problem solved.

No mystery about it at all.

As the drool continued—a natural byproduct of a new tooth—a diaper rash appeared. Mommy attributed this to the saliva entering your system and messing with your stool. Little red dots appeared beneath your chin, and Mommy explained we needed to keep the saliva off your skin. Little red dots appeared on your hands, mostly around your thumb, which Mommy said was a byproduct of your thumb-sucking ways; the saliva was interacting with your skin, and your skin wasn't happy.

On Monday you had no fever, and the drooling subsided, and all was well again.

Today, Mommy took you to daycare, and then she and I met for her scheduled once-over regarding Squeak. That appointment was quick—Dr. Ward gave Mommy and Squeak a healthy thumbs up—and we separated. Mommy went to work, and I was off to get Mommy's car an oil change.

My plans were waylaid, however, when daycare called and said you, dear one, had Hand, Foot, and Mouth disease.

I had to retrieve you.

What we thought was teething and drooling was in fact a virus.

Your condition had peaked on Sunday with your fever, and the red dots were the leftover symptoms.

Mommy felt defeated, like we had let you down, but I told her we did just fine. Sure, we missed the diagnosis, but we knew you weren't feeling well and had given you Tylenol and lots and lots of attention and love.

(We even let you watch extra amounts of Elmo on Sunday; you usually only get one episode of Sesame Street a day. On Sunday, you devoured *two whole episodes*. What a treat!)

The doctor told me that Tylenol and cuddles are all that can be done for Hand, Foot, and Mouth. It's a short little burst of mild discomfort, and fades quickly.

Had we pooh-poohed what you were going through and done nothing—no Tylenol—then we could beat ourselves up. But I believe we got to the finish line even while screwing up the actual race.

Hopefully you feel the same.

One other item of note, yesterday I received word that a high school classmate of mine passed away. Heart attack while he was jogging. Jogging. Seriously. Doing something healthy, not something 'Merican.

Ironic? Yes. Sad? Absolutely.

I had to look him up in my yearbook, because while I recognized the name I just couldn't put any face to it. Twenty-five years is a lifetime, and the mind can only retain so much information. That said, 25 years is also the blink of an eye, and no one I graduated with should be dying yet. When I heard he passed away, I immediately thought of the two children and wife he left behind. I thought of what it would be like for you and Mommy if I were to die. These were sad, evil thoughts, and I did not enjoy having them inside my head.

I do not look forward to discussing death with you, but it is inevitable. With life comes loss, and there is nothing I can do about that. You love both Kitty and Simon, and within mere years they will be gone. I will hate explaining this to you, because I will hate watching you cry; it already tears me up inside. If you haven't realized by the time you're reading this, you should know that Mommy is the strong one, and I'm the softie. I had to leave the room and cover my ears when you got your immunizations, and I'm the one who rushes in to gather you up every morning at first peep while Mommy says, "Wait five minutes, maybe she'll fall back asleep."

Death will not be a fun bridge to cross, but it's out there on every path we walk.

Love,
Dad

June 14, 2014

Dear Hillary,

I am in Fort Wayne, Indiana, and missing you dearly. On Thursday you slept in until 7:30am. When you finally awoke, I was there smiling at you, and we partook in our ritual of Morning Snuggles. I carted you away to daycare, and then departed for this city. On Friday, Mommy was ready to give you Morning Snuggles, but you were having nothing to do with it. Mommy said you whimpered, repeating "Daddy" over and over, wondering where I was. You wouldn't even snuggle with her; you were so upset by my absence.

Hearing that saddened me, and being away from you is growing more and more difficult. I knew this day would come—you recognizing my absence—but I figured we had a bit more time of cluelessness to go.

The "good" news is that in one more week I have a long swath of time to be home with you. I have a couple scattershot performances in July—all close to home—and then nothing for one month. I purposely left my calendar blank around the time Squeak will join us, so I could be in the delivery room and be around while Mommy is recovering. The projection is Squeak will come early, so I cleared the end of July and part of August. The problem, of course, is since I am home, I won't be earning any money. Which, as I've said in the past, is scary. My industry is feast or famine, and it's difficult to turn down work. My August is packed with work, though, which is nice... but also worrisome. Considering how much you miss me now, I can only imagine what my first week away will be like after the long swath at home.

Well.

Continuing backward from my last letter, where I discussed your birth, I lied a little when I said Mommy and I had no clue what to do when we brought you home. It's true we were new parents, but we did have a small inkling of what to do. A very, very small inkling.

Somewhere in the neighborhood of five weeks before your due date, the thought *We should probably know what to do in case of an emergency* crossed Mommy's mind. She found an "Infant Safety and CPR" course at the hospital and signed us up.

Within moments of starting the first class, we had the realization it was not for us. People joke about warning labels like "Do not use toaster while in the shower" and "Do Not Operate Heavy Machinery While On This Medication" (*on a bottle of dog medicine*), but the sad truth is, stupidity is all too common. A recording I heard while on hold with tech support recently imparted this wisdom: "Did you know that charging your phone for just 15 minutes will probably help if it is not turning on?" Because people are apparently so dumb they don't realize their battery is dead if their phone doesn't turn on.

In an age of catering to the dumbest common denominator, the Infant Safety and CPR course we attended was twenty minutes of useful information hidden inside a two-hour package of dumbed-down simplicity. At best, the course was designed for semi-retarded teenagers pooping out kids well before their ability to care for them. At worst, it was proof positive society is doomed and the movies *Wall-E* and *Idiocracy* are more documentary than escapist satire. Talking points included:

- Don't shake your baby.
- Really, don't shake your baby.
- Not kidding here, shaking is bad.
- You know what? We're just going to go ahead and call the police, as you are obviously unfit baby shakers.

Above all else, the instructors wanted people to walk away understanding that shaking your baby was a no-no. And not only was it a no-no, the whole world was standing in line, waiting to shake your future baby. The course offered new parents a way of making sure their babysitter wasn't an accidental murderer.

"When interviewing potential care-givers, do not ask, 'Will you shake my baby?' because people will always say no. You have to trick them. Come at the question sideways, to see how they respond situationally. Try, 'Say my baby is crying and won't stop, how will you react?' instead of 'Will you shake my baby?'"

How tricky! I bet that gets "I'm gonna shake the hell outta the thing until it shuts up!" from bad babysitters every time! Bravo, instructor. Bravo.

slow clap

Beyond baby shaking, the idea danger lurked in every corner of the world was emphasized repeatedly. "Do you have special foam corners on every edge of your furniture? Do you have special foam pads for your doors, so they don't slam on little hands? Have you put locks on the oven door, so your child doesn't crawl in it?"

(This last one made me raise my hand and ask, "But what if the kid is playing hide and seek?" I received a confused stare in response.)

An inflatable cover for the bathtub spigot was singled out for high praise, because it was both a cushion *and* a heat sensor. Like the "blue mountains" on a cold can of Coors beer, the spigot cover glowed red when warm. Just in case a parent had no clue hot water warms metal.

Measuring temperature was the secondary function of the device, however. First and foremost, it was a preventive measure regarding head-bonking. You didn't want your wee one to knock their noggin, would you?

This was too much for Mommy, who raised her hand and spoke her mind clearly. "You know, when I was big enough

256

to use the tub, I hit my head on the faucet once. *Once.* And then I learned not to do it again."

Mommy was suggesting—and quite rightly in my limited opinion—that people, even children, learn through trial and error. The thought we needed to pad *every single item* in the house was absurd to her. The instructor's response was to stare blankly, and then resume her lecture on how *every single item* under your roof was of danger to your baby.

It wasn't just the base nature of the advice that bothered me; the over-reaching nature of the course was just irksome.

"Make sure garage door has sensors that won't allow it to close if something is blocking it!"

(But how will baby play Indiana Jones?)

"Never leave your baby alone in a car on a hot day!"

(But it's OK to do so in the frigid winter days of January?)

"Keep your baby out of the sun!"

(Yeah, I've seen John McCain's nose.)

The repeated thought I had (in a very sarcastic tone) was, "My God, how did my generation ever survive? *Our* parents didn't have these nifty classes explaining parenting to them, they had to learn through trial and error, allowing kids to be kids and explore the world."

Before long, Mommy was playing a game on her phone, and I was knocking around on Facebook with mine.

Now, Mommy and I aren't sociopaths; we didn't want you to be hurt. But we also didn't want to overprotect you. We took common sense precautions around the house, like putting guards on all the electrical outlets. The though of you jamming a fork into one and electrocuting yourself was unkind to our calm, so to speak. We also tied down any large items you could possibly tip over, such as the television and several dressers. Getting trapped under one of those items could be very damaging to your wee self. We had to draw the line somewhere, however, and making sure every single item you touched was soft wasn't in the cards.

To be fair, both the infant CPR and infant choking instructions were invaluable. The problem is, those moments took up too little time. So much emphasis was placed on trivial generality that the medical training was almost brushed over. Even worse, when it came to imparting the important information to us, the instructor stopped speaking and pressed a button on her computer. No longer lecturing, she played a video for everyone. This action caused Mommy and me to stare at one another. We could have stayed home and done this on YouTube? Why exactly did we pay for a class?

Unfortunately, the CPR portion of the course came so late into the evening that I was pretty much bored to tears and trying in any way possible to amuse myself. The phrase "push hard and fast" was repeated so often, I wondered aloud if we were watching an instructional video on how to make a baby, not give one CPR. This drew uncomfortable looks from the others, and one giggle, from Mommy.

The video contained a work-along section, where people in our class were supposed to practice CPR on a doll in time with the on-screen instructor. To help with the timing of chest compressions, a snare drum was played. Mommy and I had a doll that made a wheezing exhalation noise when pressed, and did so at a tone that was similar to the snare. Discovering that, I added a polyrhythm to the beat, technically administering the CPR incorrectly, but which filled the room with a nice Brazilian samba. So as the snare would sound "tap... tap... tap..." I accented it with "tap... tap, tap... tap-tap, ta-tap-tap-tap..."

Thankfully, Mommy wasn't mad at me for my silliness; she laughed as others stared disapprovingly.

(Mommy's note: "I didn't just laugh, I was crying and almost barfed I was laughing so hard.")

The silliest portion of the video regarded instructions on how to call 911. An actress was given the role of "mother in distress." Her baby needed help, and she had to phone it in. In a very serious tone, a voiceover told people they should follow this important two-step process to get help:

- Step one, pick up phone
- Step two, dial 911

In support of these steps, the actress, using the most monotone, non-panicked voice, said, "Help. I need help." into a phone. She then turned to a doll meant to be an unresponsive baby and said robotically, "Baby? Baby? Please respond, baby."

She spoke without any hint of emotion; it was like Katy Perry singing a love song. (You won't have a clue who Katy Perry is by the time you read this, but still, oh snap.)

(Oh, and what, for the record, constituted an emergency according to the video? "If the baby has a burn, one larger than the size of your palm, seek help." Well, considering babies are tiny creatures, I'm pretty sure a burn much smaller than that would have me rushing you to the emergency room.)

As said, I don't believe the course was created for people like Mommy and me. And I don't think it was for the Asian sensation who arrived thirty minutes late, played with his Blackberry for ten minutes, and then left with a bored "this is beyond common sense stupid" look on his face.

(Time for Chinese Downhill!)

The course didn't seem designed for people who should be parents. It was almost a primer course for the kind of people you'd rather not see pouring their unique brand of pee into the gene pool. Looking around the room that day, I hoped the white, tattooed guy playing African Tribal Chief with his earlobes, or the Crunchy Granola couple who said, "We don't believe in air conditioning" (or showering, shaving, or deodorant, from what I could tell), actually got something from the course.

Because if they didn't? God help their baby, and God help our future.

Love,
Dad

June 21, 2014

Dear Hillary,

I am in Chicago, Illinois, and missing you dearly. If you've noticed, over the past year I've been in Chicago more than any other city, which is nice. It's close, and is a big enough market for me to play several locations without saturating any market or angering any clubs ("You're working for the competition, I'm not hiring you anymore!"). In my line of business, the loss of one club can hurt a lot, especially over time.

People often ask about my job, because "comedian" isn't a normal occupation. They timidly venture inquiries, usually phrased like this: "Can I ask you a personal question? Feel free to say no."

I find such leads interesting, because nine-point-nine times out of ten I have no problem with what is being wondered. Maybe my concept of "guarded information" differs from that of most people, or maybe it is others who worry too much about what is considered public, and what is considered private. In other words, as far as I'm concerned, bring it.

"Can I ask you a personal question? I take it your wife makes more than you do..."

That opening salvo came from a friend, and when he went silent part of me wanted to correct him. Not on the assumption, that was dead on. Mommy is absolutely the primary breadwinner in the family. What I wanted to correct was the format of his sentence by saying, "That's not really a question, it's more a cautious hanging statement, where you trail off at the end and wait for me to verify your belief, because you're too meek to actually ask what you want to know."

I understand polite, but I don't understand timid. If you're going to ask something normally considered "rude," then out with it. Diluting offense doesn't actually work; calling someone a "homo" with a tone of disgust isn't any better than saying "faggot." The intent to harm is still there, questionably milder language aside.

Now, all that said, in no way was I bothered by either the assumption or the question. Mommy has a Master's degree from an accredited university—a real one, no online nonsense. She has been working her way up the professional ladder since graduating with her Bachelor's, and now has the added benefit of listing "adjunct professor" on her résumé. Mommy created her very own Social Media Marketing class from scratch and presented to the young minds of tomorrow for an entire semester. At the end of the course, a majority of them said it was one of the best classes they had ever taken during their time at college; they learned more modern-day useful material from her than from many of their old-school professors combined.

(Which naturally means that the university took Mommy's course and handed it to another professor, one who used her template to teach it. Because integrity is something that's taught by instruction, not example.)

All this means is *of course* Mommy earns more than an unknown stand-up comedian. Anyone who would believe otherwise has not thought things through very well. Larry the Cable Guy might pull down millions of dollars a year, but those of us on the bottom of the comedy pyramid are not so fortunate.

This income disparity between Mommy and me doesn't offend or bother me. In fact, I've never understood the pride some men feel when financially dominant in a relationship. When it comes to the basic necessities, I pull my weight. Our bills are split down the center 50/50; I leech in no way. But there are limited occasions where Mommy absorbs the cost of an expense, and we call those instances her "wants." There are home improvement ideas Mommy has that do not interest me in the least, and Aunt Kayla set her on the path of little resistance regarding certain bills. Aunt Kayla told Mommy that sometimes it's just not worth it to argue over something. For example, if Mommy believes that the yard needs more flowers, while I wouldn't notice a flower in the yard unless it somehow clogged the lawnmower, it's easier for her to just buy her floral desires using her own money. That way, when the monthly bills arrive I don't get irritated and bellow, "Why in God's Great Name"—pause for genuflection, praise Him—"did we spend $50 at Lowes!?"

Not that this approach hasn't bitten Mommy in the butt on occasion. For the longest time, she wanted a king-size bed, a purchase I was against. Mommy, you see, likes to sprawl out at night. It is as if she cannot find peace unless she is situated diagonally across the bed, with one arm stretched out above her head, the other extended to the side, and both legs flailing haphazardly wherever they may fall. On the other side of the spectrum, I take up as little space as possible when I sleep. I'm always on my side, laying flat along the edge of the bed (because that's usually where Mommy has pushed me).

At the time of the mattress discussion we had a cat—Panda, who you got to know for one short year before she expired; she was quite old by the time you were born—that liked to sleep on my (MY) pillow, and Kitty-the-doggy who had to (HAD to) be touching me at all times while sleeping. You'd think that I would have been the person begging for extended space, but I'd rather save money than be slightly more comfortable.

I was, however, willing to listen to Mommy's reasoning regarding the need for a larger mattress.

She devised a plan. The purchase would come out of her bank account, and if I enjoyed the new mattress, then I could pitch in and pay for a portion. Mommy did some advance research, brought me in to choose from two finalists (where I reiterated my stance against spending money), and I chose both the softest and unfortunately most expensive of the lot. I didn't know it was the most expensive at the time; I just gave my opinion regarding comfort.

Mommy threw down her credit card, our bedroom was rearranged, and we settled in with a shiny new (and larger) bed. As expected, I was pushed to the edge, just as before. Mommy sprawled out in enjoyment, Panda took her perch on my (MY) pillow, and Kitty-the-doggy stretched himself out along the width of my body, leaving me nowhere to move. Basically, I went from lying on the edge of the bed with a couple feet of space to my side, to lying on the edge of the bed with several feet of space to my side.

Lovely.

After a few months, Mommy asked how much I liked the new bed and asked if I was now willing to kick in some dough to cover the cost. Like a meanie-head, I pointed out that since she was the only person benefiting from the added space, I would be holding on to my hard earned cash and using it for something important. Like the next Grand Theft Auto video game. Because I'm an awesome husband like that.

Every so often, and by that I mean ninety percent of the time, the chips do fall in Mommy's favor. When I wanted a nice iPod docking station, I didn't ask her to chip in just because she *might* use it. In that case, music was more important to me so we picked one out together, but I alone ponied up the cash. Mommy uses it to play music sometimes, yes, but it was my "want," so I spent my money on a communal household item. Because fair is fair.

The point is that I'm fine with Mommy making more than me. I pay my half of all the "real" bills, and continue to save for the future on the side. I think Mommy put it best herself, once. She called me her "little schoolteacher."

"You may not be a bigwig executive, pulling in six figures a year," she explained. "You make about as much as if I had married a small-town teacher. Plus, you love what you do, and you make people laugh. That's more important than a giant paycheck."

(Mommy, I do believe I love her.)

Mommy having the larger income of our pairing means I often defer to her judgment when it comes to mutual items. Case in point, our house.

In 2007, when I moved to Iowa to be with her, Mommy lived in a cozy two-bedroom condo. It was perfect for one person, and not-too-horrible for two. But like any ambitious woman, she wanted more. A home, a white picket fence, a dog, offspring...

When Mommy and I started dating, we somehow managed to skip the small talk phase. We were both at a point in our respective lives where the usual dating games people play were of no interest to us. We had "deep, meaningful" conversations that usually only occur in movies, where people say the exact right thing at the exact right moment, only we didn't have scripts or a director coaching us. We were winging it, and doing incredibly well.

One subject that came up very early on was that of children, and who wanted what? Zero, five, a litter not unlike the Duggar family in Utah who have nineteen kids as of this writing (meaning the mom probably has a Slip 'n' Slide for a uterus and revolving door attached to her nether regions)... one?

Given my childhood and the home I grew up in, I always looked at parenting as a burden. Children were a nuisance that prevented you from achieving your life goals and weighed you down like an anchor. Mommy agreed to a lesser degree. While she had no negative emotions toward children, pooping out her own tykes was nowhere on her radar.

That elephant out of the way, we proceeded to date, fall in love, move in with one another, and all the other things people do when walking the mating path.

But the more things developed, the more Mommy's internal tick altered. When things started to grow serious, and by that I mean "after I had moved across the country and in with her," Mommy's mood and mind began to change. She couldn't put her finger on why, at least not immediately, but when her thoughts came into focus it was all too clear.

Before I entered her life, Mommy had never been in a serious relationship. Her boyfriends lasted a few weeks more often than not, and on rare occasions several months. After years of ping-pong relationshipping, Mommy believed that a husband and family were probably not in her cards.

But then she met me.

The more she discovered what an actual, tender union was, the more she began to feel that keeping a child from such a happy circle of love would be selfish. Before me, Mommy had to focus on keeping herself happy and safe while in a partnership. With me, she wanted to share what she felt.

Logically, I understood that. I was going through the near-same emotions. Before Mommy, I had been in a mix of "not-so-awful" and "holy disastrous, Batman" relationships. With Mommy, I finally understood why the previous mergers had not worked out; they weren't supposed to last. Each relationship in my life was supposed to teach me exactly what I needed to know so I would be ready for Mommy.

So when the idea of marriage and going the distance with one another started to rear it's ugly head, Mommy knew she had to speak her mind. She had to come clean sooner, rather than later. It was completely in line with our "keep no secrets" circle of trust. Unfortunately, I hadn't changed my stance on kids; I still didn't want them.

But I wanted Mommy.

Now, I'm no dummy. I may be dumb, but I'm no dummy. When the best thing to happen to you comes into your life, you grab hold and never let go. So when it comes to choosing your battles, you choose wisely. I knew this was one I would lose if push came to shove. With little in the way of hesitation, I agreed that I would honor her wishes and become a father when the time came.

Many people in my life have stated this arrangement concerned them, because they looked at parenting as something that should be actively desired. I disagree. I believe any situation is something that should be entered into eyes open and emotions honest. You can suspect how you will feel about any situation, but you can never know for certain until you experience it. I wasn't trying to be negative; I was just laying bare my emotions instead of hiding them.

But kids, if they were ever to enter the picture, were for the future. The "now" demanded a bigger dwelling, because Mommy believed in the American Dream of home ownership.

We began looking for a house in 2008, as the stock market was tumbling earthward and home prices were supposedly plummeting. Unfortunately for us, this event was a double-edged sword. On the one hand, the University of Iowa was (and remains) an economic powerhouse, and we lived too close to it for the fiscal downturn to truly take hold. While a home in Las Vegas or certain areas of California could be scooped up for pennies on the dollar, the median house being built in Iowa still commanded a decent chunk of change and a multi-year mortgage. On the flip side, Mommy owned a condo, and those things bleed value like a hemophiliac. So we owned something that would lose us money in a sale, and wanted to buy something that wasn't as economically downward adjusted as we were hoping for.

(Hooray for irony!)

We started out looking at existing homes for sale—those already lived in—but soon decided new construction was the best path. The costs were surprisingly similar, so gobbling up something erected several months ago made more sense than throwing cash at a dwelling from 1973.

To that end, we saw a modest dwelling in a new development. It was, in fact, the only house on the block. Looking out the front door you saw an expanse of empty lots, ones filled with deer and geese. We knew such enjoyment wouldn't last—more homes would be built eventually—but we liked what we saw.

Examining the house took about 30 seconds for me, and a handful of days for Mommy. Having moved more times than any human should meant that I felt at home easily. I moved from Wisconsin to Boston, and immediately Boston was my home. I moved from Milwaukee to Los Angeles without disruption. I moved from Los Angeles to Iowa and felt no awkward transition. So I looked over the house, then lay down on the bare carpet and stared at the ceiling.

"Seems fine to me," I thought.

Mommy needed to come around a bit, and was a bit upset with me for not having more input.

I knew I could adapt to almost any dwelling, so I wanted Mommy to be super-happy with her decision. I felt my input was unnecessary, because I had no demands regarding our purchase. Well, almost. I just wanted one area of the house to call a "man cave," a place to be untouched by female decoration.

Time was taken, and the home purchased. And writing this six years later, I'm still waiting for my little sliver of solitude. Who knows how long you will call it "home," but my hope is it will remain our domicile for many years to come.

(Because Daddy is tired of moving.)

Well.

I have one final thought to leave you with. Remember the Hand, Foot, and Mouth disease I told you about last week? When I took you in, the doctor told me, "It's rare for adults to contract the disease. Unless, of course, they never had it as a child."

Take a wild guess who never had Hand, Foot, and Mouth disease as a child.

When you were contagious and playing, "I want to take everything from my mouth and put it in Daddy's mouth," you, my little love, infected me. I am now a grown man walking around with a toddler's disease. I have tiny red sores on my hands and feet, and for several days swallowing was quite painful due to the red dots in my throat.

Mommy laughs, and says that's what I get for doing whatever you want me to—especially regarding allowing you to put all your toys in my mouth. But, since it makes you giggle, I figure it's worth it. If little red bumps and an itchy feeling is suffering, I can live with that. It's worth it to witness your smile.

At least I know you won't give me chicken pox. I had that twice (if not three times) as a child. Experts say you only get that once, but I must be special.

Wait, maybe that means I'll get it yet again?

Oh Lord, I hope not.

Love,
Dad

June 25, 2014

Dear Hillary,

While I was in Chicago, Mommy's mom—your Grandma Diane—visited you. I'm told you had a grand old time, and even got to spend some alone time with her while Mommy saw a movie with friends.

Grandma Diane is going to take care of you while Mommy and I are in the hospital during Squeak's arrival, and she wants to spend as much time with you before then as possible. That way you will be more than used to being alone with her while we are gone.

(I write that with full knowledge that the hospital is only fifteen minutes away, and fully aware I will be making multiple trips home to visit you. Hopefully I will even be back to help put you to bed; we don't want you to think you've been completely abandoned.)

Now, we all love Grandma Diane and accept her for who she is. I want to make that clear going in. You light up when you see her, even if you cannot shout "Gamma!" in appreciation yet.

So, the fact we love Grandma Diane on the table, the only minor drawback to her personality is that she loves to talk. So much so, you would almost think Grandma Diane is allergic to silence. Words flow from her mouth in a non-stop torrent. It can be quite exhausting.

A few years ago, she was visiting Mommy and me in autumn. It was a Sunday afternoon, and I was sitting in the living room wearing a Green Bay Packers T-Shirt, watching the Green Bay Packers play on the television. From our front porch, a Green Bay Packer flag fluttered in the light breeze—I put it out every Sunday during football season.

Coming up from the basement, Grandma Diane took a look at the television, then at me, and asked politely, "Watching football?"

Somewhat confused (and a little distracted), I nodded in the affirmative. I mean, I was in a chair, facing the television, with a football game on said television. I was indeed watching football, not jogging, washing the dishes, or crocheting.

Unfortunately, the fact I nodded meant a silence remained in the air, and Grandma Diane was having nothing to do with that. Noting both my Green Bay T-Shirt (and possibly the Green Bay flag outside), she continued, "Rooting for the Packers?"

Because I like Grandma Diane, and sarcasm is generally considered rude, I nodded once again. It crossed my mind to say, "No... I actually want the Vikings to win. All this Packer gear is a false front, but you saw right through that, didn't you?" or something similarly snarky, but I decided against it. Again, Grandma Diane is a nice woman. She was just trying to make chitchat. However, my nod meant that once more the television was creating the only noise available to her ears, which was complete anathema to Grandma Diane.

Mustering up what she believed was a surefire conversation starter, she offered, "Is that Brett Favre playing?"

Now, it was 2013, and Brett Favre had retired in 2007, 2008, and 2010. (Which is a long, long story. Don't ask me to explain. Google it, or whatever you kids do in the future.) He hadn't played for Green Bay since 2007, and in fact their current quarterback—Aaron Rodgers—was already a household name for being a Super Bowl MVP in 2010. Not that I really expected Grandma Diane to know all of this, but even a cursory awareness of the world of football would have prevented the question. I mean, I'm not a fan of NASCAR, but I would have known not to ask anyone watching a race, "Is Dale Earnhardt driving?"

Mommy, bless her heart, probably intervened at this point, which most likely prevented a blood vessel from bursting in my eye.

Something you are already aware of (even if you cannot verbalize it yet) is that the people you love have the ability to frustrate you more than anyone else in the world. When Mommy or I try to get you to eat something that doesn't interest you, or prevent you from doing exactly what you want exactly when you want to do it, you are very impatient with us. You flail and shout and scream and cry, letting Mommy and me know that at that moment we are the absolute worst people in the world.

But we know you still love us.

Which is how it is with Grandma Diane sometimes. She has a good heart, and no one wishes her any ill will, but sometimes you want to just shout "For the love of God, woman, silence!"

Not because you are angry with her, but because peace and quiet are quite wonderful.

Mommy has a million and one stories of being frustrated with Grandma Diane, but her favorite involves the day you were put into her belly. By now, you are aware you were created using in vitro fertilization. Mommy and I were unable to conceive naturally, due to Mommy's eggs staying stubbornly inside her ovaries; they never had the inkling to travel down her fallopian tubes to be fertilized.

Our first round of IVF was unsuccessful. An embryo had been implanted in Mommy, but it didn't take. Mommy was heartbroken. I had gone with her to that appointment, but when round two arrived I was on the road performing. For moral support, Grandma Diane was kind enough to drive over from Des Moines in order to hold Mommy's hand (metaphorically) and be there for her during a very stressful time.

Going in to the hospital, Mommy was nervous. After two years of medical procedures—which, sadly is a short amount of time given the horror stories we'd heard involving infertility. Some people try for a decade or more and are never successful in their attempts to become parents—and numerous mishaps, Mommy was ready for something positive to happen.

Mommy was glad Grandma Diane was there for her, but sometimes all that's needed is the reassuring comfort of another person. Sometimes simply being there is what's important, and nothing more.

Nothing more, such as unnecessary conversation.

In the procedure room, Mommy was implanted with you (albeit in the form of an embryo), and then had to lay in bed for thirty minutes. This time was designed to allow the embryo to embed itself in Mommy's uterine lining. It is time to spend relaxed, hopeful, and hopefully worry-free.

Mommy wanted to spend it focusing on positive thoughts; visualizing the baby taking hold and growing in her belly. She was happy Grandma Diane was there for moral support, but wanted that support to take place in silence. Which, as I have already explained to you, is something your grandmother does not handle well.

Grandma Diane used the opportunity to tell Mommy of all the wonderful gossip occurring in the lives of everyone they knew; a flood of updates came cascading out of her mouth in a litany of banality. Even worse, she decided that while sitting in a hospital, her very daughter having just undergone a slightly invasive procedure and in dire need of nothing but positive reinforcement, the time was ripe to discuss all the medical ailments befalling everyone in their immediate (and not-so-immediate) circles.

"Did you know that Aunt Barbara's second cousin twice removed has cancer? She had it once already, but it's back and they don't know what they're going to do..."

"And while I think of it, back in Moulton, your grandmother's neighbor has a goiter on her neck that she's going to need surgery for. The doctor's say it's difficult, but they can handle it..."

"Oh, before I forget, Kayla ran into Sarah, a girl you went to grade school with. Do you remember Sarah?

Apparently she has been undergoing chemotherapy for about six months now..."

Mommy snapped.

"MOM!" she shouted as kindly as possible (but still through clenched teeth), "Is this really the time to be telling me about everything *bad* happening to everyone we know?"

Grandma Diane got quiet.

Really quiet.

Mommy believes the silence involved a combination of having just been scolded (for which Mommy felt slightly guilty), and an inability to come up with topics that didn't involve something tragic. It seemed Grandma Diane was best at talking about sad things happening to good people, and with that option off the table nothingness was all that was left.

For the remainder of the implantation time, Mommy and Grandma Diane sat comfortably speechless, listening to the relaxing dulcet songs of Norah Jones.

All the while, unbeknownst to anyone, you were burrowing deeply into her uterus and beginning your path toward babyhood.

Not that we would receive that information for several days.

Well.

Before I sign off, I do want to inform you of a slightly depressing addition to your personality. Up until this point, you have been a carefree, opinionless little girl regarding your clothes. Whatever Mommy and I dressed you in, you had (until now) accepted freely.

That, my little love bug, has all changed.

Mommy and I took you shoe shopping, because at your age there's nothing more fun than spending money on something you'll wear for a week and a half and then outgrow.

As it is summer, Mommy was in the market for sandals, and she found a very comfortable pair of mushy, cushy flip-flops for you. Ever-obliging, and enjoying being out of the house and exploring the shoe store (so many things to touch and pull off shelves!), you allowed Mommy to try them on your feet, and you even wandered a little in them. These flip-flops were black. Top to bottom, back to front, black. Simple. Elegant.

After deciding they fit, Mommy put them in the box and purchased them. We took them home, and the next time we tried to leave the house, Mommy happily exclaimed, "Hilly should wear her new shoes!"

They were retrieved, and Mommy attempted her best to place them on your feet. But you, dear one, were having nothing to do with it. You threw the fit of all fits, kicking your legs and arching your back. It was as if the shoes were hot pokers, and Mommy placing them on your feet was causing great pain to you.

After a few minutes, an exhausted Mommy let you scamper free, and watched and waited as you darted off to retrieve your pink tennis shoes. You brought them to Mommy and let her put them on you drama-free.

"Oh God," Mommy wondered. "Could this be a color issue?"

Several days and several more failed attempts to get you into your black sandals later, Mommy determined color was the only thing about the new sandals you did not enjoy.

"I think Hilly is asserting her girl-dom," she explained.

Looking on the shoe store website, Mommy discovered that the same style of sandal was available in a pink/black combination. They weren't in stock, however (which is why we didn't see them while shopping), and needed to be special ordered.

So special order we did, and when the new pink/black sandals arrived Mommy took you to pick them up...

...and you LOVED them. You were already trying to put them on before her car had left the shoe store parking lot.

You wear them daily.

Same exact shape/style as the all-black pair, only these have pink.

They are—and I hate to stereotype—more *girly*.

And so it begins. You are a girl, and though you may not gravitate toward dolls and Barbie yet, it might be in your future.

To this, I both shrug and cross my fingers. My hope is you will continue to love the Batman clothes I buy for you regularly. My fear is this is the first step in the inevitable march of My Little Pony, Dora, and whatever else is strictly feminine in the way of little girl outerwear.

If it is, well, such is life.

You are here to make your own decisions, not be restricted by my tastes.

But I'll always offer you Batman clothes, even if you shoot them down with an upturned nose.

Love,
Dad

June 28, 2014

Dear Hillary,

Today I want to tell you about the first step Mommy and I took bringing you into our family.

Responsibility comes in baby steps; you should never jump into any situation. When it comes to having a baby, there is a natural progression of "P": Plant, Puppy, Person. Each step is a measure of how much you are willing to sacrifice. If you neglect it for two weeks, your plant may or may not survive. If you shirk duties for one week, your puppy will absolutely pass away. If you leave a baby alone for a few hours, well, yeah. You little creatures can't really survive on your own, as reported years ago by The Onion ("Babies Are Stupid").

I'm not going to argue that dog ownership is exactly like parenthood; too many actual mothers and fathers groan at such comparisons. I'm saying that before you bring a life into this world, you take the same path the baby will, crawl before walk. Because of that caveat, I believe that having a dog is somewhat similar to child rearing in that a measure of responsibility once unknown is undertaken. You have to structure your personal life around checking on the mutt, feeding him regularly, grooming him, and making sure you get home in ample time to take him on a walk, lest you return to a urine-soaked carpet and a dog with a hung head.

I occasionally joke about the parallel between dog and child ownership on stage and once had an audience member shout up at me, "That's stupid! You don't have to change a dog's diaper or wipe its butt!"

Fair enough, maybe you don't have diaper duty when dealing with doggy, but unless you've never owned one, you know that sometimes they return from a walk with a little poop snack attached to their hindquarters. And wiping such a mess aside, if the waste is really embedded in their fur? If you've ever cut gum out of hair, you know how fun that can be. Add to that a disgust factor of 1000% and you're in the ballpark. At least with a kid you can hose everything off with warm water; skin is an easy clean. But matted fur? Not so much.

Regardless, as Mommy is one of those creatures called "woman," and as women (for unknown and insane biological reasons) desire babies, we decided to first dip our toe in the responsibility waters by inviting a puppy into our home. The "Baby Starter Kit" Mommy decided on came in the form of a mini schnauzer we named Kitty. Well, to be honest, I named him, and Mommy went along, knowing it would be easier to cave than to fight me on it.

Upon first arriving in his strange new world, Kitty followed Mommy and me everywhere. Like babies, puppies are needy. Just because they're animals doesn't mean they're born with an innate understanding of the world around them. Maybe they're higher functioning than humans, and can walk and develop faster, but up front they're still wide-eyed with fear when it comes to unfamiliarity. All Kitty knew was that he used to live on a farm with his mom and a bunch of brothers and sisters, and then one day he was with two strangers who would hopefully care for and feed him.

If Mommy or I went into the basement, Kitty would stand at the top of the stairs and cry; he was too small to navigate the steep drops. We had to carry him down so he could remain ever underfoot, the place he felt safest. When we abandoned him, if even for only a moment—stepping into the garage and not allowing him to follow, or leaving him at the top (or bottom) of the stairs while we easily went into places he could not—he cried as if it were the most painful experience of his short little life. I once took a shower, and the instant I closed the curtain Kitty started whining. He couldn't see me, and was worried that he had been deserted.

Eventually, however, Kitty matured and soon aged to the point where he would only grow anxious when it was time to be left behind at home. He learned the lay of the land, and understood the difference between my walking into the office or back bedroom as opposed to the front door. If half-asleep on the back of the sofa—his favorite place to rest due to both comfort and the added bonus of destroying something Mommy likes—and I head down the hallway, Kitty will take note and possibly arch an eyebrow of interest, but he rarely moves to follow anymore. Should I make for the front door or garage, however—places he knows I use to actually escape from his presence—panic sets in. In a mad dash, Kitty will rush ahead of me, go up on his back legs, and claw at the door madly. The wall next to the door has long since lost its paint and is covered in specks of exposed drywall because of his claws. Kitty's un-subtle inference is always, *if you're going anywhere, take me with!* Sadly, this ruse works all too often, and as I drive a contented gray and white creature gets to rest on my lap.

The thing is, if I am out running errands I will eventually have to leave him behind in the car while I pop into the grocery store or fill up my gas tank. Kitty is an intelligent little bugger, however, and figured out quite early on that when in a four-wheeled vehicle, should he happen to rest his well-padded paws upon the steering wheel, a loud noise is created that brings much attention to both him and the car. I once went into our local grocery store for several small items and immediately heard the horn beckoning my return. When I got to the counter with my meager morsels, everyone entering the store was laughing and the clerk told me with a smile, "That horn? It's a little dog pounding on it."

"I know," I nodded. "I know all too well."

I can only imagine it won't be long before Kitty learns Morse code, and I will soon hear a volley of three short, long, and short again bursts resonate throughout whichever parking lot I happen to be in.

When Mommy wanted to get a dog, I was against it. I didn't want the expense, the responsibility, the anything that came with having a dog. But that pretty much changed when Kitty arrived. I came home from a gig, and there he was, sitting on the couch. He was scruffy, and scared. He wanted to impress us, so he chewed on my feet as a sign of adoration. Or dominance. I'm not sure which.

He followed us everywhere. He nuzzled right up next to us when sleeping; he couldn't relax unless body contact was made. His ears stood up like those of a bunny rabbit (most schnauzers have floppy ears, while yours has twin satellite dishes).

The more I got to know Kitty, the more I found myself wondering what was going on inside his little puppy head. I asked Mommy what she thought Kitty was thinking so often she was ready to level me with a baseball bat.

I can't help it, though. When I look at him, he looks back so deeply into my eyes I know there are untold synapses firing around his little noggin, and I want to know exactly what they mean to him. I know he knows love, warmth, attention, and even fear, but does he know how much of that he expresses through his personality? The way he wags his little nub in excitement when happy; the way he still cries when I leave. I wonder what he thinks when I sing to him, because of course I sing to him.

There is so much love in him it is near disgusting. If I am on the couch with my laptop, he will jump up and paw at my hand until I close the computer and set it aside. He will then crawl onto my chest and plop down, staring at me intently for a few moments before closing his eyes and drifting off to sleep. Just like with you, I am apparently his most-favorite pillow.

Because of Kitty, I knew I was going to be OK when you showed up. Mommy and I had our first experience with tending to something that needed our love and affection—as well as attention and potty training—and we passed all tests with flying colors.

Again, a doggie isn't exactly a baby, but it's best to make sure you can handle one before diving into the deep end of the parenting pool. And having Kitty helped prepare us for you better than any "How To" book could have.

Love,
Dad

June 30, 2014

Dear Hillary,

Today was tiring.

We went to Target, which is par for the course, and while there my phone was dropped and destroyed. The screen didn't even crack, but the impact scrambled the electronics within.

You giggled; I shrugged my shoulders. I wasn't even upset. It's a phone, it happens.

I mean, I wasn't happy, but I wasn't upset.

It happens.

We went to buy a new phone, an expense I wasn't excited about, and that took about an hour. For being so bored in a boring store for an hour, you behaved wonderfully. I smiled and danced with you when I could, and carried and bounced you when I had to deal with the phone people.

(I also changed a poopy diaper of yours in the employee lounge. Which is what they get for not having a changing station in the restroom.)

When we got home, I put you in your crib for a nap—you had actually fallen asleep in the car—and fired up my computer.

And I saw the news.

During her entire pregnancy with Squeak, I've joked with Mommy about wanting another daughter. I figure that after raising you, I understand better how to take care of a little girl than a little boy. I also worry about the stereotype surrounding little boys: they're destructive.

Mommy has an instinct that Squeak is a boy, and when she tells me this (which she does constantly), I say, "It better not be!" and pretend to be angry. I'm not angry, of course, because I'll love whichever gender comes popping out of her. But I pretend.

Sometimes, however, I'm not so sure I want to bring another girl into this world.

And I often worry about you.

It is still, in 2014, so much easier being a white male than anything else.

When I got home and jumped online, I saw that a Supreme Court dominated by misogynistic jerks decided that, as men, they knew better *than women*, what was best *for* women.

Five men stated that the type of health care a woman receives should not be determined by women themselves, but by corporations owned by assholes who use ancient tales to cover their intellectual shortcomings.

(The three women on the Supreme Court were, of course, against this ruling. One lone man, one who probably remembered he had a mother [and possibly a wife] he loved, also dissented.)

As a father, I am at a loss for words.

I see horrible stories—universities who refuse to investigate sexual assaults, law enforcement agencies that refuse to acknowledge rape, high schools that protect athletes who commit atrocious acts against young girls—and wonder: why would I want to bring another woman into this world? Why would I want to expose her to such treatment?

As a nation, America raises a pointed finger at supposed "underdeveloped" third-world countries and trumpets loudly our superiority. In certain areas on this planet, women can be (and are) put to death at the whims of men. With an air of condescension we shout, "Look at those savages!"

But are we really the superior nation when we subjugate women using legal means, not blunt force? How does championing our fairy tales as greater than their fairy tales elevate us above anyone?

This very Supreme Court ruled, "Corporations are people."

Corporations.

Unfortunately, they don't feel women deserve that same distinction.

I am angry, frustrated, and fearful.

Which is not unlike the men who feel the need to control women; mine is just sympathetic to your plight, not cackling at it.

When you awoke from your nap we went outside and drew on the driveway with chalk. You watched Sesame Street (which is only known to you as "Elmo!"), and I watched as a storm blew through town and destroyed our gazebo.

Like with my phone this morning, I wasn't upset as I watched it get damaged. It's just a thing, and things are replaceable.

Just like women.

(According to some men.)

Hilly... I'm not sure how to end this.

I'd like to have positivity and hope swoop in, and finish by telling you that I'm going to enroll you in martial arts so you can protect yourself against predators, that I'll know exactly at what age we can talk about inappropriate pictures and how they live on forever via the Internet, that by the time you enter the corporate world women will be taken seriously and earn as much as their male counterparts, that whatever you want to do with your life and career won't be challenged by a desire to have a family, that you will be judged by your mind and not your looks...

...but I don't know what to say, and I don't know how much of that will be true.

I do believe that life is about moving forward, even when obstacles are on the path in front of you. And I know that Mommy and I are going to do all we can to give you the strength you will need to navigate the minefield that is being a woman. Many women before you have overcome greater obstacles by far and advanced the rights you have today. As I write, many women are fighting for the rights you will have tomorrow.

My hope is as you grow, women will gain more footholds than they lose.

My hope is that today was just a bad day, but that tomorrow—as the song goes—is a latter day.

(The skies are clearing and the sun's coming out...)

Love,
Dad

July 5, 2014

Dear Hillary,

Several years ago, a friend's girlfriend went off on me because she didn't like a particular band I was into. She berated the band, berated me, and then ended her tirade with what she thought was a coup de grâce, "Well, I went to the so-and-so music school, and have been classically trained, so I know music." Hearing that, I laughed, rolled my eyes, and shook my head. Arguing with her wasn't worth my time, and attempting to justify my taste wasn't anything I was about to do. Not because she had anything over me, but for the exact opposite reason, she had nothing. I could have responded, "Well, I went to the Berklee College of Music, which is prestigious in its own right, so eat a bag of hammered buttholes."

(Hammering buttholes, for the record, is how I believe you prepare them as a culinary delight.)

(Heh.)

I held my tongue, because what point would there have been in a tit-for-tat? Music isn't about critical analysis, it's about emotional connection, which is pointless to argue about. She had a classical background; I had a history of jazz immersion. Is one better than the other? No, it's personal preference. She thought she trumped me with her musical education, but didn't realize I had instruction that was just as valid on my résumé. I could have popped her bubble, but didn't care enough to. Besides, more often than not a silent win means more than chest-thumping. There is something dignified in quiet victory.

Silence is how I handle many battles. Instead of entering into them with fists swinging or caps lock firmly on (for

Internet battles), I either observe or ignore, depending on my mood. I believe my job is to make you and Mommy happy, not prove myself to anyone.

(Ironically, as I write you right now, a war is waging on Facebook, with valiant heroes saving the world through the use of anger, self-righteousness, and having too much time on their hands. I looked over the thread, typed a response, got told off, and wandered away, bored. Writing to you is much more productive than reading a litany of "Oh yeah?!" and "No YOU shut up!" Plus, according to the notifications I continue to receive, the people involved are glad-handling one another just fine without my involvement. Good for them.)

For the past twenty (or so) years, only my two closest friends heard my next story. At first it was somewhat personal and not for all ears, but it gradually faded into something barely worth space in my memory.

While in college, I tended bar at a restaurant called Pieces of Eight. It was located on Lake Michigan, and had just constructed a patio so customers could smell the fresh scent of dead fish and semi-scrubbed sewage while they got drunk (a treatment plant was about a mile down the lakefront).

I found a brown-haired cocktail waitress named Becky to be on the attractive side of things, so one day I up and asked her out. She turned up her nose and responded, "Are you kidding? Me, date *you?*"

I didn't mind the rejection—I'd already been rejected often enough to be used to it by that time in life—but was turned off and annoyed by the attitude and reason. Becky looked down on me because I was attending the University of Wisconsin, Milwaukee (slogan: "We're like high school, with tuition!"). It wasn't a very prestigious school, and therefore made me what would be in regal terms "a commoner." Becky informed me that *she* was attending Beloit College, a private and supposedly powerful university that was exceedingly difficult to get into. Because of this situation, I was somehow beneath her. Considering we were both working summer jobs as liquor-monkeys, I didn't think she was in any position to really judge, but oh well.

Bug firmly entrenched in my butt, I decided that I wanted to check out this "Beloit College," a place I hadn't even known existed. In the days well before the Internet and online applications, I made several phone calls, paid a $25 fee, and received an application packet in the mail. I filled it out, and several weeks later received a phone call; I met all their criteria, would I like to come in for an interview? Why, of course I would! How charming!

Raise glass; stick pinkie finger out

Beloit recruiters were meeting potential students at the downtown Hilton, and I scheduled a slot to allow them to pluck my brain. I showered, shaved, made my hair all purty, put on a nice shirt and proper slacks, and went in to "wow" them. I don't remember what I said or how exactly I acted, but upon leaving a fellow with a smile shook my hand heartily and said they would be in touch. Within days, they were. Would I like to be a part of the Beloit College student body? If so, I was welcome to attend starting next semester!

I declined.

I had no interest in continuing my collegiate career in another city. Becky's rejection just made me want to prove to myself that her method of judgment was silly, nothing more. I took her reasoning and turned it on its head. If she thought she was better than me because of something so absurd as the school I choose to attend, she had placed herself on very shaky ground.

Not that I ever told her. Or anyone. It was something I did for me, and me alone. Over time I told my two best friends, more in passing than as if absolving myself of sin, but other than disclosing it to them, I remained silent. It was a personal, private moment to prove to myself that no one person is ever better than another.

I later found out Becky harbored a crush on another bartender, a man named Greg who treated her with contempt every time they interacted. This information confused me. On the one hand, Becky had sufficient low self-esteem to fawn over someone who not only had no interest in her, but who also actively disrespected her. At the same time, she had a healthy enough ego to treat someone who approached her in kindness with disdain and condescension. Odd, but most people have complex, contradictory personalities. Being human doesn't mean being perfect.

Anyway, what do these two stories have to do with you? Well, I have nothing exciting to report about current events. You have been a delightful little chatterbox of late; singing, talking, talking, talking... Mommy and I aren't exactly sure what you're saying, but you do love to use your vocal cords.

One thing you have figured out is how to scold the animals. If Kitty starts barking, you quickly extend your index finger and offer an immediate, "No-no!" You then generally look to Mommy or me for approval; did you scold appropriately? The same thing happens when Simon howls a "meow." Out goes your index finger, and "No-no!" exits your mouth. It is quite endearing. (As is your attempt to mimic Simon; your "meow" lacks the "m," and is a loud "eow!")

You also recently discovered that I have nipples. Thankfully, you instinctively understand that my nipples are nothing like Mommy's, and you didn't attempt to nurse on me. Instead, you treat them like buttons. You push and giggle, push and giggle. Apparently my nipples are quite amusing. I never realized this, but what do I know?

Squeak is well. Mommy visits Dr. Ward every two weeks now, because the closer you get to the due date, the more you want to make sure everything is going swimmingly. Squeak is a kicker; Mommy's ribs feel black and blue from all the abuse. But, since movement is generally associated with health, this is a good thing. For Squeak, if not Mommy's innards.

So, all that aside and with nothing exciting on deck, I sat here racking my brain, trying to come up with something worth sharing when I hit on those old stories. The messages within are neither ideals for you to live up to, nor expectations I am placing upon you. I have no idea how much of your personality will be influenced by Mommy and me, and how much was inherent in you automatically upon your creation. You will be who you will be, and I will love you no matter what.

I will, however, be doing my best to take the lessons I've (hopefully) learned in life, and teach you to navigate rough waters with as much clarity and focus as possible.

Those lessons (as far as today's letter goes) are: there is no point in unnecessary argument, and do not allow rejection to define you. There are topics that deserve passionate debate, but only when you have things like science, history, and facts on your side. Matters of opinion are another thing. Take pride in who you are, and let no one diminish that with their shortcomings. As far as rejection goes, you can fight through it, find an end-around to it, or outright decide it doesn't matter. Rejection can make you stronger, if you allow it.

Your life is to be lived on your terms, not the whims of others.

Love,
Dad

July 8, 2014

Dear Hillary,

I returned home from the gym tonight, and heard Mommy sing-songing to you, giving you a bath.

I snuck over to the bathroom to discover the bath had actually finished, and you were being toweled off.

You saw me, lit up in smile, and happily shouted, "DADDY!"

You ran over to me, received an enormous hug, then stepped back...

...and peed all over me.

Mommy laughed.

Love,
Dad

July 12, 2014

Dear Hillary,

I have a recurring nightmare.

Twice a year I have a dream I do not exactly remember, that causes me to wake in a state of panic and slight depression. This has been happening for four or five years now, give or take.

In the dream, I am still with a woman I dated before I met Mommy, a woman named Judy. Before Mommy entered my life, Judy was the most significant relationship I had ever been in. Being with her, in fact, helped me grow into a man good enough to be worthy of Mommy. That doesn't mean Judy influenced me positively, or was good for me or my well-being. Quite the opposite, in fact. It was the situation I put myself in with Judy that taught me many lessons, not the woman herself.

To break six long years down into a small paragraph, Judy was dating a man named Jim who abused her physically and emotionally. Not only did he cheat on her several times, when his temper ignited she felt the skin of his knuckles on her face. I fell in love with the wounded dove, and wanted to rescue Judy from her abuser. Judy liked my attention, so she kept me around on the side while remaining with Jim. After Jim dumped her, Judy became my girlfriend for a while, then met someone new, cheated on me, and left.

I was heartbroken beyond words.

As said, that is the (very) short version of our tale. I do want to point out that I was not a victim in the relationship. Yes, she cheated on me and I was heartbroken, but I understand full well that it was always my decision to pursue her, my decision to be with her, and my decision to remain emotionally involved despite her unwillingness to return my affections. All too often people enjoy pointing fingers and laying blame for their own actions; I blame Judy for nothing. She did what she did, I did what I did. Such is life.

Which brings us to the nightmare.

As said, I never remember anything specific, but I always awake confused, unhappy, and alarmed, with one single, laser-focused thought running through my head, "What in God's name am I still doing with her?"

In my nightmare, I am still in a relationship with Judy.

As with most nightmares, it takes about thirty seconds to retrieve my senses. I look around, take in my surroundings, be they a hotel room or my bedroom at home, and then it dawns on me, "Wait... I'm *not* with Judy. She dumped me. I'm actually married to Lydia... and we have a daughter, Hillary... and Squeak is on the way."

And in that moment a great relief washes over me. You've heard of the concept of having a weight taken off your shoulders, and the feeling I experience is similar. The difference being I feel a full-body weight has been removed from me, not just a shoulder release. My chest goes from tense to relaxed, I go from paralyzed to mobile, and I transition from depressed to relieved, and happy.

I am uncertain what to think of this dream.

On the one hand, I'm not too thrilled with the idea thoughts of Judy are still embedded deep within me. Conversely, I believe the dream is a reminder that even if I didn't see it at the time, my life has always worked out exactly as it was supposed to. While in the throes of depression after Judy left, I couldn't imagine myself ever being happy again. The weight of human cruelty was upon my back, and instead of using it as a learning experience, I wanted to wear the martyr's cross. I tried to help someone and got burned, so what was the point in ever helping anyone?

Now I realize that every moment of my life—even the so-called failures and dark times—led me down a path that brought me to you, Mommy, and the soon-to-be Squeak.

And I couldn't be happier.

I learned quite a bit in my pre-Mommy relationships, and I told you I would be describing three of them. I've told you of Karen. Before her were Judy, and Hayden. Judy came first, Hayden second, and they were night and day different from one another.

After Judy, I spent two years in therapy. I left a lot of emotional baggage behind and rejoined the dating world, eventually meeting Hayden. With her, I discovered near-immediately what a healthy relationship was supposed to be. As you well know, music is one of the most important things in the world. Music infuses itself into every aspect of life, and enhances whatever emotion you are currently feeling. Sad? Put on a love song and revel in your depression. Happy? Put on something joyously upbeat and tap your toes to the beat. Music is a drug, albeit a wonderfully addicting one and not a damaging intoxicant.

To celebrate my love of music, I used it to speak for me when I could not muster up words of my own. I gave Judy mix tapes constantly—and yes, your dad is that old. I'm talking tapes. Not CDs, mp3 playlists, or whatever is used to store music as you read this, but magnetic, recordable cassette tapes. Because I was emotionally inept when it came to sharing my feelings verbally, I used songs written by other people. Songs I felt could express my thoughts for me. I would make Judy a playlist of love, believing the music would tell her exactly how I felt about her and our union.

It wasn't until I dated Hayden that I realized Judy had never once responded in kind. Music was as important to Judy as it was to me, and she had strong emotions for The Cure, Indigo Girls, and Sinead O'Connor; her passion for music was one of the things that drew me to her. But no matter how many tapes I gave Judy, she never said, "I was thinking of you when I made this," while responding in kind. Never did she design a chain of songs that exemplified her feelings for me.

After the breakup, I went out and purchased music I knew Judy kept close to her heart, music I knew she listened to in private, even if she didn't share it with me. Before reading the book or seeing the movie *High Fidelity*, I had Rob Gordon on my mind. To paraphrase him, "This tape I'm making for Judy... with music she likes. Things that make her happy."

I hoped she would see that despite her inability to share her favorite artists with me, I had been paying attention all along. It was to be one of those magical movie moments, where she realized that I loved her, I *knew* her, and because of it she would come sweeping back into my arms.

Instead of being overjoyed, Judy's response was anger. When I asked her what she thought of my gift, her response floored me.

"I felt violated," she seethed. "Like you broke into my apartment and rooted through my music, my emotions."

I had no response. After spending six years with me in one fashion or another—friend, illicit lover, boyfriend—instead of realizing I had been paying attention to her and knew what moved her, she felt violated, not touched.

I had no response back then, and all these years later am still unsure what to think. The obvious explanation is to say she had a very guarded heart, and though I was emotionally open with her, she was never so with me.

By contrast, the first mix CD (that's right, a compact disc. Technology had advanced beyond the mix tape by then.) I gave Hayden was met with a giggle of joy. The next day, a batch of music was placed in my hand. I was stunned. I hadn't expected a response in kind, because I had conditioned myself to being on the giving end in a relationship. Hayden taught me that relationships should involve give-and-take, not just give-and-give. This painfully simplistic observation was an important step in my emotional development.

So, lesson one to you is that relationships are fifty-fifty. They can sway back and forth, with one person putting in a little more effort now and then, but overall balance is important. Hayden taught me that. As stated, dating her was an eye-opening experience after Judy, and I must stress that you should not invest your heart in someone unwilling to invest in you. Sometimes that is difficult. It hurts, and you might feel rejected and wonder why they cannot love you like you love them, but in the long run it's always for the best to walk away from an unhealthy union. I promise you, no matter how hard it is in the moment, when you look back years later you discover how important and right it was the relationship ended. With Mommy, that is what I found, someone who matched my love for her with a love for me. When you are the only person in a relationship giving the love and putting in all the work, it will never last.

Lesson two, then, is that you should never ignore warning signs. All too often people ignore gut instincts and do whatever they can to salvage something not worth saving. And, for the record, there are always warning signs. You either pay attention to them or ignore them. I disregarded a plethora during my time with Judy, more than I could ever go into. Instead of listening to my gut and walking away, I kept trying new ways of giving, expending more and more energy, striving to prove my worth. I never asked her to be better partner; I kept trying harder to make things work.

A lack of musical reciprocation aside, the biggest warning sign with Judy came after a movie we saw together, a Tom Cruise vehicle called *Jerry Maguire*. A love story, it ends with two people who were meant to be together realizing that fact.

As the credits rolled, I turned to Judy and saw she was crying. I couldn't discern whether or not it was happy crying—her being touched by the movie's happy ending—or something else. Given where we had been, all the ups and downs of our relationship, I asked if she saw us somewhere in the movie. I wondered if she thought that's how we would turn out at the end of it all: together, and happy.

Instead of answering, Judy huffed. I don't really remember what she said, if anything. She hid her tears and grew frustrated and angry, I know that, but she never answered my question.

At the time, I should have realized something was wrong. It was many months later that I realized she was either lamenting the failed relationship she had with Jim, or hoping they would somehow end up back together. It must have been very awkward for her to be in the middle of an emotional moment and have me come bursting through it.

I tried to play off what happened, thinking it was my fault for intruding on her tears. I tried to pretend her emotions included me, instead of understanding what they really were, remnants of an old lover.

Because I didn't pick up on her guarded heart the first time, Judy did it to me again, right before leaving me, in fact. I found her listening to a song I had never heard before. I inquired as to its origins, and she quickly terminated the song and was unresponsive.

Several months later, a friend gave me a CD, telling me, "If you're trying to get over heartbreak, you need to listen to this."

The album was Jeff Buckley's *Grace*.

I immediately recognized the song *Last Goodbye* as the one Judy had been playing while lost in her head. Again, she had been lamenting her relationship with Jim, the man who had cheated on and hit her.

There was no way I could compete with that.

Allowing yourself to play second fiddle in another's heart is something I hope you never experience. I believe you won't have to, if I raise you to be confident enough to not act the doormat in a relationship. If I can achieve that, then everything I went through with Judy was worth it, if only because it helped me recognize patterns, something I can hopefully teach you.

Finally, the most important thing I took away from my relationship with Judy was knowledge—knowledge that I allowed it to happen. I was responsible for my actions. I remained on the sidelines of her abusive relationship for years without walking away. It was my choice to wait for her instead of searching for someone who would meet me on equal footing.

The worst thing a person can do is blame others for their mistakes, and in my life I have watched that happen more times than I could ever count. It is an action taken by both men and women. Instead of self-reflection and acknowledging mistakes, they shout, "This is not my fault, other people did this to me!" You will see women swearing off all men, and men swearing off all women, all because of poor dating choices they continually make.

I know I only mentioned Hayden in passing, and maybe you're wondering what happened to her. She was a good woman and we had a nice relationship, but that doesn't mean we were right for one another forever. We had a nice run, and it ended.

Sometimes that happens, too.

Hayden and I are still friends, and when I visit with her and her husband, I see him look at her in a way I don't think I ever did. He looks at Hayden the way I look at Mommy. It's just another example of what I said: when something ends, it's always for the best. You just might not realize it at the time.

All this writing aside, the best thing Mommy and I can do to help you pick the best partners in life is to raise you under the banner of a healthy marriage. If you witness us interacting in loving and respectful ways, you will grow up instinctively understanding what a healthy relationship looks like. That way, as you enter and exit your first few unions you can make adjustments in what you look for in a partner. I hope Mommy and I can give you foresight enough to trust in yourself, and do so better than I did when I was younger.

Love,
Dad

July 19, 2014

Dear Hillary,

I almost sat down to vent and complain about how annoying people can be, but as I started typing, I realized something.

Here's the backstory.

Several weeks ago, three women did their best to ruin a comedy show. Rude beyond words, they talked and texted through three comics before management threw them out.

There was a time I would have ripped them a new one the instant I hit the stage. But ever since you were born, I've been trying to do a better job of controlling my irritation with the insolent few who walk among us. Instead of attacking, I watched silently as employees, the other comics, and audience members tried to quiet the disrespectful three.

After my set, I sat at a table to watch the next comic, and though the women talked and texted and made entirely too much noise during his set, I vowed to let the situation resolve itself without my involvement. Two tables surrounding the women tried to shush them to no avail. When one customer finally said he was getting management and left the showroom, one of the trio asked, "Jesus, what's his problem?" This prompted a woman from another table to respond, "You're being rude is the problem, and I wish you'd shut the fuck up."

(Forgive the language; I am simply reporting things as they happened.)

A manager arrived and asked them to pay up and leave, which caused the women to act belligerently surprised. "Us?! We're just trying to have fun! What's wrong with having fun?"

The fact their loud talking and texting was bothering others was of no concern to them.

As they stood to exit—making a performance of it, of course, disrupting the show again with their actions—one of the women approached the man who had complained. She got in his face and leaned in on him, slurring, "You know, we were just trying to have fun. Maybe someday you'll be a good person and learn what it's like to have fun too!"

The man put his hands up defensively—palms out to prevent her from pushing in too far—causing the woman to yell, "You touched me! Maybe I'll press charges for that!"

I had had enough, and snapped, "Maybe he has witnesses who saw he didn't do anything," I said flatly.

"Maybe you should mind your own business!" she yelled at me.

"Maybe you should go be fat and obnoxious somewhere else," I responded.

Her jaw dropped. She was stunned for a moment, but when she recovered it was like the detonation of a nuclear bomb.

"WHAT DID YOU SAY?!" she shouted. "WHAT DID YOU SAY?!"

"Please leave," I said, bored with the proceedings. "Just please leave."

She put her middle finger right up against my nose, shouted, "FUCK YOU," and stormed out.

The people around me golf-clapped their appreciation.

The show continued, and I sat and pondered my words. Had I gone too far? Maybe. Attacking her weight was unnecessary, but had the woman deserved it? Again, maybe. She obviously hadn't responded to kind requests to stop being rude, which means she needed something fierce to really grab her attention. Now, because she deserved to be insulted, did that mean I had to stoop to her level to deliver the slam? No.

And therein lies the problem. Just because someone deserves poor treatment doesn't mean I want to be the karmic come-around. I didn't feel bad about my actions, but neither did I feel proud; there was no "I sure told her!" high-fiving going on in my mind. If anything, I felt resigned. It happened, so be it.

After the show ended, while standing in the bar outside the showroom, one of the more-polite women from the group approached me. We began a nice conversation regarding public etiquette, because she still didn't understand why they had been asked to leave. "I hadn't seen my friends in a year, and we were just trying to catch up," she defended.

I felt it somewhat confusing and sad that I had to explain, to an adult no less, that talking and texting during a live performance was inappropriate. She seemed to come around, and we were getting along quite well. I admitted that I had lobbed my insult at her friend because I was overly annoyed by her behavior, and since civility hadn't been able to burrow it's point into her noggin I wanted to say something mean to provoke a reaction. The woman agreed they should have quieted down and remained silent after their first warning.

A resolution to the whole sordid event was in the works, when the angry one returned and started calling me an asshole. I shrugged and walked away; no one wins a shouting match.

So.

At the beginning of this, I sat down to write about how clueless people can be, how some people shouldn't be allowed in public and so on and so forth, when something dawned on me, the last time I witnessed audience members as disrespectful as these three was almost one year ago.

One year.

I wondered how many people I had been in front of since then, how many thousands.

I wondered why I wanted to focus on the negative, the offensive, and the clueless/classless, when the obvious focus could/should be the majority of people—the wonderful masses. Hell, that night alone I had been in front of 250 people, and of that only three were bad. And of those three, only one could be completely written off. That's less than 1% of the audience.

That means 99% of the people in attendance were upstanding, there-to-have-fun folks.

The last time I wrote about an event involving obnoxious audience members, it also involved three people. That means that out of—and I'm just spitballing here—6,000 people I've been in front of in a year, only six were really, really obnoxious. Yes, there were drunken louts and idiots, but when it comes to people who had to be removed from the showroom: six.

The percentage of less-than-stellar citizens becomes microscopic.

One drop of poison can ruin water for everyone, however, and that's a problem. The minority can disrupt the majority; the few can harm the whole. But overall, people are good. I need to remember that when dealing with people who are socially dense.

I think I'm getting better. As said, time was I would have begun the proceedings with an inappropriate, cutting remark, but these days I'm waiting until the bitter end to pull out the big guns. Which might not sound like much, but hey—baby steps.

If I do anything right in my role as "parent," it will be to teach you to be courteous. In public, in private, and in general. If you're in a movie, watch the movie. If you're in the library, or at a play, be quiet. You don't have to always be talking; you don't always have to be piddle-farting on electronic devices.

Respect your surroundings.

Love,
Dad

July 22, 2014

Dear Hillary,

While you were playing in the kitchen—one of your favorite games is "Everything out of this drawer and on to the floor, now!"—I went into your bedroom to straighten up. I had the immediate thought, "Wow, it smells awful in here," and then realized I had left a poopy diaper sitting on the dresser.

Sorry about that. I'm sure the stench made your nap "pleasant."

Love,
Dad

July 26, 2014

Dear Hillary,

I have been home several weeks now, which you absolutely love. This "Blocked-off-for-Squeak's-Arrival" time means I get to have Morning Snuggles with you every day, which is a billion times better than waking up in a hotel room in a faraway city. It does make me worry, however, that my return to the road in a couple weeks will be all the more difficult for you. You have become quite the Daddy's Girl, much to my enjoyment. In fact, if Mommy gets you out of bed, the instant you see me, you lunge. Mommy becomes chopped liver—Daddy is who you want. In fact, at breakfast the other day, Mommy was playing a game with you.

She asked, "Hilly, do you love Daddy?"

You smiled sheepishly and said, "Loooove."

Then Mommy asked, "Hilly, do you love Mommy?"

You shouted "No!" quite definitively.

I laughed as I raised my arms in the air, victory! When I disappear again in a week, I hope you handle the absence well.

Squeak, upon arrival, will be also difficult for you to process. Mommy and I realized this the other day, during a visit to one of your favorite play places, The Campsite.

Mommy arranged for a play date with you and our neighbors; you have "friends" who are conveniently the daughters of Mommy's friend Shelly.

(I say "friends" because you are only just beginning to co-play. Up to this point you've played side-by-side with children we introduce you to. Which, Mommy tells me, is normal. She reads all the parenting books, so she would know.)

At The Campsite, everyone was running around and giggling, when out of the blue Shelly's two daughters—Alice and Jane—ran up to Mommy and piled onto her with big hugs. Mommy was surprised, but laughingly welcomed them into her lap and returned the affection with joy.

You, little one, were less than pleased with this event.

Standing in a foam canoe, you watched with horror, and then burst into tears. Why was Mommy sharing hugs with other little girls? Mommy's hugs were made for *you*.

We all laughed, and Mommy opened her arms and invited you over, but you were too traumatized to move. I had to lift you out of the canoe and let you scamper to her. Once there you buried your head into Mommy as she tried to abate your sniffles.

It was a very telling moment.

When Mommy and I introduce Squeak to the family, we have to be very careful of your feelings. You have to understand that the addition of Squeak does not mean we love you any less. How we will impart that upon you I do not know. You understand love via attention; when you ask it of us, we give it to you. But with a new infant under the roof, there will be times when Squeak will need a bottle or diaper change at the exact moment you desire our affection. You won't understand our inability to pick you up is no slight against you, you will simply understand you didn't get picked up.

That saddens me.

I know I'm just being a big softie, because this is a "problem" untold billions of people have dealt with since the dawn of time. Every single second of every single day a family adds someone new to their roster. The sibling (or siblings) who were there first have to put on their big boy panties and deal with it. Getting a baby brother or sister is not a big deal.

As a toddler, you don't know that. All you'll know is that you have "competition." You don't realize that in a few months you'll be fine with everything; time isn't a concept you grasp yet. It will be our job to ease you through the transition from "only" to "one-of-two" as smoothly as possible. If you're reading this in your college dorm room and not a homeless shelter or prison cell, Mommy and I probably did OK.

I might not be here for Squeak's arrival, by the way. I've had an important booking scheduled long before Mommy was even pregnant. It's a semi-convoluted story, but the short version is that I filled August 7 – 9, 2014, on my calendar way back in September 2013. Mommy went in for implantation in November 2013, and much to everyone's joy, the first embryo transfer was successful. Now we had a due date that landed right atop my booking. The comedy gig could have probably been canceled at that point, but Mommy and I discussed things and laughingly (and ignorantly) believed that since you came three weeks early, Squeak would also be making an appearance well before I had to leave town.

Now we're not so sure.

To cancel the gig at this late date would be unwise. I'd burn an important bridge and gain an unpleasant reputation as being unreliable. Plus, having taken several weeks off for Squeak's arrival, I haven't been bringing in any income. This week is important for that reason alone, as a weekend I'm home is a weekend without a paycheck.

On the flip side, Mommy would like me in the delivery room supporting her, and that's where I want to be, too. We were oh-so-certain that Squeak would come early... shows how smart we are.

We're not at a crossroads yet, because there's still hope Squeak will decide to come out before I hit the road. But if Squeak isn't here by August 4th, Mommy and I have an important decision to make. Should we induce labor, so I can be there for the birth?

A few weeks ago, this seemed to be the path we were on. But the more Mommy learned about induction, the more she started to realize that natural birth—allowing Squeak to decide when to come out—is safer for both her and Squeak.

It's not that there are horrific odds—"One in three inductions result in death or other serious complications!"—but the fact of the matter is you are "Playing God," so to speak.

Is it selfish of us to evict Squeak from Mommy's warm womb, just to placate our desires? We're leaning toward "yes, it is."

Fortunately, in a moment of pure happenchance, Mommy met a young woman training to be a doula, a "birth coach." The woman—Keri—is putting herself through school as a hostess at a restaurant we like. She commented on Mommy's very-pregnant belly, they struck up a conversation, and before you know it an offer was on the table to help Mommy through the delivery, free of charge. As a doula-in-training, Keri needs experience in the field, and Mommy loved her enthusiasm. Mommy asked me if I was OK with bringing Keri into the fold, and I thought it would be good karma to help out someone in need. So even if I am not around for Squeak's arrival, Mommy has a support team lined up to replace me.

I don't think this whole letter should be a mess of confused emotions, do you? To end on a positive note, I'll call back to something I first mentioned several months ago. In May (I think) I told you of a comedy contest I entered. After my set, I was approached by a man named Tony, a man with connections in the comedy world; a manager who said he liked what he saw in me, who wanted to help with my career.

I like Tony. He isn't a shark, someone who is all business and talks to me like an employee. Tony asks about you, he asks about Mommy and the pregnancy, and tells me stories about his life and daughter. We have conversations, which is important to me.

Since the contest, Tony and I have been in constant contact, putting together the right set for him to pitch to his connections. Having been in the business for over thirty years, he knows what works, and what doesn't. Tony has always been confident and supportive of my material, but not everything that's appropriate in a comedy club is acceptable for television. Any joke of mine involving a corporation? Can't use it; they might advertise on the show. Any swear word? Can't use it. They don't want to hear you say, "I promise not to use that word on television," they never want to hear it in the first place.

And so on.

After many months of back-and-forth, with many near misses in the mix, Tony finally got what he needed. I recorded a show where everything clicked. I kept it clean, the audience responded fantastically, and all the chips fell into place. Tony and I had a fantastic conversation about my new tape earlier this week, and it looks like things are going to start moving forward. He wants to submit me to comedy festivals and television shows, both of which could be a huge boon to my career.

I don't know what will come of this—maybe nothing—but I remain ever hopeful.

Love,
Dad

August 2, 2014

Dear Hillary,

There is an old quote, maybe even a cliché, that goes like this: "Worry is like a rocking chair. It gives you something to do, but you never get anywhere."

Over the past few weeks I've been worrying about missing Squeak's birth, and how you're going to react to having a baby in the house.

All for naught.

Truman Baxter Timmel was born on July 31st. You, my little bug, are a big sister.

I was in the delivery room, and your mom—who was an absolute rock star—said I was a good coach. I held her hand, held a leg, and said whatever words of encouragement I could.

(Which weren't that many, because the doctors and nurses were fantastic cheerleaders. They carried the weight of "Go Lydia!" better than I ever could.)

It's a long story, but a shortened version is that after two false labors—instances where Mommy believed Squeak was on the way and took off for the hospital—the third time was the clichéd charm.

Grandma Diane (Mommy's mom) was here on standby, and we were all on a walk. You were in the stroller, Kitty was on the leash, Mommy waddled, and Grandma and I meandered slowly along. We stopped so you could visit with your friends Jane and Alice, but mostly so Mommy could talk to her friend Shelly.

Mommy lamented all the false labors and wondered when Squeak would ever leave her belly; Shelly was a kind and sympathetic ear, tossing back words of encouragement. We started on our way again and had gotten approximately ten feet from Shelly's house, when Mommy started laughing.

"Shelly!" Mommy shouted. "My water just broke!"

Grandma Diane and I paused.

Well then.

It was officially go time.

Grandma Diane started walking off with you; she wanted to keep you distracted while Mommy and I stole away. She tried taking Kitty, but he kept pulling toward Mommy and me, so I grabbed him and we made our way home.

Everything was packed up, so after putting Kitty inside the house, Mommy and I hopped in the car and away we went, hospital bound. Once there, we were put in a triage room in Labor & Delivery. They wanted to make sure Mommy was really in labor before putting her into an actual delivery room.

After being checked at 8:20pm, it was determined Mommy was absolutely in labor, and that her cervix was dilated four centimeters. A point of information: when having a baby, you begin pushing at ten centimeters, and a general rule of thumb is that you dilate one centimeter per hour. This meant we had six hours of sitting around to do.

Mommy and I walked up and down the hallway, Mommy bounced on an exercise ball, and I rubbed her lower back during each contraction.

And, being hungry, I ordered a pizza. With six hours of waiting, I wanted to get some food in me.

At about 9:40pm, my phone rang. The pizza delivery guy was pulling up and I needed to meet him in the lobby.

I left, got the pizza, and returned at around 9:45pm to find a room full of doctors and nurses swarming everywhere.

One of them looked at me and laughed, "I have some news for you, you're about to have a baby."

But... Mommy was only four centimeters an hour ago. There was no way she dilated six centimeters in an hour, right?

Wrong.

Mommy's cervix had hit the fast-forward button and sped through the process in record time.

I set the pizza on the TV and got behind her to comfort and coach (which, as I already stated, involved more comforting than coaching).

Your Mom began pushing at 9:54pm and eight short minutes later, a perfectly healthy seven-pound baby boy entered the world. He was a bit of a purplish mess, just like you were, but he was beautiful. Mommy cried, I smiled, and all was well in the world.

And, bonus, since it had only taken eight minutes, my pizza was still warm! I retrieved it from the TV stand, and while Mommy was examined and being stitched up, I alternately ate and fed her.

The doctor was incredulous. "I've never had anyone eat pizza when I was delivering their placenta," he noted.

It was a very surreal moment. We were surrounded by all things disgusting, including (but not limited to) blood, placenta, and feces. Through it all, I munched away happily, noting, "Well this is gross."

Once our room was ready in the maternity ward (somewhere just past the midnight hour), we transferred to it and settled in for a short night of no sleep and many feedings.

To help you maintain a schedule, on Friday morning I sped home around 5am so I would be there when you awoke. I did this on Saturday, too. With your world about to change, I wanted to keep some semblance of normalcy in your system. I had been getting up with you for the past several weeks and administering Morning Snuggles, and I didn't want to change that pattern.

After our Saturday routine, I went back to the hospital and got Mommy. With her and Squea... sorry, Truman. With her and Truman under the roof, our second fear—how would you react—was as quickly assuaged as our first.

My little dear daughter, you have reacted to your baby brother with glee and grace. You point at him and say "Baby!" in the most delightful, joyous voice. When in his bouncy seat, you cover him with a blanket and look to Mommy or me with a smile across your face. You have even tried sharing a pacifier with him, but you usually try doing this a little too forcefully, or while he is asleep. Regardless, it is wonderful watching you taking an interest in him.

Best of all, out of the blue and for no discernible reason at all, from time to time you reach over and touch his nose with one hand, your nose with the other, and proudly exclaim, "Nose!"

Kitty, for the record, reacted to Truman the same way he reacted to you. When within range, Kitty walks right up to the sleeping baby, shoves his nose into Truman's face, and sniffs vigorously for several seconds. Determining all is as it should be, he then turns to us with the look on his face, "Seriously, again?" Kitty is well aware his sleep schedule will be disrupted for months to come.

From here, my stories peter out.

There was a fun moment in the hospital when the room phone rang. Considering both Mommy and I have cell phones, the idea someone would be calling us on the hospital phone was odd, so I answered by saying something stupid like, "Thank you for calling Pizza Hut, may I take your order?"

A confused voice at the other end asked if they had reached the right room, to which I responded in the affirmative.

They needed to fill out an intake form for Truman, and began asking questions:

"What religion is Truman?"

I began laughing.

"What ethnicity is Truman?"

"Honky."

There was a long pause.

"Would you like to do this with my wife?" I asked.

"Please," a kindly but curt voice replied.

And that was that.

Oh, I almost forgot!

Without going into too much detail, after hearing the name we attached to our new baby boy, a particularly narrow-minded family member mentioned something silly regarding both of your first names. They tried attaching political affiliations to them, which is both absurd and tells you about their mindset. But, since it came up, I feel I should tell you something in case it ever comes up again: Hillary, neither you nor your brother Truman were named after anyone.

Mommy had three criteria when determining how you should be addressed, the most important of which was that the names should be common enough to be easily spelled and understood. After that, Mommy wanted to make sure they were not overly popular. Mommy wanted something unique, not the trendy "name-of-the-day." Mommy also wanted your names to carry weight and a sense of power. Looking up both Hillary and Truman on name registries, she discovered both names met all three of her desires easily.

Over the course of time, people may or may not want to align you with more famous women named Hillary, but that is on them, not you. Neither your mother nor I wanted to burden you with the weight of idolatry. To me, there is something slightly obscene about holding someone in such fascination that you want to call your offspring that name. It adds a level of expectation that is unfair. "You were named after this quarterback/musician/homosexual, fictional vampire, so live up to that!"

(Of course, it was suggested that I name your brother Truman Martin Riggs Timmel, and I almost went with that. Martin Riggs meant more to me as a teenager than he probably should have, and I do have a bit of a tender spot in my heart for that particular fictional character. But not enough to throw it on a legal document. Which is unfortunate, because I'll probably regret not doing so for the rest of my life. Dammit.)

Anyway, both you and Truman are expected to be nothing other than who you are. We have neither expectations nor delusions of grandeur; we will raise you to be kind, respectful people, and beyond that let you create your own paths in life. To quote another fictional character, all we will ask is that you "choose wisely."

Love,
Dad

August 5, 2014

Dear Hillary,

You are a toddler, which means two things:

- You enjoy digging in every nook, cranny, and drawer you can find, destroying everything in your path and grabbing everything possible
- Sometimes, to save time, you shower with Mommy or me

So, that said, I must inform you that there is nothing more awkward than you climbing into the shower with me and handing me the Astroglide you just pulled from the bedside drawer.

I plan on telling that story to all your friends when you are a teenager and acting uppity.

Nothing knocks a person back into line than abject embarrassment.

Love,
Dad

August 8, 2014

Dear Hillary,

I am in Royal Oak, Michigan, and missing you dearly. Today even more than usual, because today is your birthday. It is one of many milestones I have missed due to my job.

(Yes, it's technically Mommy's and my wedding anniversary, too. I'm a stellar husband/father, aren't I?)

By now you've read about your birth and the ways we prepared for you (getting Kitty, attending a silly class...), but what I've mentioned in passing (yet haven't discussed in detail) is how you came to be.

One of the most awkward moments a child can have is the realization that at some point, their parents made love. It's something no child wants to imagine, and I am here to tell you that you, my little turtle poop, can remain as blissfully ignorant (or in denial) for as long as you want.

You, dear one, were created via the wonders of medical science. In vitro fertilization, to be specific.

For reasons our doctors couldn't explain, Mommy was unable to ovulate. She had plenty of eggs queued up in her ovaries and ready to go to work, but instead of traveling down the fallopian tubes and fighting to be fertilized, in the ovaries they remained.

For two years, different approaches were taken to try and get them to "hatch." Mommy took Clomid, a medication that didn't help her ovulate, but did cover her ovaries in cysts. Strike one. She tried Letrazole, which didn't have any negative side effects, but neither did it have any positive ones. Strike two. Finally, she was prescribed a combination of Letrazole and injectable stimulation medications. Strike three.

With the main go-to methods failing, the doctors recommended in vitro fertilization (hereto referred to as IVF). IVF is a process in which eggs would be taken from Mommy and fertilized in a lab using sperm donated (*cough*) by me. The neat thing about this process is that the scientists put my sperm in a centrifuge after donation, spinning away all the weak and deformed ones. That means they're left with the best of the best. The Marines of sperm, so to speak.

When we were filling Mommy with drugs to help her ovulate, everyone joked, "You're going to have triplets!" One possible side effect of fertility drugs is having more than one egg fertilize. With IVF, everything is more controlled. "One egg = one baby" was a much more likely outcome, which is exactly what Mommy and I wanted.

IVF is a multi-step process; it doesn't happen all at once. First, the doctors had to harvest Mommy's eggs. Because she was a good little egg grower, they were able to pull twenty (a nice high number) out. Then I had to donate my swimmers. Following that, the best combinations of each were paired up in Petri dishes and left to do their business, meaning their cells would divide and multiply.

There are medical terms aplenty I could look up and throw out here, but medical terms are obnoxious and I'm not qualified to use them. The long and short of it is, when the sperm and egg meet, they either multiply, or they do not. If the cell expands and grows, the chance for a baby is stronger. Using high-powered microscopes, the doctors measure cell walls, shape, growth rate... anything and everything they can. Examining the data, they determine which embryos have the best chance of becoming a baby, and line them up in order of strongest to weakest.

Out of Mommy's twenty eggs, eleven were fertilized. This was considered an extremely high number. With eleven on hand, we could freeze the unused portion and have it on hand for future attempts.

The first transfer used up three embryos. Two were determined to be "good enough," but one was fantastic. It, the supposed healthiest embryo, was implanted in Mommy in September 2011, but did not take hold. When Mommy had her blood test, it showed no signs of pregnancy. There was no rhyme or reason why it did not work; simply put, it was just not meant to be.

Mommy was devastated. At this point, we had been trying to conceive for nearly two years. With each new hope—"Try this medication! Now let's use IVF!"—came an even greater letdown.

I maintained a more even-keeled attitude. I don't know why, but I just figured everything would work out like it was supposed to. Having been through more than my fair share of "failure" in life, I'd long ago discovered that rarely does something worse follow something bad.

On December 9th, 2011, Mommy went in for a second implantation. I, as you already know, was out of town. According to my calendar, I was in (of all places) Chicago.

(My favorite city; I am forever in Chicago.)

Two weeks later, Mommy went in for her first blood test. By measuring her HGC (human chorionic gonadotropin—don't ask me what that means) levels, doctors could determine whether or not Mommy was pregnant. According to the charts, they were looking for a number between 10 and 750. Higher was better; normal would be around 300.

Mommy came back at...

...13.

Things did not look good. Such a low number indicated the pregnancy existed, but likely would not hold. Miscarriage was probably imminent. Mommy was asked to take another blood test in two days.

She did, and the doctors wanted to see a 75% increase. The minimum desired number was 23.

Mommy registered 22.

Now she was below the acceptable levels for a strengthening pregnancy. While still going upward, she wasn't progressing enough. Technically, she was still "pregnant," but with little hope of it lasting.

"Don't get your hopes up," the nurse told Mommy.

The woman was just doing her job, and trying to prepare Mommy for the worst, but hearing the words were devastating. Mommy wanted hope and positivity, not negativity.

The professionals recommended Mommy wait a week and a half for the next checkup, an ultrasound to look for a heartbeat, but she didn't have the patience. Mommy demanded another blood draw two days later.

This time, the minimum to register pregnancy was 36.

Mommy registered 75.

While the number wasn't fantastic, the leap was. No one expected her to jump so dramatically.

This was extremely good news.

From there, everything averaged out. You continued to grow inside Mommy's belly, gaining in strength, becoming more and more healthy. Eventually, despite your very humble beginnings, you began measuring right up there with the best of babies.

When you arrived (three weeks before you were supposed to), you were seven pounds and one ounce. You measured 21¼ inches long.

Mommy held you and cried as you cried, but her tears were of joy where yours contained confusion. Mommy whispered how much she loved you into your ear, and explained how you were her little survivor, the embryo that started out at a lowly 13 and exceeded all expectations.

The doctor delivering the placenta paused and stared at Mommy. The perfectly healthy baby she had just delivered had started as a 13 HCG? That was near unheard of.

But that's what happened.

I cannot tell you what to make of all this; I don't want to add undue pressure to your life by saying, "You were put here for a reason" and force you to figure out what that "reason" is. That said, it cannot be denied: *you are a survivor.*

You fought all the odds, and you made it.

Whenever an obstacle is put in front of you, whenever a door is closed, or someone says "no," you need to remember your earliest origins.

You beat the odds.

Mommy never gave up on you, and you should never give up on yourself.

Happy birthday, my beautiful baby daughter pants.

I love you so much.

Love,
Dad

Acknowledgements

Truth is, I have too many people to thank. If I were to sit down and family tree a list of everyone in my life deserving kudos, the ensuing pages would double the length of this book. I have met way too many kind, generous people while traveling the road telling my jokes. I have met more kind, generous people via the graces of social media.

When both Hillary and Truman were born, a flood of munificence came pouring in from places unexpected. Gifts were showered upon each of them from near and far; toys to teddy bears, art to ensembles. People I only know through online profiles asked for my address and sent handmade items of clothing; others sent the most adorable (and I say that in the most macho and manly of ways) outfits: onesies for the present, T-shirts for the future, socks, hats, outfits... both of my children were tended to by the Blanche DuBois kindness of "strangers." It was beyond unexpected, and hopefully a sign that I've done something right with my life to be surrounded by such wonderful people. Sometimes I fear I don't express my gratitude enough, but I hope they know how much I learn about life and benevolence through them.

Added to those kind folks are those who support my career. From people who buy my books, fire up my comedy on streaming services, promote me via social media—"Friends! Check out Nathan Timmel!"—and come see me when I'm in their nape of the woods, neck of the nape, whenever I'm near (not an exact quote, but I love references) to those who book me into comedy clubs, I give a Japanese bow and English tip of the hat of respect to you. Danke.

Of course there are the friends I interact with locally and personally; they too show great affection to my family, and I am eternally humbled by it. After the birth of each child, all too many of them brought us the most delicious meals to eat, knowing full well we would be too exhausted to cook.

Beyond that, I try to thank those who are closest to me on a daily basis.

Kitty, of course, for being patient as all get out as Hilly enters her Terrible Twos. The other day she got a hold of a fabric toy and started swinging it at him. His ears went back, and he wasn't happy, but he dealt with it as Mommy rushed in and put an end to the abuse. Hilly had to apologize to Kitty and give him hugs and a treat, and I try to give him as many belly rubs nightly for his ever-pleasant attitude toward all things kiddo.

Lydia, for, well, being Lydia. Again, it would take a whole book to thank her properly for the way she changed my life. To make things easier on the eyes reading this, I'll just continue to buy her specialty cupcakes from the local bakery. Because nothing says love like tubbing up your spouse. Upon reading this page, her first words were, "Really? You put the dog before me?" Only because I know you'll understand, sweetie. Only because I know you'll understand. And forgive.

Finally, my children. Though this was written for (to) Hillary, both make me think of John Donne's 'A Valediction Forbidding Mourning' whenever I get behind the wheel of my car to away to another city. Though I leave home often, my love for them is the tether that keeps me sane, and their "firmness makes my circle just, and makes me end where I begun."

And there you have it.

The photos adorning the cover and back of this book were taken by Dreamday Photography. Lindsay McGowan Photography shot the photo of Hilly and me at the end of the last letter. My Mrs. designed everything and edited and re-edited this manuscript. If there are errors within the covers of this book, they come from me noodling around and screwing things up after her meticulous eye had fixed everything.

If you enjoyed reading this, I hope you line up for my next offering. I'm thinking of writing a piece of fiction, something about a rogue shark that attacks swimmers on Martha's Vineyard.

What? You're kidding. Well poop.

About the Author

Nathan Timmel has been writing since he could scribble using crayons. As a comedian, he has released four CDs—three of which are in rotation on Sirius/XM radio—and has appeared on The Bob & Tom Show. Nathan currently lives in Iowa with his wife Lydia, a gender-confused kitty, Simon, his doggy (named "Kitty"), his beautiful daughter Hillary (who was born on Nathan & Lydia's wedding anniversary. Neat, eh?), and his son Truman.

Nathan is an avid fan of Billy and the Boingers, and enjoys a fine pair of pants.

Nathan is the author of two novels and seven mini-books:

- *I Was a White Knight... Once*
- *Touched by Anything But an Angel (and Other Word Salads)*
- *The Four-Legged Perspective: One Dog's Take on Burp Rags and Baby Sisters*
- *An Inattention To Detail: A Comedian Lobs Jokes in Iraq*
- *The Accidental Substitute: How a Stand-Up Comedian Became a Part-Time Teacher*
- *Same Same: Why Gay Doesn't Matter*
- *Go Home Happy: The Serious Side of Stand-Up Comedy*
- *Are You There, Xenu? It's Me, Nathan.*

Please visit www.nathantimmel.com for anything and everything Nathan related, including his weekly podcast, but not his naked pictures. Those are available for only $19.95 a month on his alternate website, www.engorged...

You know what? Never mind.

Thanks for reading, now go see Nathan perform comedy live. You'll giggle and have a good time, promise.

Follow Nathan on Twitter, "like" him on Facebook, watch his videos on YouTube... Please, become his next stalker. He's had two already, and is always in the market for another.

Made in the USA
Columbia, SC
11 July 2019